Huntin' and Fishin'
with the Ole Man

We love the outdoors! More great titles from Islandport Press.

Leave Some for Seed
By Tom Hennessey

A Life Lived Outdoors
By George Smith

Backtrack
By V. Paul Reynolds

This Cider Still Tastes Funny! and *Suddenly, the Cider Didn't Taste So Good!*
By John Ford Sr.

Birds of a Feather and *Tales from Misery Ridge*
By Paul Fournier

Where Cool Waters Flow
By Randy Spencer

My Life in the Maine Woods
By Annette Jackson

Nine Mile Bridge
By Helen Hamlin

These and other books are available at:
www.islandportpress.com.

Islandport Press is a dynamic, award-winning publisher
dedicated to stories rooted in the essence and sensibilities of
New England. We strive to capture and explore the grit, beauty,
and infectious spirit of the region by telling tales, real and
imagined, that can be appreciated in many forms by readers,
dreamers, and adventurers everywhere.

Huntin' and Fishin' with the Ole Man

Tall tales from the Maine outdoors

By Dave O'Connor

Illustrations by John Hulub

ISLANDPORT PRESS

Islandport Press
PO Box 10
Yarmouth, ME 04096
www.islandportpress.com
books@islandportpress.com

Original Islandport Edition published April 2015
Portions of this book were originally published in 2009
by Maine Outdoor Publications.

ISBN: 978-1-939017-56-7
Library of Congress Catalog Number: 2014911181

Publisher: Dean L. Lunt
Cover Design: Karen F. Hoots / Hoots Design
Interior Design: Michelle A. Lunt / Islandport Press
Author Photograph: Kevin Bennett, courtesy of Islandport Press
Interior Illustrations: John Hulub

To my father, Edward "Steamer" O'Connor—
I wish you were here.

To Roger Thurlow,
a truly inspired deer hunter and togue fisherman,
my mentor outdoors.

To my wife Nancy,
for friendship,
and for all of her help with this project.

Contents

Acknowledgments

I'd like to thank Melissa Hayes, my copyeditor, for her responses to the manuscript that were the guide to bringing my stories to life. She was the crucial first and last reader before the book went to press. Many thanks to her and all the people of Islandport Press: Dean Lunt, Michelle Lunt, Genevieve Morgan, and Shannon Butler, who helped me get this book to the readers. I'd also like to thank V. Paul Reynolds, who first saw the potential. The Ole Man would be proud, too.

1

Our Lines Got Tangled at the Beaver Dam

IT WAS A SOFT MAY MOMENT in northern Maine. I had a sack of fiddleheads already bulging with the tender green ferns I loved so much. I picked them near the old mill site and put them away in my pickup. Now all I needed on this lovely day was a mess of brook trout to complete a light noon lunch with my wife.

A guy at work, Loren Ritchie, had told me about the Swift Brook Meadows area and about the plentiful fiddleheads and great brook trout: "There's never anyone out there. You'll be all alone, and both the fiddlehead ferns and the trout should be ready about now." The brook was not huge; it could be fished by walking along the edge or by wading. The current lived up to the name—swiftly moving water, what I called "a brook in a hurry." The meadows were upstream. The lower reaches had three feeder branches all combining into one seventy-five-foot-wide brook, creating a stream.

Beautiful country, just beautiful; I was going to like living here. We're going to like it here. Access from town was via

a logging road to the remains of a lumber mill, now just flat grounds, a sawdust pile, and rusting mill equipment. The old dam the mill used for power was breached, leaving quaint-looking tumbledown debris now. This was where I parked my pickup just as Loren Ritchie had suggested. No one else was apparently interested in this brook on a May day, I thought, as I started up the singing brook. Great trouty-looking water, and I was alone. Well, not quite.

As I walked north along the edge of Swift Brook I noticed moose tracks, deer tracks, and man tracks . . . all freshly made. I was excited by the prospects. Who was the man? Maybe we would meet. This looked better and better, with undercut banks, swirling pools, midstream boulders with pools below, quiet straightaways. I would fish some of these natural trout holes on the way back down. Right now, it was exploration time. I carried a light Orvis Battenkill rod with a very light floating line. My book of flies was mixed wet and dry, with a center page of favorites. I chose an all-purpose Chinese manufactured fly I had purchased from a tiny back-of-the-magazine ad in *Outdoor Life*, where for $10 you got twenty flies, all hand-tied. The collection of flies was called "Great American Trout Flies." This fly was bright yellow with a moth-like appearance. In the water it just flashed yellow. I was a novice to fly fishing, but I liked it a lot.

First downstream cast on a swirling eddy near an under-cut bank, and I had my first trout. "I like Swift Brook already," I said out loud, to nothing or nobody in particular. The fish was fat and about eight inches. Good for lunch, I thought, and slipped it into the creel. I was exploring every nuance of the brook. The next corner was quite sharply turning north and it was channelized by eons of water squeezed between outlying granite. I walked gingerly, and as I fully rounded the corner I found a tiny moose mid-stream—about twenty feet away. This was clearly a moose born early in the season, perhaps only days or hours before. This creature took a look at me and bleated. Being quite innocent and unthinking, I kept on trying to wade by the young creature. Suddenly, *very* suddenly, THE BIGGEST COW MOOSE IN THE WORLD appeared and headed my way, closing ground so fast that my survival looked doubtful. I've never been that scared—never. Not close calls on the highway, not upside-down white-water rafting, not on my one and only skydiving expedition.

The hair on Mom's neck was strictly vertical, her eyes were bigger than the devil out after a lost soul. She simply flabbergasted my sensibilities. As she brushed or pushed by me, I felt her muscled rib cage glancing off my shoulder and I fell over backwards, neatly snapping the tip section of my beautiful and quite expensive Orvis Battenkill rod. The rush of her passing breath was dreadfully scented with foul odors, and, it was hot, not warm; it was *hot*. This all took place in a quarter-section of a second, with a thousand flashed photo memories locked forever in my mind.

Mama had placed herself between me and the newborn. Orders had obviously gone out to the young one, because the little creature was already retreating into the woods about seventy-five feet away. I was struggling to get up and the cow moose was moving away, but keeping a very close watch on me. Her neck hairs were up, but not quite as intimidating as they were a minute ago.

I started to take stock: My new digital Nikon P-500 camera with Nikkor lens and 36x zoom was in two feet of water. It must have been shaken out of my backpack. The tip section of the Battenkill was washed ashore, and my ashwood creel handmade by a Penobscot native was going to need repair next time I went south to Old Town. I had blood running down my leg from where I'd banged a river rock on the way down to moose submission. I had a right elbow that was pulsating with pain. The moose had brushed me aside like I was a single autumn leaf, but she had clearly made her point about who and what was valuable, and who and what could be crumbled. I was grateful to her for understanding. Things don't always work out this well. A Maine moose is a gentle creature, but a mother is a mother, and you had to be proud of her defense of her youngster. I never gave a thought to retreating to home ground. I just pledged to be more careful. I tied the rod-tip section to the creel with mono line. I'd fish without a rod tip. I put the probably ruined camera in a lunch bag and stowed it away in the small backpack. I always carry a tiny first-aid kit, and I used two bandage strips to cover the wound on my leg. The elbow was already purple. The single trout had stayed in the crumbled creel, and I wanted to get a few more.

Next to a quiet pool I noticed the man tracks again—nice boot tracks like those on waders. They were fresh. I got a nice trout in this pool, just about nine inches, I'd guess. This one I got on an "American Classic fly" named Grateful Gertrude. This fly was tied on a #6 hook and consisted of a dyed red-feather body wrapped with silver tinsel, and had a green head with black-and-white paint spots placed down near the hook-eye. Those Chinese flies sure were wild, but they fell apart after a couple of contacts with rocks or fish.

Upstream beckoned because I had heard rumors that the beaver dam on the south side of the meadows was the best fishing on the whole stream; perhaps fellow-worker stories were more than rumors. Actually, I discovered there were several beaver dams in place to control different feeder trickles from the main flow. This was a real introductory morning's fiddleheading, exploring, and trout fishing as an introduction to paradise. The beaver had been quite busy with flood control—at least, their version of flood control.

They seemed to have a few old lodges and a couple more under construction.

I was trying another American Classic fly called Bear Hair Buddy that the Chinese made from stuff quite closely akin to cheap black twine wound with gold-colored tinsel and liberally glued to a #4 hook. Not very attractive, I thought, but I whipped it out there, and when it plopped on the water I gave it a slight jerk every now and then. Suddenly a splash, and I had a really nice brilliantly colored fish on the line, a nice brook trout, I believed. I was paying so much attention to the fish that I didn't notice the approach of a stranger. He looked like a veteran angler with beat-up hat, good-quality waders, and a very expensive-looking, obviously custom-made, seven-foot fly rod.

I landed the fish, admired him properly, took the fly out of the trout's mouth, guessed to myself the fish was nearly twelve inches long, and carefully snapped the creel shut. I looked up as the man loudly asked, "Who in hell are you, and what in hell are you doing on Swift Brook Meadows?"

I was lost for words, but he wasn't lost at all.

"That's the dumbest-looking excuse for a trout fly I ever saw. Who in blazes taught you to fish, anyway? Whoever it was, they wasted their time. And how'd you break a perfectly good Orvis Battenkill on such an easy stream to navigate? I'll bet that Jake Goodwin or Loren Ritchie told you this was good fiddleheadin' and troutin' grounds, didn't they? Huh? Huh? Cat got your tongue or something? You do speak, don't ya? Huh? Huh? God bless me, I've got a know-nothin', tongue-tied, poorly equipped, sassy out-a-stater gooky creep . . . What say?"

My voice came to life but sounded squeaky and far away. "I'm new here. I just arrived here with my wife. I work at the plant. I only know a couple of guys, but the name Loren Ritchie sounds familiar; seems like he might be the guy who told me no one ever fishes here, or picks fiddleheads here, either. I love it . . . we love it . . . my wife and I. I like the job, too."

He looked like he was studying a new book, hot off the presses.

"Loren Ritchie! I thought as much. He knows less than you, and that's sayin' somethin'. There's a feelin' about you, almost a smell of the newborn. Are you a devoted fisherman and hunter, or just a boy-man lost in the glories of those pioneers who came before these accumulations of years and such?"

I didn't know what He was talking about, but I took an instant liking to Him, and I'd have to admit, I needed all the outdoor training and experience I could get.

I said, "I'm really glad to meet you, sir. I mean, I love hunting and I love fishing. Actually, I like just about everything there is in the outdoors. I guess I look kinda funny, but I'm just inexperienced, that's all. I need help."

He answered, "You sure do, boy. You sure do. Come on, and I'll show you a shortcut back to the old mill lot where I've got my Jeep parked outa sight. I've got to get home for lunch; Herself will be waiting."

And, that's how I met the Ole Man. It was a fateful meeting at the Swift Brook Meadows.

2

The Big Buck

THE ALTON BOG WAS DEER COUNTRY. Everyone who carried a gun knew the whitetails spent their lives within these wild square miles. Cedars were meshed with runs of young hardwoods, and mixed in were hemlocks, white pine, spruce, fir, birches (white, yellow, gray, paper), and a host of lessers, such as alders, ash, ironwood, wild thorn . . . typical northern New England forest mixes.

From the first day I met the Ole Man, He was clear on one thing: "If you really want to hunt deer in a wild setting, far from the crowded fringe country, you need look no further." To Him the discussion was ended. There were miles of swampy deer cover with a few hardwood ridges, and there always were dozens of deer, including some big-racked bucks. Because there was water and swampy ground, almost as a natural moat surrounding the best areas, it was a given the Ole Man would want to hunt there. No crowds.

For forty years and more, the Ole Man had hunted The Bog with annual success. The limited access kept away the hordes over the decades. Right from the tarred road it was a long walk through tangled alders for a half-mile; then, just about the time you were okay with alders, it turned into a broad swale to drown your legs in chilly November waters. Every step was a torture. Waders or other waterproof gear, knee-high, are required. We usually wear the waders from the tarred road to the interior edge of the swale, where we switch to boots that we've slung over our shoulders. The waders stay on the inside edge of the swale until we return from the hunt. Then we reverse the process to go home. As I said, it isn't easy access.

On the other side of this swamp there is a slight rise in the level of the land. Deer hunting begins as soon as we leave the swale. If there are three (or, rarely, five) hunters in our party, it is here where the hunters begin to choose an area of The Bog to hunt for the day. The final impediment is a massive acreage of firs generated so closely together it makes getting through a real chore. Most hunters skirt the edge and pass through.

The first morning I followed the Ole Man through this maze from the far distant highway under flashlight conditions, with a light freezing drizzle, I swore I would never, never return there again. Never. I sure hoped no one got a deer.

Who the hell would want to shoot a deer back here? How would you drag it out to the road? I thought this, then realized we were not far from town; we were alone, and it wasn't likely anyone would come out here. Very unlikely. The Bog was the Ole Man's hunting preserve. Someone owned it and paid taxes on it, but only the outer edges were usable for logging or farming or residential housing. The Bog was largely a natural wetland providing an aquifer reserve and wildlife environment for both man and nature. Perfect deer hunting. The Ole Man was right.

We each got a nice buck the first time I hunted there, and I have been back hundreds of times since. Although every deer shot means a sweaty, difficult haul to get the deer back to the road, we always gladly do it, because hunting in The Bog is exciting. I always learn something I didn't know when I hunt there. New details. Things I file away.

One hunting season a few years ago it seemed like neither of us might get a deer that season. We hunted hard, but luck seemed elusive. To make things worse, Jake Goodwin shot a nice ten-pointer and had it prominently hanging from a tree limb near his shed. Everyone knew. Jake boasted downtown to everyone, "The Ole Man's been asking me for deer-hunting lessons, but I'd have to start with the basics; probably take too much time. Maybe if He paid me by the hour . . . ah, maybe." The joke was out. The gauntlet laid down.

The Ole Man responded by saying, "Jake Goodwin has more success than most people because he ain't married. If you ain't married, you don't have the distractions caused by women in general, wives in particular. They want fences painted, lawns mowed, leaking water pipes fixed, garbage taken out, oil changed in the car . . . oh, the list is endless. Useless things taking time from huntin' and fishin'." He adjusted his stance, adding, " 'Course he can get deer like that, 'cause if he wants to hunt, he just goes. There ain't any question the unmarried guy can outdo a man who's bound and tied."

I never mentioned that Jake got the deer on the first day of the season, or that we hunted more days already than any other man, married or unmarried. The Ole Man refused to say that luck played a role. Skill counts, but hunting is often blind, dumb luck. It was well known Herself hardly recognized the Ole Man the first couple of months of hunting season each fall. He hunted partridge, woodcock, ducks, geese, and, of course, deer. A lot of work for one man. What with earning a living, He was a busy man.

Now, the deer season was down to a single week. It would be a stinging defeat if the Ole Man failed to tag a deer. Jake made sure he made everyone aware of how the tides were running. If the Ole Man needed pipe tobacco and stopped at the store, Jake was there. When the Jeep needed gas, Jake just happened to be there. Nothing was said—at least while He, the Ole Man, was around. It was the knowing smirk, the gesture, the feeling of being second-class.

To counter, the Ole Man took two extra days of vacation at Thanksgiving, giving Him four days of straight deer hunting, "nearly as good as being single." He oiled the .308 Savage 99. He did it as though the gun was somehow responsible for failing to get a good buck this hunting season. The stock was scratched from hundreds of days of dragging deer in the bog, the metal's bluing was worn, and the metal surfaces showed signs of a huge amount of handling. Still, He handled it with pride. The gun was not at fault.

When I got to His house at 3:30 a.m. on Wednesday morning, I found Him up and ready to leave. He was sitting at the fireplace with two pack baskets filled to the brim. "I already told Herself to call your wife and tell her we won't be back until Saturday night, unless we both find success before that. Might even be Sunday morning if we got one late before the season closes at Saturday sunset.

"The big pack has all the food; Mine has the tent and sleeping bags. I'll cut tent poles in The Bog."

All this was said as we loaded the Jeep. He never seemed to leave me a choice. My option was to hunt four days, stay in The Bog those nights, or . . . start a war. I chose the easier way. I was ready for a day's hunt. He was ready for a major assault.

If walking into The Bog was terrible under normal conditions, this time, with all the extra gear, it was trial by water torture. He was determined. "Out here, like this, we're nearly like bachelors. We can hunt like the unmarried guy." Could be true for real if we missed too many holidays with the spouses.

Our forward progress was nearly as rapid as Benedict Arnold's expedition to take Quebec. Ours was just as heavily laden but a few days shorter in duration. My pack was heavy beyond reason. I asked what was in it, but He only said it was "food and necessaries for the four-day weekend." I struggled to manage as I stumbled through the maze leading to The Bog.

After the alders the watery swamp looked easy. It was worse than I thought. I stumbled, fell, quickly dousing my flashlight as it got covered with mud. After, I had to follow the flickering light ahead as He sloshed through the muddy waters. So consequently, I stumbled a few more times, but was able to recover without falling by grasping a handy tree or bush. In time, I swore the pace of advance was actually increasing. As I hardened to the task I found myself actually anticipating the coming hunt. I wanted a deer.

By the time we got to First Ridge I was beginning to think the pack was actually getting lighter. The first lights of dawn were clearly beginning to awaken our part of the world with the crisp feeling of late fall. Leaves snapped, twigs broken roared back at you. It was the time and place to hunt.

"Since I'm the best hunter in this party, why don't you ferry the dunnage over to the rapids on Birch Stream," the Ole Man said. "We'll camp there. I'll meet you for lunch. That should give you plenty of time to get camp set up and a noon fire going for hot food."

I was left to carry out the assignment. He was off deer hunting. I knew this was all part of His plan. I also knew He was the better hunter.

My own strategy was to walk slowly and try to be quiet while carrying each load to the Birch Rapids. It would take two passages. I was struck by the quietness of the morning. It surrounded me as I trudged forward. The red squirrels broke the silence to announce my coming. It felt useless to advance with stealth, but that's what I did.

The only real obstacle to my getting to the rapids was a long hill of paper birch. It was a favorite day haunt of the bucks; both the Ole Man and I had caught decent bucks wandering or napping here during past hunts. I needed to be careful. I had two trips to make. I angled across, keeping the wind in my face as best I could.

That proved impossible unless I wanted to circle around the whole ridge. I decided to try a straight pass, up and over. It was the shortest way to the proposed campsite. The strange thing was, I almost changed my mind because the pack basket felt lighter and lighter, at least in my mind. Maybe I was getting my cruising-speed wind.

An hour passed, and I reached Birch Rapids, setting the pack down. I didn't need it now. I needed the tent. I guess I would be cutting the poles, not the Ole Man. I noticed that the pack looked odd; it had fallen over when I put it on the ground. It looked like bricks, red bricks, had fallen out. They *were* bricks! I had been carrying bricks. What in hell?

I tore at the pack basket just as I heard the crack of the Ole Man's rifle, back on Birch Ridge. It was a single shot. I knew what that meant. Several shots—a deer, maybe. One shot equals one deer with the Ole Man.

I went back to my job. I had a few more than a dozen bricks packed in bubble wrap, so I never guessed what I might be carrying. In the bottom was a small bag, now almost empty. I examined it closely to see a small spigot, partially open. I smelled the dripping fluid. *Deer musk.* It was straight deer musk, dripping out as I walked. Now, I knew it wasn't food I was carrying. It was a package of used bricks on top and below the bubble wrap was this flask of fluid. The "bag" was a wineskin equipped with a spigot He had set to slowly drip. Things were getting clearer with the passing moments.

The bricks were dumped. I loosely shouldered the now truly light pack. It was a record-setting pace I took to reach Birch Ridge. He was there. He was grinning ear to ear. The deer was a stupendous buck with an atypical rack. There were clearly twenty points, and an argument could be made for several more.

"See what waiting all season can bring ya?" The Ole Man was excited, justifiably so.

What could I say? I was the beaten one. He clearly had no intention to hunt for four days. He wanted to be home for Thanksgiving. He did not tell Herself to call my house. He hadn't even brought the tent and sleeping bags. I later found His pack was overfilled with a feathery lightweight tarp, and nothing else. No wonder He could set a record pace. No wonder He stayed so far ahead of me.

The spigot? He never opened it until just before we separated, with me as the walking musk factory and He as the knowing hunter. It worked.

"How much of the deer musk was I carrying when I first started out?" I demanded to know.

"About three GALLONS by the formula I concocted. Must have been a little heavy, I guess," He said with a snicker. Heavy it certainly was when added to the bricks, but it had been very effective. Just not for me.

"I would have cut you in on it, but I figured I needed a deer and you needed a deer-hunting lesson . . . with musk." He laughed and laughed.

As we dragged the deer He formulated a plan.

"This buck requires a newspaperman's write-up," he said. "It ought to be front page. A twenty-something-pointer is unusual enough for a good news story, and you add a few bonus details . . ." Ha ha ha.

It came to pass.

He invited the local newsman for free drinks that night, filled in the story; the man sure thought it was a funny story. It got printed, front page, above the fold, photo of the Ole Man, his rifle, the deer, and me. All the details printed, too. The deer weighed 228 pounds. Much heavier than Jake's.

I got a nice buck, hunting alone, the day after Thanksgiving. I was hunting in The Bog, near the Birch Rapids "campsite."

Jake received a dozen copies of "The Most Amazing Hunting Trip to Deer Camp." They came in the mail, one at a time, a month apart. One copy of the story was posted at the gas station, at the diner, at work, at the church . . . I mean, the Ole Man really gets around.

3

Scuffin' Smelt at Lower Shin

NO MATTER WHEN YOU GO OUT AT NIGHT, it seems illegal, immoral, or maybe improper. Hunting or fishing should be a daytime activity, shouldn't it?

Yet, there are aspects of the outdoor sports traditionally done under the light. Thrashing through corn with the blue-ticks after a raiding coon or dipping for smelts in ice-cold springwater are examples of nighttime activities that usually bring out the best in the sporting crowd . . . Even the Ole Man likes to go.

The fact is, He goes smelting to get the winter kinks out of his legs, or so He says: "My legs get ridges sagging in the muscles by the time the ice is going and the smelt are running at Lower Shin. The doctor says I need to get out fishin' more." I doubt He has seen a doctor professionally in twenty-five years. But, I let Him tell me this fairy tale every year.

Ramming around in the middle of the night with a ten-foot fine net, a bucket, and a flashlight might not sound social, but it certainly can be. Often we meet our outdoor friends "when the smelts are running." The spawning season only lasts a few weeks each year, and there are only a few nights when the majority of the small silver fish make their move to leave the lake or pond and swim to the spawning beds in a brook or stream.

The people who live near a spawning run are the best ones to say "They're runnin' now." They see flashlights in the night every time they glance outside. Busy spots are especially eerie, with up to two dozen fishermen and fisherwomen flashing in the dark. The kids try smelting, too.

Osmerus mordax, the American smelt, is the prime feed fish for all coldwater game fish. Salmon, togue, and lake-driven brookies are fed right, and properly, on the huge schools of the delectable baitfish. The early settlers of New England were quick to join with the native inhabitants in a spring eating festival centering on frying huge numbers of these fish after first sloshing them in an egg batter and crumb dip. Ahh, perfection in taste. You can even leave the bones in if you choose. They are quickly cooked.

The last time I stopped at the Ole Man's he asked me to keep an eye on the smelt news. As I walked out the door that night I noticed that the leaves were still not raked up from last fall. He had been "busy with woodcock," a thing he does every day of the short season. I couldn't help but smile. House- and yard work were not high on the Ole Man's lists of things to do. Trapshooting or trout fishing or even a Saturday poker game came far ahead of most anything Herself would have as a priority item on her list.

I heard they were runnin' and stopped to see if the Ole Man wanted to go.

"Want to go? Hell, man, I thought you must have been hospitalized or somethin' when you didn't come here by dusk." The usual greeting. I was late by his judgment. Forgot my waders, too. Not a great start.

He has a way of disarming guests, friends, and enemies with outbursts. I had come over on one of my near-daily visits. I thought I had news. I thought He might want to go smelting. It had not been previously discussed that we were going fishing. We both knew it would be soon, although nothing was definite. He now had his smelting stuff out. I guess we were going.

Without a pause, He said, "Smelts are runnin' at Shin. Bud Patterson got his two-quart limit in twenty minutes last night. I don't know how you can be so damn stupid about these important doin's. You know how I like to see those fish all fried in deep fat with corn batter just crispin' its way into every scaley pore. Ain't nothin' I like better. They aren't those starved smelts, either. Those needle smelts aren't worth catchin' or eatin'. Bud's ran big last night, over seven inches on average. Damned fine fish. Damned fine. Nearly ninety percent were males; females were already passed upstream. Peak is passin'. Now, let's get goin'. There's no time to fritter."

In ten minutes we were in His sagging, worn-out Jeep and on our way to Lower Shin Pond. He called his vehicle "Reliable transportation for the places you really want to go." In reality the useful future of the junker was sure to be much shorter than its past. He spent half His spare moments worrying over a noisy bearing or a raunching thump or some other disabling ailment.

At speeds approaching a high of thirty-two miles per hour it was a long twenty miles to the scene. I had to listen while He scolded me for never being prepared for "these obvious emergencies." He lent me some waders, an extra flashlight, and a half-gallon plastic milk container with the top cut away to be able to throw in a handful of smelt at a time.

Our first pass by the bridge showed a "crowd" of maybe six cars and a truck or two parked by the side of the road. It was early in the evening. Nearer midnight the crowd would grow. Smelting is still a popular sport in some places. There was plenty of time to get a limit of smelt in spite of the snips about "being late." According to the Ole Man's own theory, the best runs come after the smaller females have made their way through the stream to the spawning beds. Shortly after dark they make their "first run." The spawning charge often gets much heavier as the night wears on. By dawn there is not a single smelt to be found in the stream. They have returned to the coldwater ponds or lakes and to depths of thirty to a hundred feet, where they spend most of their lives.

The total length of the run varies greatly from lake to lake, but the largest numbers of the smelt population usually spawn in a single week to ten-night span. On any given night the females move up the stream and are closely followed by the males. They ascend the first hundred yards of the stream, rarely going much farther from the lake. This crowding makes for huge concentrations of silvery fish. It is during this

time that the hopeful fisherman wades out in the stream with flashlight and net in hand to try dipping. The use of the light must be minimal so the angler is really "fishing in the dark." On a good sweep you will find a dozen smelt. The average number of dips will generally be much less. Fishermen always hope for great nights with "a three-dip limit," meaning two quarts in three sweeps of the net. Fantastic fishing, but short-lived. You're done fishing in five minutes.

I prefer slower but steadier fishing. When it is slow fishing, one hundred sweeps of the net will yield ten smelt. That makes it more like work. Somewhere in between is preferred.

We didn't stop immediately. We drove up the road for a "thinkin' and schemin' " session. The battered Jeep pulled off on Cyr's logging road and came to a restive halt. It was obvious the Ole Man was up to something. The soft chuckle and twitter coming from His side of the four-by-four was a matter to be reckoned with.

I made some pretty plain offerings to see if He was going to fill me in, but they passed by without a single comment on His part. He wanted to let me in on the plans only by letting me see them develop. After a half-hour of small chuckles and banter about nothing, He decided to turn the Jeep around. "All the game hogs will be gone by now. Won't have to put up with anyone crowdin' us in," He said, as the clunker came into full high at a crunching speed of nearly twenty-five miles per hour.

Back at the bridge a surprising development had taken place. Where once there was a half-dozen cars and a pickup or two, there was now at least three times that number. You could get a quorum for a town meeting. In fact, thinking about it, most of the fishermen in town must have been there, probably with their families.

The next development was even more surprising to me. The Ole Man seemed happier than ever. He actually seemed to enjoy the gathering of a true crowd at his favorite smelt hole. Most unusual. Most unusual, indeed. I can't ever remember him being joyous about any gathering of people, unless it happened to be one brought together to admire a trophy trout He had taken, or perhaps a giant ridge-running buck.

With kind of an uneasy feeling in my stomach I followed Him through the ritual of getting waders in place, checking the flashlight, and getting out a net with the jug to hold fish. He uses a telescoping net with extremely fine netting. They fold up to less than three feet and extend fully to ten feet. His works very well and He treasures it as a valued smelting companion. My net is the conventional ten-footer, which can be tricky to maneuver in the kind of heavy wooded growth where streams tend to wander. He can't resist telling me, "You need to invest in a *GOOD* net. Yours is a terrible excuse for a veteran . . . more like something a kid would carry. Humph."

We sloshed around the first bend in the stream to where the horde of people was in high spirits. I really expected the Ole Man to back away when he saw more than a few people. There were flashlights everywhere, probably nearly two dozen people on this stretch alone. They were busy slamming their nets in the water and working a near froth. I doubled my expectation when I heard the smelt were not running well tonight. Not a single person had gotten a two-quart limit. That explained why so many vehicles were parked back near the bridge.

The Ole Man picked an open spot, near a small ripple. That was His usual place anyway. For some reason no one else found it attractive. I even found my special submerged log was unoccupied. It seemed that no one had been aware of how the spawning smelts were likely to pause in these places to rest out of the main current. The waiting smelt dipper can get a bundle with each dip when the smelt are really running.

My first dip got me nearly a full quart. I couldn't imagine how I could have been so lucky to be in just the right place. Not wanting to make a big fuss and wind up with ten nets thrashing my waters, I eased the fish into my container, which was attached to my waders.

I was standing nearly chest-high in some light currents. The chill of the spring evening was passing through the waders with surprising ease. Water temperatures at this time of year hover awfully close to the freezing mark.

From what I could see, no one was doing well. Time after time they plied the waters and seemed to be getting only a single or two. Occasionally someone would throw a handful in a bucket, but not with regularity. I still was not a believer. This kind of luck never comes my way. In half a dozen passes I now had nearly my limit. Another lick or two should yield me a limit of fish. Then I could stand on the bank while the Ole Man finished up. He wasn't doing as well as I was. That would mean I would beat Him and get to restfully smoke a pipe before He was done fishing. I would enjoy the moment to the fullest. That chance doesn't come very often.

The fact that everyone was easing my way didn't interest me. And then it happened! All hell broke loose. The bottom fell out of my milk container. My fish were all returned to the water instantly. And, as if on some magical timer, my waders began to leak in several places at once, just as the back fell off my flashlight and the batteries fell in the stream.

As if by signal, every light I could see was turned off and bellows of laughter broke forth. I splashed my way safely to shore, but not until after I'd tripped twice over some rocks in midstream. I successfully squeezed in a few rude, crude, and elemental English words, bringing on even more laughter. It was dawning on me that I was the butt of some kind of communal joke. No triumph here.

Wet, cold, humiliated, and fishless, I was back on the bank of the stream and back to square one. Actually, I now had no functioning equipment except for the net. Suddenly I heard the Ole Man in a loud voice say, "One . . . two . . . three." At *three*, the lights came on and every flashlight in the crowd was trained on my disheveled body. It's nothing to be too proud of in regular circumstances, but under these conditions, it was unbearable.

Sheet after sheet of communal laughter rose from the woods. Most of my friends and neighbors were all doubled up in poses that would stick in my mind for years to come. Some had tears in their eyes. Others, the look that spells outlandish joy, just like going 250 straight at trapshooting.

I tried to recover as best I could. My first chore was to get my waders off. They were filled with water. And, it was here that I discovered part of the ploy. Bubblegum, the dime variety, was stuck to everything I had on. It was not as soft as when it was applied, but it was still messy. My bottomless fish container was edged with it. The rear end of the flashlight had bubblegum oozing from the battery compartment. And, my leaky waders had a dozen spots where gum, the ordinary chewing variety, had been used to seal cuts in the material.

I had been had. Someone had gone to a lot of effort to pull this off. It was obvious, to me, that the Ole Man was in on it. His soft chuckles back at the Jeep were now ringing with full-blown sails as He stood some five feet away with side-splitting gales of noisy laughter.

I now noticed, too, how everyone had their limit of the silvery smelt. Full pails were showing from every direction. Suddenly, I noticed a familiar face. My better half was standing there with the broadest grin I'd ever seen her muster. What was even more strange was her being there in the first place. She never went smelting. Never.

She stepped forward and instantly the crowd quieted down. She brought down the house with a simple statement: "Happy anniversary, dear! Thought you'd like to have a little party to celebrate the event."

I never, never forgot again.

4

The One-Gallon Day

NOW DON'T GO GETTING THE WRONG IMPRESSION. The
Ole Man just isn't a hard-drinking man. He will down a few
"social drinks." He will drink a few beers and sit by the fire
while swapping stories. I've even seen Him when He's had a
couple too many.

But, on the average Wednesday afternoon He will be more
straight sober than you or I. I've even seen Him refuse to take
a drink (although that was only once, and then just about the
time He was getting ready to go trout-fishing for the first
time in the spring of the year—a sacred, purifying time).

There was, however, what the Ole Man called a "full, one-
gallon day." It wasn't that the gallon jug of blended whiskey
was to be consumed by Him or me or both of us at a single
setting. It was more the feeling of having plenty to drink—a
casual drink . . . a required drink . . . a drink while feeling
blue. "It's to drink and drown, or get a glow on. It's a platform
from which anyone can launch a campaign, or exchange tri-
umphs or woes with good friends," He said in a quiet voice.

The feeling was like throwing an extra half box of #6's in
your pocket on a special hunt for partridge, even though

your belt was full. Or having a second compass, or a spare dog collar tucked in your game bag. A sense of being ready, aware, full of life, but aware of the possibility of needing a Plan B. The truest form of basic happiness insurance.

There was a one-gallon day I shall always remember. It stands free and clear in my mind. The Ole Man would, I'm sure, think of it as an all-time low in his life. He went from sad to mad, to clearly violent, and even (I think) shed a tear or two along the way.

The loggers had a garden planted on the three-acre plot of ground occupying most of the island. There's no evidence of any previous human activity there now. The second-growth spruce, fir, alder, and maples fill in the void. The look of wilderness.

For us, it's Togue Farm Island. In the years I had known the Ole Man, the waters off Togue Farm always produced truly huge lake trout. Often, we returned them all to the water because He would say, "Too big for just the two of us for lunch, chummy . . . need to keep lookin' for one we can swaller in one gulp." Sometimes they all ran too big, and we wound up eating beans or canned ravioli.

Our trip was planned over an entire winter of blustery nights. Every detail was gone over and over again, to be sure nothing was missing. Eagle Lake is remote, wild; there's no way to run home to get something. "If it ain't there when we get to Eagle, it ain't comin' with us," the Ole Man said many times during the winter.

Thus, little things no bigger than a speck on the horizon got discussed and listed at least three times. We had a functioning list for everything. Breakfast list, lunch list, tools list, cooking ware list, fishing gear list . . . and everything to be taken was packed, loaded, and only then checked off as accomplished.

It's a wonder we could make our way up the lake. Things such as a third Coleman stove were hard to justify. The Ole Man's camp-cooking philosophy was easily summed up: "Everyone who's a decent camp cook knows you need two stoves to cook a meal with, so the third stove is just insurance. We'll find a place to stow it aboard."

The mountain of duffel and eatery was discouraging to see on our day of departure. We had two-layer sleeping bags in case it got chilly at night. I took three flashlights, each with a different purpose. One was a headlamp to be used after dusk for cleaning fish, or any use where you needed both hands. One was an all-purpose 2D-celler He called "Your Plain-Janer light." The third I used for reading at night. It was a super-long-lasting LED with a "focused light" to shine a spot on the book's pages. It works well in a tent where the tent mate is asleep.

The Ole Man took two Leonard fly rods, a pile of Murray Spoons, and his best (and second-best) trolling rods.

His stack of trip duffel was downright awesome. While I had more money invested in camping and fishing gear than my mate would have wanted, mine paled next to His. Maybe with age and a lot more money I'd someday have the range and quality of outdoor equipment the Ole Man already had stored away.

Eventually the boggy days of April gave way to the promise of May. No job obligations or family ties were to stand in the way. Departure Date would soon be set. We were off to a very smooth day in which the gods of business gave us outdoor catalogs—really, dream books filled with promises of expertise and outdoor success.

The sun was out. The temperature hung around sixty. Mac Swallow came in to tell us the ice was moving at Chamberlain Lake (our nearest accessible waterway). Departure Date was now. A gang of friends came to wish us well (I hope it was good cheer and not jeer). Old decrepit Loren Ritchie even came with a tear in his eye because he was no longer able to travel. He was a well-known fisherman in his day. He came from down Greenville way.

Loren was a close friend and rival to the Ole Man. They used to hunt, fish, camp, and sport around together. I thought he had a better backcast and was better on quick timberdoodle shots in heavy cover than the Ole Man—a thought I kept to myself.

Ahead was some time at the Togue Farm. Eagle Lake was calling. As we rode in the overstuffed Jeep with canoe atop and boxes tied to everything with a flat surface, we must have made a funny sight, bouncing down the tarred and then gravel roads to Chamberlain, where access to Eagle was by water.

The Ole Man was just full of impossible promises and theories as to the best time to hit The Farm. He even went so far as to predict we would soon get the biggest lake trout to be taken all summer by anyone hereabouts. A winter of

serious planning made His head wide with overinflated confidence.

Although He wouldn't show me His super weapon, I knew he banked heavily on a tiny Black Gnat fly creative imitation for brookies. He brought the fly into being on a Fuzz Ball #16. He added a single white strand of hackle on the center. The white was slightly taller than the fly. He felt he had made a "Killer combination primarily for brook trout but sure to kill togue, too." We'll see someday.

The Ole Man used a magnifying glass to tie small flies. His eyes were showing age. But, to me, the tiny flies in #12, #16, or even some #20's were simply too small to cast from a boat. Get a light breeze and the fly has no weight. He thought otherwise, and I had seen Him be effective with some mighty tiny flies tossed artfully to waiting fish. Time and time again I watched with a degree of respect and amazement.

Our last stop was for gas for the Jeep. Wilderness was now ours to enjoy. We needed to put sixty-four miles behind us. We were supplied for a seven-day minimum with a maximum of ten days, or even two weeks. The ladies at home wouldn't yell for help for two weeks if we failed to reappear. Gives you a feeling of freedom . . . say what.

The Ole Man told Herself, "I'll be home when I get here. Don't expect to see me until then." I tried to be a little more diplomatic domestically.

The owners of pretty modern cars and pickups and SUVs were not thrilled by our slow progress. There was a liberal use of their horns as we poked along. One of the guys we knew later told us, "I thought you were packed for Africa for a summer's safari when I saw the pile of junk you folks managed to squeeze into that wreck."

Inside the Jeep was far noisier than a 747. Much more cramped, too. There was a fear of fly-rod backlash or flying mustard jars at every turn or bump of the wheel. The canoe racks moaned and groaned under the load. The glove compartment bulged with last-minute thoughts. Even under the hood there was a small, specially installed rack holding three extra quarts of oil, just in case. Also under the hood was the toolbox, which was always kept stocked because of a trip several years ago when things went awry because there was no wire to replace a broken muffler hanger. We made it home after seventeen stops to replace monofilament line used in place of wire. We didn't have wire and the line worked fine until it burned through. Not fun; definitely not fun. So, the toolbox always went fully loaded on any Jeep adventure.

Deep down in the packing was a full gallon of Canada's finest rye whiskey, ready for any emergency. It was not there to use as regular daily fare. It was the spare of all spares.

Matagamon, Webster, Telos were soon passed by. The gravel road was now a lesser path. We never went down the main-drag logging road most people used. Why take the easy way? When we did chime in on the main logging road, it wasn't too far to Big Indian Brook, our access for life at Togue Farm on Eagle. Relaxation was getting easier with every inch gained. We were psyched; maybe too much.

It soon became clear we could not take all of these "necessaries" on the fifteen-mile trip up Big Eagle Lake in a canoe. We needed a naval transport ship. Something must give. A lot of somethings. Our alternative was two trips. We would use some of the extra gas we brought with us. The Ole Man propelled the canoe with a four-horse outboard he called the "little kicker." We used it off and on, mixed with a lot of paddling. When he said, "The little kicker won't use much gas," I knew he had decided on two trips up the lake.

It was hours before dark, time for two runs watching the wildness slip by with every dip of the canoe in a light, breezy chop. Trip one's payload held lots of heft, but the load was distributed evenly. It was safe travel. There is a time to be somewhat reckless. This wasn't one.

It was a long, long day . . . memorable, but filled with so many parts, we just wanted to get camp set up and all goods delivered. The blue sky was unreal in a deep color fringed in nature's best greenery. The mission was going well. The temperature was still warm, high enough for us to feel the spring heat.

The Ziegler campsite was perfect. The setting is high, dry ground with huge spruce, pine, fir, maple, yellow birch, and hemlock, and it was empty. We piled our stuff in one giant heap, laying claim to the best waterfront site. All was perfect for run number two to get the remaining stuff.

We decided to make a one-time pass by Togue Farm trolling grounds to see what our glorious future held—at least, what was coming for the next week or so. This would be our opening burst of memories in fishdom. A new tale to tell.

Our sewed-on live bait barely touched the gravel bottom of Eagle, off Togue Farm, before we knew we were in the exact right place. We both felt the jolt of a hard-hitting lake trout, a two-at-one-time deal. We allowed the canoe to swing with the wind while we played the fish to the surface. Mine was a four-pounder. A nice start. I quickly released it and grabbed my camera for a fast click of the Ole Man's six-pound "cooler-size" togue. He held him up for a second and, as usual, said to the fish, "Live long, grow bigger, keep on producin'." Back to the water.

We rarely keep many fish from Eagle. A few get eaten every extended trip, but the 99 percent majority get returned to the water a few seconds after landing. No harm done. The Ole Man said, "If we kept too many fish from the Togue Farm, how would we ever know whether the fishin' was not good on any given day, or whether the lake was just plain fished out?"

Except for the fishing swing by Togue Farm, the second run down the lake to get the rest of our stuff was uneventful—simply a nice May day under the sun, with a slight breeze, the land of spruce, fir, pine passing slowly by. We kept to the edge of the puddle.

As soon as we got back to the Ziegler campsite we got the tent up. A spiritual sense of happiness settled over both the Ole Man and me. Nothing quick, just an unspoken sense we had arrived—after all the planning, all the hours of preparation, we were in the one spot on the planet where we wanted to be. Nirvana.

Gone were the thoughts of trophies, competitions, business, bill-paying—everything. The Ole Man took out a Leonard rod and I grabbed an Orvis Battenkill. I liked to fish brook trout on a little Rusty Rat. I already knew He would be using the special Black Gnat creations with the strip of white. We eased the Old Town canvas canoe out into Eagle to try a few casts on a little stream nearby. It's called Belle Bottom.

The trout of Belle Bottom run above average, getting a few takes after only an hour or so of wading and careful casting. We'd release all of the beauties. It was already agreed. The Ole Man stood by a small riffle he liked because "The trout can move around but I don't have to." He could cast downstream or up-. He caught the first fish and quickly started bragging about his winter's creation. "Gosh darned if I ain't got a real winner here. Boy, oh, boy. This is sure to be a national favorite. It's destiny!" That flushed away the previous feelings of peace on earth. I moved upstream.

By dusk we paddled slowly back to camp, saving gas for the "little kicker" for the more-serious chore of trolling at the Togue Farm. The Ole Man turned to me and said, "This has been a real one-gallon day, it certainly has. I hope I have a few more of them left in me." The Canadian whiskey was still back at the Jeep. We didn't really need it.

5

Herself Spring-Cleans the Freezer

EVERY YEAR AS WINTER TURNS to the pleasant afternoons
of spring, the Ole Man's household comes alive with pails
of water laced with white vinegar and pails of water laced
with ammonia. The drapes come down to be dry-cleaned
and the household disruption reigns in every room except
the cozy cavern where the boys play, and even that will
eventually get sandblasted with abrasive cleansers once the
boys get out of doors more often. Finding an empty den
isn't hard once the spring ice moves around and West
Grand Lake becomes fishable. Herself has much to do and
the last step will be, as she says, "To cleanse the freezer of
things you never should have brought home from the wild
in the first place." She had several things in mind. Nearly
every fall the Ole Man "snagged" a couple or three American mergansers to add to the larder, often a couple on every
early duck hunt, jump-shooting narrow passages in snake-
like streams and wide brooks.

"Mergansers make good paddin' for the season's tally when Jake, or some other know-it-all, insists on a SEASON'S TOTAL TALLY," the Ole Man would snicker toward the end of each waterfowl season. When these mergansers were wrapped in freezer paper He labeled them with a code. When the duck was really a wood duck, He put that on the freezer label. When it was a merganser He'd scrawl "mangled woodie" or "smashed teal" or "heavily damaged pinhead." Herself knew His crazy shorthand well, and also knew she was expected to produce a gourmet dinner from these creatures which she referred to as "FISH-EATING, FOUL-SMELLING droppings you expect me to save for the table." With only a slight shift in body demeanor she'd add, "Why you put such meat in the freezer is beyond me. There are plenty of good ducks to bring home, and you bring TRASH QUACKERS. It's beyond me," and she'd turn and leave the room in a huffy exit. The Ole Man pays no attention except to add, in a soft voice and with a snicker, "Herself ain't always blooming with love, is she?"

Jake Goodwin made the whole exercise necessary because when the season finale always left the Ole Man as the top gunner, Jake would pull a freezer inspection to personally size up the Ole Man's claims. Except for American mergansers or the occasional hooded merganser, or some fish-eating specialists such as the American coot from inland or costal hunts, a TRUE *COUNT* of either Jake or the Ole Man was always very close. Fish eaters were not counted, except by the creative label scrawls of the Ole Man, making sure He won the seasonal tally.

When spring cleaning was nearing an end, Herself would casually say, "It's time to clean the freezer." It was a marital code where it was understood He would invite the guests and Herself would "fancy up your marshy woodland trash food." He would later let it be known how many, and when.

In addition to spring-cleaning waterfowl, there were sometimes packages of bear meat, raccoon roasts, or even the occasional attempt to turn trapped beaver rumps into good food. Nothing was beyond salvage if the Ole Man got it for free, on a bet, or for any other reason that seemed to give an advantage over another outdoorsman.

There was the time Mike Bayberry homesteaded on a logging road close to the trout-rich Swift Brook Meadows. Mike was trying to make a go of it in a long-abandoned trapper's cabin his grandfather had used at a time when furs were a common trim, lining, collar, or main material for clothing of all types. The prices back then were high enough to make a good subsistence living. Today, things were different. Prices were lower because of diminished demand. Whether Mike could make a living from the proceeds of trapping was questionable. The Ole Man and I stopped to talk to Bayberry one afternoon in the early fall when he was working on raccoon furs. One thing led to another, and they left with several hindquarters from freshly taken coons.

About six months later Herself put up an awful fuss over these neatly wrapped packages put at the very bottom of a top-loading freezer that normally held berries, apples, fiddleheads, asparagus from the garden, as well as homemade bread, a pie or two, and sometimes cookies. Meat of any kind was never, never kept in what Herself called "the heart of home cooking." I mean, it just wasn't done. She demanded to know what she was supposed to do with something labeled "coon haunch." The Ole Man seemingly had been expecting this confrontation to happen, because without hesitation he said, "I got a chance to get *free meat* from a trapper friend, and thought it would go right well with your annual wild-stuff-freezer-cleanser meals for our neighbors. I was trying to help you out by adding variety, so I tucked these coon packages on the bottom of the freezer where they would be safe until spring came. I see you found them."

Herself was not amused. "What other surprises, pray tell, have you got squirreled away somewhere?"

"Well, now that you ask, I've got an offer from the widow Trask . . . Jim got a nice bear during deer season and then had the heart attack—remember?"

I thought there would be an explosion. Instead she said, "Lydia already told me you were storing bear meat in her freezer and asked me about our CLEAN-OUT MEAL. Is that it? Nothing else. You're like a vulture grabbing carrion off a highway." The Ole Man told her there was nothing else. "This year's CLEAN-OUT is going to be lacking variety with just mergansers, some salty coot, the raccoon haunches, and a few pounds of bear meat. I got to figure out who gets an invite. What else you making to spice up the occasion?"

Not a single word was said in answer. Herself was still mumbling when distance made the room silent. "She's a pretty good cook; I'm sure there will be plenty to eat," the Ole Man said.

There was never a debate about Herself's cooking skills. She came to the marriage with a family history of home cooking. Her mother taught her basics like making white bread. How much kneading was needed or when to add extra flour, how to check the yeast, even the choice of cooking pans, with glass preferred above metals, pottery, or ceramics. Her mother told her, "Glass has uniform heat and makes the bread more uniform in height and color." These marriage-entry cooking skills included cranberry/walnut muffins that she made, as she made nearly everything—from scratch. Biscuits made with the Bakewell recipe right off the can were always fabulous. The Bakewell secret is cream of tartar, and good cooks everywhere know how to use that in home biscuits, with or without the New England traditional use of a few spoons of Bakewell when you double or triple

the basic biscuit recipe. Good home cooking. Some very fine eating.

The Ole Man decided to concentrate on the guest list. One year wives were invited, but it proved difficult, even with Herself cooking the wild food, to get everyone interested in eels fried in sautéed onions, a touch of garlic, and steeped in locally made farm-fresh butter. The Ole Man's solution was to "tell them it's a special seafood that's a part of every Hollywood party. If they think it's highfalutin, they'll all gulp it down and ask for more. You know how them Hollywood wowsies are."

The response was quick: "If you think our friends should be fooled, why don't *you* cook the food!"

The eels reverted back to eels and were actually quite popular with some guests. The men gathered in the den near the beer keg and the women gathered in the kitchen and living room. By evening's end it was decided the spring-time freezer clean-out meal would be mostly male outdoor friends who enjoyed the odd food and swilled their way through gallons of beer and Old Stump Blower by the half-gallon, and for a few wives who didn't mind helping Herself in the kitchen with a couple of glasses of wine, and the conversation often featuring the men in the den.

Assuming I was invited, I dropped in one night after work. The time for ice-out was coming. The clean-out dinner should normally be before ice-out.

"CLEAN-OUT DINNER is Saturday night, with cordials beginning at 4:30 and eatin' at 6:30, or thereabouts, depending on how long the before-dinner booze lasts," the

Ole Man said as I entered the lair. "I already asked everyone else I want comin', but you have to keep a short stockpile of booze until after the meal. I mean, their lies and tall tales can become boring if they drink too much on an empty stomach." I guess I was invited.

When I got home my wife said, "Herself is a terrific cook, and when she called me to help with the dinner, I found I was one of a crew of six wives helping out. When I asked how many guests, she said, 'Well, I guess about thirty, but some will drink, taste the food, and leave, having met their social obligation, but others come and stay forever. A few are not invited but come anyway. Once the party gets started, no one cares about anything except the upcoming fishing season, food, drink, and storytelling."

I nodded my head. We both knew. It was a spring party after another long, long winter was past, officially marked by the Ole Man's CLEAN-OUT festivities.

Pickup trucks, sport utility vehicles, and even a few cars filled the front lawn and driveway to the Ole Man's house at the appointed time. There was still a little chill in the April air as I found a parking place. My wife had driven over earlier to help Herself in the kitchen. Judging by the odors, the food preparation was reaching a climax. I always tried several dishes because they were different, and a chance to eat a bear burger or have a slab of roasted coon hindquarter glazed with homemade pear butter, cooked with carrots and baker-sized potatoes with skins still on. The baked potatoes were grown the previous summer in this backyard, along with the carrots, turnips, squash, and other veggies.

The pear butter was just one of the many preserves Herself put up each year to keep the pantry full. Tonight much of the food was home-based. All was home-cooked. I went around to the back to join the men in the den.

The sliding-glass door was open, so I heard Pearly Wheaton ask Jake Goodwin about a dip Herself had just dropped off to go with the plates of cheese, crackers, potato chips, pretzels, olives, salsa, mixed nuts, peanuts, and now a pile of pita bread. Several guys were trying this mound of small meat bits covered in marinade and special sauce. They took the pita bread, heaped on the good-smelling meat bits, and threw on grated cheese. Since some were making a second round, I wondered what it was. I tried a small dose.

The meat was dark, soft, and was flavored with brandy. In the pita bread with Canadian grated cheese, it was *very* good. It was not until much later I realized that Herself had taken a French chef's recipe for cow's liver to be served as bits in a sauce and served as hors d'oeuvres that I found we were actually eating mergansers and coot with a lot of fancy doctoring. It was good. I liked the brandy taste with duck. The taste of a critter whose diet is mostly fish was soaked away with sharp spices, alcohol, and time. Even the women loved this concoction.

I never did hear how Jake answered Pearly's question, but I did see Jake go back for seconds of the meaty dip. I asked, "What do you think this meat-sauce-dip thing is anyway?" Jake shrugged and answered, "That woman can cook any wild meat and make it taste great. From the texture I would say it was originally a duck or goose; more than that, I can't tell. It makes a nice snack when you pile on the strong Canadian cheddar. It's a hit with me."

A head count would have shown more than thirty people were here, mostly hunters and fishermen and their wives, but Warden Clements stopped by for an appearance, as did Deputy Mac Dobbins, who was always looking for good gossip to add to his repertoire. He turned down the drinks but loaded up with a plate of bear roast, coon haunch, mashed potato, baked potato, fiddleheads, and carrots. All the food was on the dining-room table, and the people just roamed everywhere.

When Mr. Keegan arrived, there was a swirling whisper around the rooms as each group passed the news to the other. The Ole Man came out to greet the new guest, saying, "Well, now, this is a pleasant surprise! Mr. Keegan, I believe this is your first appearance at our annual SPRING CLEAN-OUT DINNER . Can I get you a drink?"

Mr. Keegan was all smiles, happy to be invited, as he was normally passed by at social events, so he said, "Yes, I'll have some coffee with just a little cream. No sugar. Thanks." Without missing a beat the Ole Man led him to the kitchen, where there was a borrowed church hall–size coffeemaker.

"Fresh coffee we have," He said, as the room full of women greeted the boss man. Most of their husbands worked at the plant, and Chub Foster's wife, Linda, who worked there too as a forklift driver on the loading dock, said, "I'll get you a plate in the dining room, Mr. Keegan; there's more food than we can eat."

The Ole Man faded away. It was a pretty slick coup, inviting the big boss. A grinning Ole Man returned to the den. All was well.

Chub Foster was discussing a new trout fly featuring closely trimmed grouse feathers with Peter Qualey when the Ole Man came back in the den. "Hey, Chub, your wife's squiring the boss around the dining room. You ought to get extra brownie pay next week. Already, you get two checks." There was a laugh and Chub said, "Linda's good at that kind of thing. I leave the politicking to her. I'd rather stay right here with the snack food and the booze, if it's all the same to you."

Some of the guests were friends from work; most were outdoorsmen, and the sprinkle of guests like Mr. Keegan and Warden Clements just added to the party, especially when they left and the hard-core got down to tales and stories. Spring planning was afoot, and each story was angled in a different direction. Pete McNally just wanted winter to be over. "I like ice-fishing and I love snowmobiling, but I hate *driving* with ice and snow. About this time of year I just want green grass, trout biting, and I like to get out to Matagamon to open up the camp for the summer. Know what I mean?" They all agreed, but each had a different version.

There were really two party gatherings developing speed, as the men clearly preferred the Ole Man's den and backyard, while the women graced the kitchen and living room. Claire Cody asked Herself about the creamed asparagus served in a casserole dish. She said, "I just wonder where you got that much *fresh* asparagus at this time of year.

It's hard to find in the store right now—and that spicy sauce was delightful." It was this kind of thing that made preparing this dinner all worthwhile.

While the Ole Man's men friends just shoveled in the food and booze, the women were more respectful and appreciative. Herself answered, "Well, Claire, I think it's because we take such care of our garden food. Putting up the seasonal food is half the battle of good meals. The asparagus I used tonight was actually last year's crop from our hundred-foot double rows of Martha Washington asparagus. We've had the same planting for many, many years, and I pick the stalks every day in late April through the middle of May. I take cuttings of no more than ten-inch-high spears. They are the most tender. I sort them in bags in the freezer so that all the asparagus in each bag are precisely the same. I make sure each stalk is dry before being put in the freezer bag, and I throw all the culls in the refrigerator to be eaten soon after harvest. Asparagus, fiddleheads, and rhubarb are serious spring crops. They take a lot of time, but are sure worth it in the long run.

"Paying attention to details is very important. For instance, fiddleheads must be processed in the canner and stored in Mason jars. Fiddleheads simply slapped willy-nilly in the freezer stay fresh for only a few weeks. We grow seventy-five tomato plants and process from fifty to seventy-five quarts and pints of tomato sauce, simmered for six hours on the stove, processed for forty-five minutes with our home-grown oregano, basil, dill, fennel, Stuttgart onions, and with a few cut-up sage leaves added. We make about seven to eight quarts in a batch and label each batch."

Suddenly realizing that not only Claire but several other women were listening, Herself filled in the details about the sour cream and dill sauce on the asparagus, and how much rhubarb it took to make three pies. With barely a breath she explained why the Maine shrimp and pasta salad was made better by adding celery, olives, and onions, and topping it with EVOO (extra virgin olive oil) and three-quarters of the dressing with Modena, Italy's balsamic vinegar, as the remainder.

It was a Herself performance of great knowledge, and it impressed the younger women in the same way the Ole Man captured the younger outdoorsmen with embellished tales of catching a trophy brook trout.

Basic knowledge honed sharply by decades of practice, the spring freezer clean-out party was the talk of the town for weeks. A couple of the men had to be driven from the den by their wives, who then drove them home. Too much booze made a few unaccompanied men sleep over on the den couch and floor. But, they were fine in the morning. The winter's ice cover was getting ready to fully clear West Grand Lake and SPRING FISHING was at hand. Bless the ICE-OUT days. It was a short season of gushing water and full creels, with the freezer dinner as a starter gun.

6

Collectin' Used Flies

MY BUTT WAS GETTING SORE from sitting in the Ole Man's den for three hours. I was waiting for Him to get off the midnight shift. It was a command performance that He'd ordered: "If you're a friend of mine, I'll expect to see you in my den as soon as I get off the shift. It's important." I wanted to be there; the mystery intrigued me.

Herself was out to some woman thing, so I used my key to get in the back door. I had a key to His house and He had one to mine. Made it easier if something came suddenly on the scene.

I arrived early because it was easier to tell my wife I was going to drop over to the Ole Man's early in the evening than it was to explain to her why I was going out so late. You know what I mean? So, when I saw Him half running, half fast-walking, coming down the street, I knew the Ole Man was up to something. He was never that happy unless it was something related to hunting or fishing. Perhaps an early start on trout fishing was in my near future.

"I can't believe we ain't there yet. We oughta be already gone," He spouted when the door was barely open. He

looked at me as though I should already have my hip waders on. "They must have used worms, or some other trick.
Maybe dynamite or something to get those lunkers," He
said, while whirling around the den, gathering gear.

He threw His work coat in the corner as He continued
to gather stuff, piling fishing gear up as He said, "There isn't
a decent fisherman in that crowd, and they can't be that
lucky. No one is without some kinda voodoo. Shoulda seen
me sneak into Charlie's cellar to get a really close look.
From the color of the dorsal fin I'd say those fish came from
Hurd Pond; no place else around with that deepa shade of
black. One of them would go five pounds . . . I shoulda
brought along my own scales."

The Ole Man was really excited, all right, but I didn't
have a clue as to what the story was or what He had
planned, since it seemed to include me. Finally the details
tumbled out. Grabbing me by the shoulders and pulling me
close He got back to the beginning.

"I was over to Roger's when Harry came by with a three-
pound trout to give Roger. Now you know Harry never gave
anything to anyone unless he was braggin' or overstocked.
Well, sir, I forgot all about the gun tradin' I was doing with
Roger. See, Harry mouthed off some more about there being
plenty more where those came from, and how there were
bigger ones taken, too. He said Jake Goodwin was the
leader of the expedition, swearing them all to secrecy." The
Ole Man was full of this fish story. Getting more animated
by the moment. More agitated by the second. Nothing

made HIM more crazy than to think Jake Goodwin was one step ahead of Him.

"So I left Roger's with the excuse of a headache and snuck over to Charlie's cellar for a closer look. There, on top of his chest freezer, were some uncleaned trout. The fish were still fresh, very, very fresh. The colors were faded, but not by much. I think they must have come home and headed out to brag before even cleaning the fish. I told you, they ain't real fishermen—never even stopped to clean their fish. Amateurs."

He wasn't done yet, making it clear there was more to come.

"Every trout was a real lunker, and Charlie left a note to his wife that read: 'Sweetie, when you get these fish cleaned, be sure to mark them only with the date and Jake Goodwin's trip. I want to be able to grab them to show my friends.' Ain't this amazing, how these guys pulled this off?"

His eyes were glowing with fire, envy, excitement, and revenge. Not much could equal being stomped by an archrival.

"Ahhh, I said to myself. I got this all figured out. There was a fly book lying there right by the mess of fish. I took a little peek. There it was, a new fly, and it was still wet. Evidence, I tell ya. Evidence. It's a variation of the Sparse Gray we always use on Dead Stream. I took a little more liberty and took three wet samples with me so we can make exact copies."

He whipped out the liberated samples; a handful of more poorly tied flies you have never seen. A rank amateur must have tied these flies, with the lights turned out, and while recovering from a hangover of mammoth proportions. But the Ole Man's mood was unshakable; he had His theory.

We immediately got out the vise and tied up some copies, a few like the ones the Ole Man liberated, a few of better quality, but better in execution and detail. The Ole Man was pleased with His investigation. He hurried to say, "I was smart going to Charlie London's house, because he and Jake Goodwin are both sneaky, conniving, miserable, rotten, creepy, crazy yahoos who are fishermen. Nowhere near as good as you and I."

He was as psyched as the night he drank a whole bottle of Old Stump Blower in one sitting. I mean, He was fun just to watch get ready to go fishing. It would be hilarious once we got out on the road to Hurd Pond.

"It doesn't even need to be light. We can go early, right as soon as you get your stuff packed," He said while putting the new flies in a small box for His fishing vest. Mentioning home reminded me I needed to tell my wife we were going tomorrow; actually, it was already the early morning hours of the next day. This day we would slay the lunker brook trout at Hurd.

The Ole Man was breathing scales as He impatiently waited for me to gather my gear. My wife was totally unconvinced this trip was "absolutely necessary," as I told her, but in the end she allowed a somewhat favorable smile as we waved our good-byes.

Jake Goodwin's success was the tragedy in the Ole Man's life. It needed to be corrected, changed in outcome, rectified

in local lore. It *must* be outdone. In three hours we had the old Jeep within three feet of Hurd Pond. It was still pitch-black. That didn't stop the Ole Man, who was churning up the water within seconds of arrival. He worked as if every cast was going to produce a new star on the angling horizon.

He tried letting the fly lie dead on the water for fifteen seconds, then giving it a twitch, creating a slight ripple. Variations included popping it in the air every two seconds, just high enough to create a surface disturbance, or keeping the fly twitching in an erratic surface loop. The battle raged in darkness, in early dawn and the full light, but the search for a lunker was still going on. We each had caught and released several good brook trout, up to fifteen inches in length, but no lunkers matching, let alone besting, Jake Goodwin's tribe. My arms were getting tired from casting.

The Ole Man even tried some of the flies Charlie London had "donated" for our trip. Nothing; at least, nothing big. We were not doing well. Right place. Right time. Right flies, taken right from the gift horse Himself, by Himself. Still, something was wrong. He fussed and fumed through the next several hours. It got to be noon, and since last night was His last round on that shift and this was a day before the next shift began at work, He could fritter time away.

Fritter, flop, splash, retie, redo, retry, retake, twist, turn, wiggle, flick, or cast, we were unable to come anywhere near the Goodwin Party record. It occurred to me that we might be fishing on the wrong pond. Maybe the Ole Man was wrong. Oh no, I wasn't voicing that thought.

At dusk his mood was already downright mean. He had not slept last night, and He had worked before skipping the sleep. I was dead on my feet. The ride home would be silent. We had caught nice brook trout, but none were mates of Jake Goodwin's. *Brrrr! Brrrr!*

When we got back to the Jeep it got even worse. There was a neatly typed piece of paper under the windshield wiper on the driver's side. He took it and asked me to read it aloud. It read:

Glad you liked the flies so well as to steal them. I only paid a dime at a church yard sale for the whole lot. It was tied by a seven-year-old who then gave up fishing. Next time you need exercise, I'll bring over some more trout from Labrador. You remember how some of us had our best brook trout quick-frozen by the commercial plant up there last fall, on our caribou hunt? Well, we certainly have enjoyed them this spring. We took them out of the freezer to behead, clean, and get ready for family dinners. We're getting together tomorrow to show our Labrador pictures.

We decided to plant some ideas in your puny mind, Ole Man. It worked better than we ever thought, thanks to you guys. You're invited to our dinner at the community hall tomorrow at high noon. Bring a guest. We'll be showing our slides and bringing our photo albums.

It was signed "Jake, Harry, Charlie, and the rest of the gang."

There was a P.S. to the letter. Handwritten, it read, "You need to hold your arm higher on the backcast and try adding a little classier hat."

The ride home was less than silent.

7

There Are Only Two Kinds of Firewood: Rock Maple or None

SEPTEMBER IS FIREWOOD MONTH. We cut the wood, pile it after a careful splitting, and let it rest for thirteen months. By then it is ready for duck season. It will be seasoned, making it dry enough for a quiet fire. The Ole Man likes quietly burning wood in his fires unless He's just getting one going with kindling. "Quiet fires give off more heat and don't waste time with sizzlin' or snappin'."

This annual trek to get the firewood ready is as much a part of duck hunting as buying a duck stamp. We peer into every overflow, sneak up on every bend in the road, or paddle every reedy cove as though the ducks were waiting and the guns were ready. Preseason rituals have a habit of growing larger rather than falling by the wayside. It's built into the sporting fraternity.

The weather this time of year is pleasantly ideal. It's still too warm during the day for serious thoughts about hunting, but the nights remind you that winter is not too far away. Frost can come at any time, making the vegetation die back to its various hues of brown. Then the hunter feels his blood stirring.

A walk after dark along the shore of a marsh requires a warm sweater and a fast pace. Even then the chilling winds can cut short your night dreaming of good times that have been had out there among the marshes and pines in the daylight hours.

The Jeep wound its way around the last twisty turns, leading to Home Base, a name the Ole Man had given to his duck-hunting haven. He purchased it from a retired Boston banker who could no longer muster the energy to brave the blustery fall days when "the blacks were drivin' for home base." I think He bought it so cheaply because the aging banker wanted someone who loved duck hunting, black duck hunting especially, as much as he did. Someone who would really use it. The Ole Man never talks about Home Base except to say that it deserves a dynasty of another thousand duck seasons to finish out its career. "It got started by someone who loved to hunt, and it will die when someone stops coming here with a cache of well-oiled guns, grub, and Old Stump Blower. Someone like us." He'd pace and add, "That's just the way it is. Takes time every fall to get things ready for open season."

As buildings go it is no great monument. The cedar logs are full cut and held in place by huge spikes. All the corners are notched, and the rafters are simply peeled whole spruce logs. White pine boards are laid on the floor and roof. Split cedar shakes are closely layered against the fall and winter weather. Seen from a distance the curly smoke from the fieldstone fireplace is a fixture when the sportsmen are here. The fireplace rocks were all gathered on-site, many with solid colors, such as the white quartz and coal-black mica, a hard smooth rock often used for jewelry by some craftsmen.

The fireplace inside gives out the heat with an old fashioned Atlantic damper as the only brass adornment. There is a combination kitchen–living room, with two bedrooms off to the side. The kitchen has wood heat, too. The stove is a Glenwood Number 35 with light green panels; a water tank on the right holds ten gallons of hot water, and the oven is just under the four burners above. Each burner has a cover allowing the pot or pan to receive direct heat or to be protected by the cast-iron cover.

Each of the bedrooms has two double beds of the type that have high iron corners and slouching, sagging mattress centers. You can sleep only by allowing your body to be rolled to the center of the mattress. The metal springs creak and groan at your every sigh. The quilted blankets are leftovers from the previous owner and date to the middle of the last century.

A lean-to-type woodshed covers about half the length of the camp on the back side. It is three-sided and, like the camp beds, a little bit of sagging shows in the middle. Winter snow loads on the roof have not always been quickly tended by the owners, including the present one.

Still more to the rear is the permanent home of the gracious and well-received Sears catalog (or any other catalog with a certain kind of soft paper). Various reading materials are stored there, too. I've seen some frosty mornings when I would have given a tidy sum to be a little closer to something more similar to a Best Western facility and made a very short visit to this outdoor experience.

The Ole Man says the woodshed will hold "a strong three cord, but we need to cut five." I think we actually cut about seven cords of rock maple every fall, because there is a growing pile of seasoned wood that inches closer to the back door with every passing season. We never do seem to burn as much as we cut. It is one of the few excesses the Ole Man ever does when it comes to hard labor. I think, if the truth be known, it would be because he enjoys these firewood trips, and doesn't want to see them end too quickly, even if we already have plenty of wood. I made such a suggestion once, but got such a spirited tirade back I decided to lay off any further suggestions.

"You're gettin' so you sound like my wife. Always lookin' for ways to criticize me when I am willing to put in a day's work. We're here to cut wood; now let's get to it—right after we check out the Black Hole, where that whole flight settled in last fall. Remember the time when you got lucky and doubled on them the first fall you ever came out here?" I did, indeed.

The Black Hole was well named. It is a shallow cove with a narrow sandy spit, a bunch of scrubby pines, and, most importantly, a beautiful natural blind out near the point. The black ducks scoop in over the sandy point to get to the delicious wild rice beds and "duck grasses" lining the other shore. Prevailing winds usually bring the waterfowl right over the natural blind.

It's the absence of cover that makes ducks unwary of the barren approach across the narrow point. I have always suspected the Ole Man carefully planted that cover shortly after buying the camp. It's just too perfect. But, He swears it is "an act of nature that is just naturally an aide to God's hunters."

What makes me suspicious is that the small firs are the only ones of that species for a mile in either direction. Even more dubious is the fact they never seem to get much taller. He says, "They's jest a wee bit stunted, that's all; probably poor soil out there on that point."

In any case, on this day we edged up to the blind and found two families of black ducks, and one wood duck pair with a blue-winged teal wedge feeding along the grassy bed. Suddenly, the Ole Man jumped up in plain view and the ducks set their wings for the roof. He never said a word, but I knew as we watched them drive for another county that He was thinking the real test was only a few weeks away.

"Let's go cut wood!" And we did.

We could have purchased some cheap stumpage only a half-mile from the camp. The wood was mixed beech, birch, and a few lesser trees, for firewood purposes, like white ash and hornbeam—so-called "ironwood," often used by handle makers for the best handles on hand tools. But the Ole Man was adamant about having only maple—and not white maple, either, just red or sugar or "rock" maple. Rock maple dries quickly, splits easily, burns quieter, and burns hotter; at least, that's what I have been told.

Because of the "absolute need" for rock maple, we endured a twenty-mile ride in the bucking Jeep with an overloaded utility trailer thrashing around behind for the return trip. The maximum number of trips per day was about three, although once I recall we did four when an approaching special early teal season was announced by the state regulators. It caught us unaware.

That was the year we were going to get a "parcel of those early birds." It didn't quite work out as planned. The first trouble was with the Jeep on the way to Home Base. As we flashed our lights around the engine and considered the solutions, it was obvious we needed a water pump. Getting one in the middle of the night is a real trick anywhere, but for a model Jeep the military had dumped decades ago, it was even more effort. It involved getting the parts dealer out of bed (he's a duck hunter, too), and it involved taking a water pump off an even more beat-up old Jeep in what the Ole Man calls "the permanently parked" area of junkers, behind the parts dealer's place of business. As I said, it gets complicated.

We arrived at Home Base well after sunrise. The Ole Man mumbled, grumbled, and seemed about ready to throw a fit. Going duck hunting after dawn is always weird, but going without any sleep is just another strange way to get out on a good hunt. When we arrived we found someone had "permanently borrowed" our duck boat, so we had to go back to town to get mine.

When the Ole Man saw my craft, he always said, "Now that's a second-class boat to hunt ducks from; the sides are

way too high. It'll scare the dickens out of any respectable duck, even a merganser." He thought mergansers, particularly the American merganser, were cluttering up the duck population with their terribly fishy meat. "They even smell like fish when you throw them in the bottom of the boat," he said. My boat stayed where it was. The Ole Man decided my aluminum canoe was a better second choice.

Even the Jeep seemed to be running hot when we arrived back at camp with an aluminum canoe to get a very belated chance at the very early teal season. He said, "Those silver bullets are a poor excuse for a hunting craft." I didn't bother to state the obvious. With his regular duck-hunting boat among the missing, and my high-sided craft disliked, it was down to the Silver Bullet, a rather plain aluminum canoe.

The final ripple in the gathering storm was when we found that the missing boat had been returned to its rightful place, and that the person who'd "borrowed" it had brought it back with a few teal feathers still left on the bottom. The Ole Man never did find out who the person or persons were who took the boat, but he had it figured that it must have been someone He knew, someone who wanted to get a devil's revenge. The Ole Man was widely known in the sporting community, and He had pulled off some real tricks against others he saw as "needing a lesson." The bird had come home to roost.

Tim Judson was a possible trickster because the Ole Man had switched his trap loads for buckshot in a club championship shoot-off. Tim did poorly on the round and lost the $100 cash prize, realizing too late what (and who) had happened. Or Roger Thurlow, whose togue spoons were "exchanged" for brook-trout spinners on opening day as the ice left West Grand Lake for the year. Just two of the possible duck boat thieves.

We did each get a limit of ducks that day, but only after considerably more mileage and effort. The Ole Man was even blaming them for the bad water pump in the Jeep and the high banking shot to the right that He missed on a rising drake. "Those boat thieves disturbed my concentration for the next week."

Duck season is tied to wood season. "Having rock maple in escrow is simply good business," the Ole Man said when

I asked him why we needed so much wood every year. On the evening of the teal hunt we sat there at Home Base with a roaring fire going—rock maple, of course—while we reflected on the hunt. "You can't get out duck hunting until the firewood is cut and split and stored. You can't." I guess he was referring to firewood for home and firewood for the duck camp. His logic wasn't that direct. He always managed to blur the lines.

When we go to cutting rock maple for Home Base it's the beginning of the fall hunting season. We visit the Black Hole and usually the Pintail Special and remember our history-making hunts. It's a fall ritual. Rock maple is a good firewood, one of only two choices. The Ole Man loved to say, " There's only two kinds of firewood, rock maple . . . or none." It's time for a drop or three of Old Stump Blower.

8

Rain Ain't Nothin' But Water

LONGFELLOW IN "THE RAINY DAY" SAID IT BEST:

The day is cold, and dark, and dreary:
It rains, and the wind is never weary:
The vine still clings to the moldering wall,
But at every gust the dead leaves fall,
and the day is dark and dreary.

That's a good duck hunter for you. He recognized all the good things that happen when fall approaches, and allows us the chance to duck-hunt under the best of conditions.

Perhaps it is stretching things a little to think Longfellow was actually thinking of us when he wrote the above stanza, but he sure captures the feeling. Nothing is better than a day of dreary rain, a meteorological deep low, bringing not only the rain, but also the wind and the blowing fallen leaves, too. The ducks will not stay put for long on days like that. The hunter loves to see the waterfowl constantly on the move. Out of the constant flux will come a better chance for incoming ducks to choose our decoys. Ideal conditions. With their eyes fogged over with rain and low visibility, perhaps the ducks won't see us move cramped muscles or light a cigarette.

It's days of rain and bluster when the call is greatest to go to Home Base where the waterfowling begins—and ends. The duck camp at Merrymeeting Bay will see a whirlwind of activity. With Jeep, decoys, guns, food, and a supply of Old Stump Blower for after the hunt, we all blow in on the evening tide. A blazing fire is set, a couple of drinks, no more, because it is early to bed. Dawn will come early enough, even if we do tend to toss and turn as we dream of perfectly banking doubles on incoming blacks.

An hour and a half before a lightened sky we will be up. The pine-board floors will remind your feet it is very cold out there in the real world. The gun on the rack will some-how not seem as magical as it did in the dream swings last night. Water is poured in the coffeepot, eggs fetched from the refrigerator.

Only minutes have passed since the first light from the kerosene lantern hit the eyes. An aroma of fresh coffee brewing whiffs through the air, mixed with the smell of rock maple wood burning, and the day's weather report is on the battery-operated radio sitting on the shelf near the stove. "It is still raining hard this morning, according to the radio; looks like the day will be good for us," the Ole Man said as he poured a cup of coffee, even though it was not quite ready.

Wasn't a big deal or a long story, but the story was told in a few words. The wind could be heard through the pounding of the rain on the board-and-shake roof. No one was ready to leave the warmth of the womb yet, but the musty odor of human life was starting to lift from the air around.

After three cups of coffee we bottled up the rest in a thermos jug to take with us on the hunt. I made up some one-pound sandwiches of homemade bread, pickles (in a sealed bag, so as not to get the bread soggy before we ate), mustard, mixed with a slab of roast beef. I threw in a bag of quarter-pound molasses cookies my wife had called "necessary" when we were packing.

The grind of the sneak boat on the gravel shore was like a violation of the grayness surrounding all. It hung in the air, echoed off the walls of pine and fir, with mixed spruce and birch. We were headed out hunting in full regalia.

Decoys were waiting in cedar boxes on the deck. The little four-horse engine coughed into life on the third pull. The Ole Man was running the "kicker" while I nestled down against the driving rain in the cover of the bow compartment. The package of our shells, lunch, calls, toilet paper, and the like was stuffed under the roomy bow, too.

He had seen fit to throw in a "confidence bird," a cutout seagull form, and the dowel shank was resting smack-dab in the middle of my cowering posterior. The confidence-bird idea is to make the decoys look real by mixing in other sea-going birds commonly seen with ducks—sort of an "everything's okay to come in and sit for a while" sign to the quarry.

Our nose was barely visible around the sand spit of Black Hole when dawn arrived. Our two dozen mixed decoys were out, in a modified "V" about twenty yards to our front.

A full dawn was only seconds away when the first flight of pins caused us to freeze and hunker down. Out of range, but we didn't want them sending flaring signals to every duck around.

The pintails are very popular ducks with us. They are elusive, hard to hit, excellent on the dinner table. The Ole Man likes them with wild rice, locally picked mushrooms, served with light white Zinfandel wine. I have to admit they taste like gourmet food. Shooting time was upon us.

A threesome of blacks wheeled to slip over our heads, within range, coming from the rear. They had flared wings set when the Ole Man gave the signal to stand. I took the easiest shot to the left. I missed on shot number one, but connected on number two. He had a far harder fetch shot to the right, but managed to crank one home on the first try.

Getting two blacks from a floating blind boat will raise the morale in any duck hunt. We were off to a good start. Blacks are wary, skilled, and very hard to cleanly kill. I skulled the boat up the point to pick up the downed ducks.

As always seems to happen in duck hunting, I was surprised by an incoming wedge of teal that nearly took my hat off my head in one of their weird dips. They fly with a complicated motion, en masse; what appears to be a single unit can break up into ten pieces, or suddenly drop feet to sit. The change is instant. These birds simply overran me and then disappeared across the land spit. No chance for a shot.

"The hell divers of the sky got by you, didn't they?" the Ole Man said as he chided me about an opportunity missed. He never fired because I was in the line of fire. This wedge never saw us again. They weren't gone very long before I had my hand back on my gun again. More teal poured in close on the water. Hard shooting. The angle makes the shot look easy, but the speed of the birds exceeds your swing.

I missed my shot. The Ole Man got one of two. The rain came down in sheets, giving very limited visibility. I saw two Canadian geese over on the far shore, but they were wise in the spot they chose to rest. We searched the sky in sweeps. A lull. The rain mixed with hail as the temperature was dropping after dawn.

Through this water bath came several small groups of ducks. I couldn't identify every one as they passed or settled, but out of range, out of clear visibility. One group saw our decoys and turned toward us but turned away just as we both said aloud, "Pintails."

When a genuine lull was upon us, I crawled under the bow to get the thermos. I poured each of us a cup. A lone duck flew at the fringe of sight, passing across the sand spit. The Ole Man asked, "Well, how do you like duck huntin' in the rain?" It was more an affirmation than a question. We sipped at the coffee, bearing the rainy onslaught. Suddenly, a wedge of blue-winged teal gave me a chance to even the score. I picked up one for two shots. The Ole Man sucker-punched one at close range just as the wedge popped ten feet higher.

In the far distance other gunners were firing away. We might soon get some of their ducks as the fowl flew away from them. Two snuck into our blocks without us seeing

them. He said, "I think we ought to put the coffee cups away and pay attention to business. Those ducks didn't swim across the bay to come see us. We were just caught looking the wrong way." I thought we ought to let them stay to add a touch of reality to our decoys and confidence seagull. There wasn't time for a long discussion as three blacks winged by one side of the boat and a lone adult male woodie, trailed by an immature female wood, flew by the other side. We both proved we were not market hunters.

The Ole Man laughed. He cut a funny sight as we moved to the beach blind. Whether crouched, standing, or sitting, He had a cap, waterproof, pulled down over His ears. The olive-drab rain poncho was flared at the edges with His double Parker edging out of the right flap. The L.L. Bean Maine Guide boots were just barely showing below the rain pants.

I suppose I looked the same, but there was something visual in my mind as we settled in on land. He thought aloud, "The ducks are both cooperating and setting us down, but good. Maybe the blind will prove us able to limit out . . . shoot better." It was said with a smile. We were doing well, for two wet, on-the-outside, devoted duck hunters, trying to act at home in a bleak fall scenery.

When we were one duck each from the daily limit—the teal were bonus ducks that season—the Ole Man said, "Let's keep the last one for afternoon. We've had enough fun from the early hours shootin'. Funny, ain't it, how rain ain't nothin' but water, but we make it a great big deal?"

It does seem different in November at Home Base when we look forward to stormy, low-pressure weather. We did limit out at dusk and decided to stay overnight, right here at the camp. Later, as we settled in, He said, "Back home the poor people are slaving away at the midnight shift. We're rich . . . out here."

9

His Tackle Box Is Full

IF FLY FISHING IS A HIGHER ART, and the Ole Man sure thinks it is, then deep fishing for lakers must be an art, too. The lake trout, better known as "togue" in some northern parts of the continent, can be a lazy fish hovering near the bottom, feeding off schools of passing smelt, or it can be an elusive mystery fish.

The mysterious part is the legend on which thousands of anglers spend so much time, effort, money, and resolve, all to catch a trophy laker. The fish will be old, at least a full decade, maybe two decades. All that swimming and eating and avoiding trouble with hooks makes them veterans worthy of our respect. They have encounters with danger from above and manage to swim away.

Cool northern lakes lead to cool brooks, streams, rivers, or the ocean. This coldwater habitat is ideal for salmon, brook trout, char, grayling, and all the other species loving oxygen, water temperatures under 55 degrees Fahrenheit, and structured terrain. Togue love boulders, rock piles, gravel bars, even shifting layers of deep sand. Their special structure of attraction seems to be the sunken tree washed deep in a basin lake. I can testify personally to how many lures, spoons, and hopes I have expended on a fish able to tangle himself up in a half-ton sunken spruce washed free of the land in a spring breakup.

Lakers give the Ole Man the most trouble. He has spent a lifetime looking for the twenty-pound togue to come to His waiting net. He has a spot on the mantel all reserved for this trophy. In the meantime, there are photos of great fish taken over the years, but not the real trophy fish. The photos He calls "blank spots where the *real* one's supposed to be have been there for twenty-five years at least, since Herself and I drew up the plans for the house. I was younger then. I thought I'd have one by now."

It was a rainy afternoon when I watched Him rummage through those old house plans. The bluing in the architect's drawings had changed colors over the decades. There was a yellowish tinge to the papers. The trophy was etched in on the drawing of the den with a notation from Himself. The note read, "The pegs to hold the togue should be at least thirty inches apart and at least a foot above the mantelpiece." They were installed before the house was completed. The pegs were covered by a photo hung on each. Blank spots.

"I should have caught him by now—even twenty years ago. Jake Goodwin has a twenty-eight-pounder he caught on Moosehead nearly fifteen years ago. He didn't even find a special spot in his den for it. In fact, he just tacked it up in the shed. I think he did that just to irritate me. I think of it every time I go over to Elm Street. I swear." He was getting worked up just thinking about it.

Fact is, every season He gets plenty of lakers in lunker size. Over the years, this would add up to hundreds, perhaps even thousands, of big fish. Yet, the elusive super trophy was still something in the future, not the past. He wanted a memory. It's just because He and plenty of other good anglers do not have the connection to a landed fish from the top 1 percent of available fish. I asked Him once if He ever came close to the target.

"Sure have. Twice I've hooked on to *the* fish—the togue I've been waitin' and practicin' to get. Once, I even got the danged thing in the net." I thought I might ask what happened, but His face grew grim and I was not going to get the answer right now.

Suddenly, just as I thought the story was buried, He said, "Once I was over at West Grand back before the Civilian Conservation Corps (FDR's make-useful-work program of the Depression era) built those nice roads we ride on right now. It was a hard trek; even with the little kicker it meant going down Bottle Lake, to Bottle Stream, Junior Lake, Junior Stream, to the campsite at the entrance to West Grand, right where Junior Stream dumps in. We camped there because it was near the entrance to The Narrows. The CCC did a lot of useful work."

He was caught up in His tale now. A telephone rang in the background, and kept ringing, but He never budged an inch. I heard Herself say the call was from a friend, but He never acknowledged the telephone bell or His wife's voice. There was a distant look in His eyes. "Happened right after ice-out one spring when I was down there with Jake

Goodwin, Loren Ritchie, and a few other fishing-fool
friends of mine. We stayed up too late playing cards the
night before. That was my downfall. Kind of had a shaky
hand on that day, too, from the tension of holding those
cards the night before. I lost quite a bit of money."

He got up to pour Himself another glass of Old Stump
Blower. It seemed to help, or at least clarify. I looked at my
glass, still full. After adding a log to the fire He breathed a
little light around the subject by saying, "You see, me and

Jake had a side bet on the biggest fish of the day. I was hoping to get back some of the money I'd lost playing cards. My money. So, I made a pretty good wager. Jake, he tripped me up by landing a six-pounder in the first twenty minutes of fishin'. Did it by himself, too. I was still trying to get a bait sewed on just right."

The Ole Man believes the baitfish has to be running just perfectly in the water to fool a big fish. I've seen Him take a good half an hour, maybe even reject a baitfish that refused to truly imitate a wild bait in the water at boatside. He would say, "This bait ain't designed right by the Maker. It has too much belly hangin' out. It will go flip-flop all the time we drag him around. No good."

He was a fanatic on bait being perfect. "I got the right bait out in the water just in time; Jake and I were just passing over the gravel bar that sticks out in the water halfway across The Narrows. Right spot. You know the place, where you got the nice lunker a couple of years back. I never thought of losing the fish. Not from the first time I saw how big he was. I could already see him hanging on the mantel in the den. It was a twenty-pounder, maybe more. Certainly not less. I just knew He was a trophy for the mantel right from the time he struck. Hard strain, quick. He was pulling this way, then that, then deep, then shallow, right from the time he took the bait. Never felt anything like that from any fish. He was in control. Not me. The fish stayed on for at least ten minutes, maybe more, I lost track. Suddenly, he was gone. The line broke. I remember it well, even now."

He almost seemed to be retelling the same story. "The Murray Spoon was running straight and true. It was about fifty-five feet down, near bottom. The bait was right. Bang! He was on. Every time I got him close to the boat he managed to elude the net. I had to manage the net by myself. Jake was sulking, feigning he had a hook stuck under his fingernail. He thought I should have helped him land that six-pound minnow earlier, but I was busy with getting my bait just right. Now, when I needed help with a *real* trophy, Jake was faking trouble with a hook.

"Just then was when the trouble caught up with me. The fish was near the net, and I somehow got the hook caught *on the outside of the net*. That was all this monster trout needed. He broke the line instantly and with a flick of the tail was headed back to the bottom. For twenty years and more he had lived there. He was returning. My chance was gone. Simple as that. I'd like to blame Jake; in fact, I did back then. Now, I see it was the poker the night before that did me in."

He stopped right there. I never asked Him about the second time He lost the mantelpiece lake trout. Certainly not that night in the den. The Ole Man only told me that Jake topped the day off by saying, "Pay up, Ole Man! Right now! I caught the biggest fish of the day. You owe me." The Ole Man looked tired as He added, "I guess I did pay. I don't rightly know. I have no memory of the rest of the trip." He looked tired. He looked beaten. He looked old.

10

Ruff: Cheaper than Chicken

"YOU AIN'T GOT A LICK OF LEARNIN'," the Ole Man said
to a complete stranger who was shopping for door hinges
in the hardware store. The man had just finished saying the
partridge is an easy target, "Easy to shoot, easy to kill.
Ruffed grouse are simply not a first-class game bird like the
quail. It's a stupid bird who likes to hang around an apple
tree until someone finally puts him out of his misery." The
guy was bringing shame and disgrace to an American idol.

I guess the stranger deserved the comment. In fact, he
ought to consider himself lucky the Ole Man didn't pop a
right hand to his jaw. This was sacred ground. The Master
feels strongly about the partridge as the essence of a well-
designed game bird par excellence; a bird with a shroud of
mystery crossed with a beauty of a covering with usable
feathers for fly tying. "On top of that, the partridge is better
eatin' than the best chicken ever raised." He was thoroughly
irritated by the thought that someone had demeaned a classic target of the fall hunt. It might be safer to speak poorly
of Herself or His favorite rabbit hound, Queenie. With the
ruffed one there was no room for discussion.

The stranger did say one thing of rationality: "Grouse are possibly better eating than chicken. That bird even tastes like a well-cooked, well-seasoned chicken." The Ole Man thought about what He had just heard and seemed to like the idea, even if it did come from an ignoramus whose previous statement was clearly wrong. A lightbulb smile was brewing in the Ole Man. The stranger moved away, but the Ole Man's mind was clearly burning with a new strategy or theory. He had to leave the store immediately. Something was afoot.

The Ole Man left the hardware store without a purchase. He forgot why He'd ever gone there in the first place. The dash down the street would take Him home. No time to look, shop, buy, or waste more time with small talk. His mind was clear. The old Jeep had to cough up blood to keep the pace for the trip home.

I wanted to see a new drilling, a three-barrel gun with two shotgun barrels and a rifle barrel in a single gun. This sporting gun was made popular by World War II soldiers bringing them home from Germany as souvenirs. While they were, and still are, popular in Europe, they only have a very small, although very dedicated, American population base. The idea is to be able to switch from bird shot to lethal deer bullets with the flick of a lever on the receiver. Dakin's Sporting Goods had one in stock now. I couldn't afford it. I just wanted to hold it a minute. But that would have to wait. I wanted see what was up at the Ole Man's.

By the time I opened the door I saw that stacks of checks, ledgers, and all things in private finances from Herself's desk were spread out over most of His den floor. Some were for past years, some for the current year. It was a good thing Herself wasn't there to see the way He had scattered the bills, checks, receipts, and other such in stacks without a monthly order. He was full of "Aaaha!" and "I knew it!," and I was sure it must have something to do with His project.

"The crazy dude at the store got me wondering about food prices. I believe I can prove to Herself that ruff is cheaper than chicken. I've been looking at grocery receipts, looking at checks made out to the meat market for freezer chickens, trying to figure exactly how much a chicken costs. The ruffed grouse just takes one shot, two at the most. Pretty low-cost bird, especially when you figure what good eatin' they are, and how much fun they are to hunt:

crafty, wary, hardly stupid like he said. Anyway, I think I can prove to Herself just what a bargain grouse are."

Knowing some of his past purchases to support partridge hunting, I thought He was stretching it to limit the total costs to the price of a single shotgun shell, but I didn't tell Him that. There was the Brittany pup named Lady He paid $500 to buy as an eight-week-old. A Parker double was in His gun rack, along with other shotgun names like Winchester, L. C. Smith, and Browning. They would not go for cheap prices in any gun auction. They were not considered as part of the partridge price-per-pound structure, though. He also had a Purdey, but He would say it was free because it was handed down from His father, a longtime hunter in his day.

In addition, there was the grouse trip to northern Quebec where He and I went for seven days of some of the best grouse hunting around muskegs I ever experienced. My share was not cheap; far from it. Even on the Quebec trip we stopped at L.L. Bean in Freeport to get some last-minute things. We both bought a field vest for a hefty price, along with a couple of new chamois shirts. Prices not included in this pricing project, either.

I ventured to tell Him it wasn't going to be easy to prove a theory to Herself if it wasn't nearly all-inclusive. "Well, look, it's simple; I have a bill from Dakin's for a box of express loads. Can't count that 'cause it's for ducks. Got another one here from Dakin's for $78.27, but it don't say what it's for . . . Miscellany . . . can't count that stuff for partridge. Don't even know what it was."

Looking over His shoulder I saw a bill for nearly two hundred dollars. Anyone, even the Ole Man, should know what that money was buying. I said, "Now, surely you can account for that, can't you?" All He said was that I was getting to sound "more foolish, ornery, downright anti-hunting than Herself, yes, you are." I backed off.

I located the newest *Field & Stream* and read several articles before He was again ready for me.

"Now look, I ain't never spent a red cent on partridge. My wife spends more than a hundred bucks a year for chicken. And I ain't spent one cent." I thought He would be grinning knowing I didn't believe a word of His logic. Instead, He was getting even more frisky.

With fire in His eyes He said, "The Parker gun I bought for $50 cash, and it's now worth near a grand. Pretty damned nice profit, I'd say. Her chickens ain't making a cent when Herself buys $50 worth of chicken. They never grow profits like a Parker. No sir. Never will. The L. C. Smith was part of an estate gun collection. I bought all ten guns for $475, or something like that. But, I horse-traded nine of the guns away; over the years I made perhaps $1,500, or even more. Let's see a box of freezer chickens make a profit like that!"

By the time He was done telling me about His shotguns, He made over $5,000, on these items alone. I was beginning to get hauled in by His direct logic. Traveling to Alaska twice and a few trips to the Yukon must have made profits, too. My bank account should be really fat by now.

"I made some wise investments is all. She wastes money on chicken. Never goin' to be a profit in chicken. Gettin' stuff for partridge huntin' is like buying saving bonds or Treasury notes. Surprised I haven't made more profits over the years. I must be forgetting some profits I got stashed away somewhere." He bought guns when prices were low and sold them in a rising marketplace. I guess He's got it right.

"You might say I'm something of a gun tycoon. I could have made millions if I had concentrated all my assets on buying grouse guns instead of wasting it on food, house, doctors, clothes, and other trash. I'm a potential gun J. P. Morgan in the shadows, by God. I think I should tell Jackson over at the bank. Maybe he doesn't know the secret: Buy more guns, make lots of easy money."

The turn of events led to the eventual bubble. Every time you invest on the margin there's someone who comes along to take the wind out of overblown sails. The false hope of easy wealth falls victim to bottom-line logic.

Herself came in. One look at the den and the spillover into the living room made her want to take immediate action. Papers scattered everywhere, two empty whiskey glasses, our muddy boot tracks in both rooms (I can find mud in Death Valley in July). She even took in the pipe ashes where they'd spilled over the edge of the ashtray. The Ole Man always used a knife to sharpen pencils. The scrapings were on a coffee table.

She said, "Hurricanes and floods do less damage to a house than the two of you grown-up mess machines."

Throwing both arms in the air she started to clean up, but the Ole Man wanted her to listen to His theory on how cheap roast partridge dinners were, and so He told her about the stranger, the ledgers on the costs of chickens and shells. She might have bought an item or two in this store—she did love the taste of roast grouse—but He ruined it all when He told the tale of His gun purchases making the family rich.

Somewhere around J. P. Morgan she exploded. I thought, for a moment, she was going to throw both of us out of the house.

"You old goat! Don't you see how you never actually sell *any* of these so-called Necessary Shotguns. *Never*. All you ever sold was a gun or two at a time, but you forget, you came home with a much more expensive gun. You even had a name for it: *upgraded*. You upgraded by selling a cheaper gun or two and THROWING AWAY MORE MONEY to get this Rolls-Royce of a new gun. You do it so damned much you probably have more money in partridge guns than it cost to build and furnish this whole house. Now, I've heard everything! You making a profit on selling guns; my word, how much did you two hombres have to drink today? Hah! Profit on guns. My everlasting word. Profit on guns! Well, if there's so much profit on guns, I want to ask, how many you selling tomorrow? Why wait, when there's so much profit to be made? Huh? Huh?"

The Ole Man was floored. His face showed something close to fear. Why did His theory fold like a pair of cheap camping chairs? He'd thought He was standing on sound ground, a fifty-dollar gun worth nearly a thousand; that's a profit. Yet, right now, Herself was clouding up the issue. It was all her unclear thinking and her lack of appreciation of a fine grouse double gun. But, before He could speak, Herself said, "If you just added up what you spend under Miscellaneous, it would buy a considerable percentage of Getty Oil stock. You say it's hard to tie those expenses to one outdoor sport, because you use the same knife for several different things, such as cleaning a rabbit, gutting a deer, or cleaning a duck. Maybe it could be all for the good, as far as it goes, but to me, there are just two categories for every expense you have: hunting and fishing. By my tally I can testify we spend 61.3 percent of every dollar coming into this house on just those two things. Throw in your bill for Old Stump Blower, and it's a wonder the bank hasn't foreclosed. You foolish old goat. PROFIT ON GUNS? What a crock."

The Ole Man sort of crumbled away. I headed for the door.

Herself had spoken. There didn't seem to be much of a set of facts to be raised and discussed about the relative price of chicken and ruffed grouse.

11

Matagamon Lake Has Two Extra Salmon

THEY MADE A REALLY, REALLY BIG STINK ABOUT IT sometime back. All of the newspapers were full of the great debate over Louse Island. It seems Henry David Thoreau camped there while exploring the East Branch of the Penobscot River two centuries ago, and now some folks felt the island should be renamed in his honor. The opposing side eventually won out in the state legislature; thus, it remains Louse Island, just as the natives have always known it.

I brought this topic up to the Ole Man. The response was an unexpected answer: "Who cares about some man what walks over this land hundreds of years ago. Was he a good backcaster? Could he make a double on rising partridge crossing left to right in pretty heavy cover? Could he hold the crosshairs right on a buck running broadside two hundred yards away in a potato field? Did he ever do anything simple like those things?"

I was quite taken aback. Normally, the Ole Man was quite respectful of the memories of those who have passed on. It wasn't like Him to dislike anyone He never knew personally.

The topic passed. We went on to other things. I probably never would have known the whole truth about Louse Island if I hadn't seen Jake Goodwin a few days later. In the process of talking about recent events in town, I asked him what his thoughts were about the Louse Island debate. It was still making the papers at least once a week.

Jake, well aware of my close relationship with the Ole Man, started to chuckle, increased it to a laugh, stepping it up until he had a real side-splitter. I waited while tears formed in his eyes. "I haven't thought ab—" The laughter was getting old for me, but Jake now grabbed my arm to be sure I stayed around. I thought maybe Jake was referring to something funny about me, or maybe my well-known appreciation for the works of Thoreau. Still, it probably was just something long ago forgotten in which the Ole Man was a star. He'd done some pretty strange things when He was younger.

Jake began the story: "About twenty years ago, when we were all a little younger, something that the kids of today would call a 'happening' took place on Louse Island. It was springtime. The landlocked salmon were hitting well with some big fish coming to the net. Loren Ritchie and Tom Banter were camped there on a four-day trip to Matagamon. They came back to town with the nicest string of salmon seen, by anybody, for many years before. They were beauties." All at once, the storyteller began to wave his arms in arcs about three feet across.

"The Ole Man and I went there the next morning, early. We put up a tent and made camp on the leeward side of Louse Island. There was a tiny cove we could use as a safety valve. You see, we wanted to only keep two fish apiece, to take home, but we wanted the absolute biggest salmon we could catch. To take out the guesswork we needed a way to determine which fish was the biggest just before packing our bags to head home, so we placed a ten-foot drop-and-gather net with good bottom weights in a cove about the same size. It was a secure holding pen with good water exchange so we'd have no fear of the fish dying early from stress."

Jake was still moving his arms, but he looked more suited to the role of quiet yarn spinner than evil enemy of the Ole Man. He continued. "We named the little cove Sure Bet. Then, we went fishing. I didn't know, at the time, that the Ole Man had placed a huge bet on bringing back a stringer with at least one salmon bigger than any of theirs. The bet was based on Loren's superior-grade L. C. Smith—old, but an excellent gun in twenty-gauge. Perfect for early wood-cock gunning when there's a lot of leaves and a quick gun is essential. I'd like to own that one myself. I don't think the Ole Man even thought about what would happen if He lost the bet. He only focused on the L. C. Smith and the salmon. But, hey, I'm getting away from my story here."

I thought I was going to need a bullwhip to get the whole tale out of Jake. He was gesturing, reliving, smiling, being pleasant—being Jake.

"Finally, there was a good salmon chop that day on Matagamon," Jake continued, "an ideal day to troll my

Whiskey Finn." (This is Jake's version of the Mickey Finn, with an amber feather stripe on each side of the yellow-red buck hairs; it works.) "I could have used my special Gray Ghost"—another striped fly, this time with a little crow quill on each side—"but I tied on Whiskey and away we went. The Ole Man was using an oversize Gray Ghost, tied on a number-four hook. Big fly. He even had versions with tandem hooks. Too big for me. All right, so I get a good, fat three-pounder right off the bat. The Ole Man lost a good one to a broken leader. He mumbled about the poor quality of catgut these days. Then, He tied in to a really nice fish."

Jake was in full storytelling mode, even though we were still in the street.

"The canoe was sliding along well, and I kept it offshore so He wouldn't get His line snarled on a bottom sweep. After a great battle I got a net under it, and wow—it went a full seven pounds. That's a really big landlocked salmon— bigger than anything Loren's party had brought home. We kept the fish in the net, over the side, and took it back to Sure Bet for safekeeping. I mean, we were just getting started, right? With one fish in safe harbor on Louse Island, we went right back out fishing.

"Late in the afternoon of the second day I caught on to a huge salmon. It jumped, it flopped, it twisted, it turned, but in the end, after a battle, I had my fish for Sure Bet. It tipped the scales at eight pounds and one ounce. Beautiful salmon. The Ole Man was so happy we were beating Loren's party record that He even complimented me. Not once but twice He said I did a good job and the fish was beautiful."

Jake paused to poke me on the shoulder and cock his head a little to the right side. I thought about buying him a beer just to stave off dehydration, because his animated performance must be causing him to run low on water, but before I could say or do anything, he went back to the story.

"Ya see? We had our fish. They were bigger than Loren's. We could have quit right there, and unknown to me, the Ole Man would have had Loren's Smith gun. Right there. Unknown to me, at the time. Ya see? I forgot to tell ya, we had three fish then, didn't I? Well, the Ole Man had a six-pounder tucked away at the Sure Bet corral, one He caught after His big one. Well, now, all we needed was number four, one for me, and the looking and fishing was done. Easy fishing. Easy winning. After lunch on the third day . . . Hey, you getting thirsty?"

I went back to Elm Street to Jake's den where we popped a top and settled in for the finale fish tale.

"After lunch on the third day I tied in to another giant salmon. This was a fish to end all fish. I mean, he was tore up. He trashed and bashed and ran away and ran deep—all sorts of escape episodes, to no avail. I had him. The catgut must have been stretched to the limit. The Ole Man was excited, too. He must have been, because He was praising me again. I mean, come on . . . Well, by golly, the Ole Man practiced landing the fish again and again, like a bullfighter with a cape. It was a sight to see. Finally, He got His chance to sweep under and hoist. All went super well. After the fish quieted down in the net, we went back to Louse Island and to the Sure Bet depository."

Time out to open beer number two; then he continued: "Now we had our four fish. Wondrous fish, all of them. Loren wouldn't be able to beat the Ole Man now. I thought it was all about fishing pride. I didn't realize, of course, at the time, that the L. C. Smith double was on the line. We certainly had Loren's party beat, real good. Yes, we did. I was suspicious when I saw the Ole Man standing by the pen with the four salmon in it because He kept throwing His arms in the air and swinging an imaginary gun as if sweeping the sky. I couldn't see the connection. It was sure going to be nice.

"You might want to know why the fish had to be fresh. Well, you see, the fishing bet was based on one day's catch. So, the Ole Man wanted the fish to be real fresh when we got back to town. Nothing obviously dead a day or two. A little trickery built in here. You know how the Ole Man sizzles when He has a deep, dark secret. It was one of those kinda things. Man, was He sizzling, I'll tell ya. Wild, sizzling grins with wild eyes a'gleaming."

Jake was waving his arms around like a wild man, but I knew what the Ole Man looked like when He knew He had bested a competitor. I was sometimes the loser, too.

"Now, the Ole Man decided He wanted them alive, not just fresh. So we went to see Bill Robinson, the forest ranger on Matagamon. The forestry people had water tanks, small ones, they used for spot forest fires. Just right for transporting four live salmon. The tank was mounted on an old eight-wheeler frame. The tank capacity said five hundred gallons in big white letters on the side of the forest green tanker.

"Bill was cooperative and liked the idea, but said he'd have to get some gas in town. Come back in the morning. The Ole Man said that was okay by Him, because He wanted to celebrate the upcoming homecoming anyway. One more night at Louse Island. We partied a little but went to bed early; I mean, how many ways can you tell the same fish story, ya see?

"Early in the morning we struck camp, gathered up the net to sling over the side until we got to the forestry camp. The canoe was loaded; the kicker ran well; the twenty-seven pounds of live salmon was a sight to behold in the sling of netting over the side. Four fish, mind you; four fish, four salmon at that, and they weighed twenty-seven live pounds! Wow, man, I tell you, it was a sight to behold. It really, really was.

"Bill had the fire truck all filled with gas and the tank filled with water. The Ole Man took great pride in hoisting up the net so Bill could be the first to see the fish, and we could be the first to brag. Bill greatly admired the fish, each and every one of them, then he let them flop into the tank and screwed the top down tight. All was secure. Oh, it was a real tale to tell. Oh, yes sir, it was. And, the Ole Man was at a crowning height in His glory. Really up there with the rock stars and Hollywood types. He was bowing and tilting, bending His knees, telling the tale and waving His

arms. I thought we'd better get going or He was going to
have a heart attack.

"It was decided to dump the water and draw a crowd
right in back of Dakin's Sporting Goods, right in town. The
Ole Man told the Dakin's clerks and He started to gather a
crowd. People started coming from all over town. I mean,
there were people there to see the four lunker salmon that I
hadn't seen outside their houses in ten or fifteen years.
Wow, it was a sight to see. I thought the Ole Man might be
stretching the truth a little when He retold the story so

many times about the size, girth, weight, and such, but they were huge fish. No doubt about that. No doubt at all.

"When all was ready to commence with dumping the fish out in the parking lot for everyone to see, I would say about a hundred people were right there. Loren Ritchie was there, too. He brought the L. C. Smith with him. The Ole Man finally told me about the bet on the way back to town. I don't know why He waited until then, but you know how He is, right?

"The Ole Man had His cash money ready, too. He went to the bank to withdraw it while telling them He would be bringing it right back for redeposit. He announced to the crowd that the four fish of Loren Ritchie and Tom Banter weighed exactly twenty-two pounds and four ounces, and ours were going to weigh over twenty-seven pounds. Vote for the winner. He made a joke of it. They all laughed, except for Loren, who wasn't wanting to lose his valuable gun, but was still willing to honor his bet. Tom Banter just waited stoically for the ax to fall.

"The forestry truck was used for firefighting, but served a dual role by allowing state fisheries biologists to stock a lake or pond with live game fish. So it came all equipped as a fish tank with a big spigot, which, as the crowd gathered around, the Ole Man proceeded to open. Out came the water in a bigger gush than some of the people gathered had planned on. They jumped back to keep from getting their feet wet in the parking lot. I mean, five hundred gallons of water creates a big splash all of a sudden.

"The first fish came out, flopping around; it was the biggest, and the crowd cheered. Now, out came another and another, and then the fourth. Loren Ritchie already passed the L. C. Smith double up to the Ole Man on the forestry truck because it was obvious these four salmon were bigger than anything Loren and Tom caught. The weigh-in of four fish would just be a formality. The Ole Man had already weighed them on His postal scales.

"The Ole Man was grinning from ear to ear, the righteousness of it all. He was the top angler in town. He and I made a great team. He started to address the crowd to thank Loren for the gun, when ALL HELL BROKE LOOSE. What's this? What? What are those? You see, don't ya, there were now six fish flopping around in the water from the truck. The tank had six salmon released. Oh, ho, oh, ho, I'll tell ye, ah, I mean it was wild. Six fish is TWO EXTRA. There were TWO TOO MANY salmon. It was illegal. Against the law. Yes, it was. Two each was all the law allowed. We had three each. Loren had not completely released the Smith, and he now reclaimed it and, to make matters worse, wanted the Ole Man's envelope of money. Ah, yes, there was HELL TO PAY, I tell ya.

"It got even worse, yes it did. The two extra salmon were about ten inches each. They were too small to keep, in addition to the fact they were over the limit. People called them short salmon, meaning they needed to be put back in the water because of minimum size restrictions. Someone ran for a small fish tank or bucket to hold them until they could be released into wild waters again. The Ole Man's jaw was flopped open worse than the four big salmon. He quickly tried to say these fish were just leftovers from the last salmon-stocking program. It was obvious, He said. Well, Bill Robinson was right there, and he thought back to the previous week. He allowed as yes, they did stock a few leftover salmon in Matagamon Lake that came from the state hatchery. So, it could be these two little guys came from that stocking delivery.

"Loren and Tom were quick to point out that the deal was for four salmon, not six; it was illegal. There was no way to tell which ones were the four from the Ole Man's trip and which ones were not. No sir, a bet's a bet. 'Where's my pile of cash before we start calling you the Ole Thief?' Loren said; he was defiant. He had the Smith to protect. Maybe even some extra cash.

"Dismal doom was looming in the Ole Man's eyes. When they weighed things in, the folks kept all the fish alive, in a bucket for the two small ones, and several makeshift tanks made out of kids' plastic swimming pools for the big ones. The debate was on. The four fish of Loren and Tom *averaged* over five pounds and nine ounces. The *six* fish of the Ole Man and I—we were forced, by crowd logic, to accept these as *ours*—averaged a measly bit less than five pounds apiece. The Ole Man and I clearly lost with the crowd logic. Cries of 'It was only fair' were heard all around."

Jake was clearly down at this point in the tale. But there was also a smile. He wanted to be on a winning team, but the idea of the Ole Man giving Loren cash swung him over.

He could enjoy the whole event. It was the Ole Man that really lost out.

Jake added, "The local newspaper photographer took plenty of pictures, but the one of the Ole Man handing over the envelope of cash to Loren Ritchie, the one the paper used on the front page the next day, was a locally known classic. People saved it to show their friends all over the state. The title of the story and the photo series was 'Local Men Lose Fishing Bet.' LOCAL MEN LOSE FISH-ING BET. It was bad enough for me—some people laughed—but for the Ole Man, it was brutal. He had not gained a shotgun. He had lost a considerable amount of money. Herself would want to know how much. And, he had lost prestige. He had been made fun of by the very people He was trying to impress. Brutal, I tell you. I think this is why he hates any mention of Henry David Thoreau and Louse Island. Ya see?

"It gets worse. We took all six salmon back to Matagamon Lake. The crowd wanted us to, and I agreed, because the Ole Man said if we kept the four big ones now, it would be like eating crow pie. Ya see? Well, by the time we released all six salmon, the crowd had grown to nearly two hundred. People were coming from other towns to join in the release ceremonies. A politician was there, too." Jake took to laughing. I hit the road.

I never mentioned Henry David Thoreau to the Ole Man again.

12

Poached Mooseburgers

WARDEN CLEMENTS WAS A NICE GUY, well thought of by the sporting community. He was well versed in the law, knew and appreciated the outdoor life, was a hunter and fisherman himself, as he waged a hard, diligent war against every lawbreaking poacher he could find. On that issue he was unwavering: No poaching in his district.

The Ole Man didn't like him. No way. No how. The warden never made any arrests of the kind you might call "dubious," and he never bothered, certainly never arrested, the Ole Man. Why the hate? The Ole Man said, "Those guys just make me nervous, always sneakin' around trying to catch you accidentally or technically violating the law by half an inch. They try to shrink fish under the legal limit, just to catch the innocent." The fact the Ole Man hung pretty close to the edge of legality probably explained His pure, down-deep hate for all enforcers of the laws of hunting and fishing, most especially Warden Clements.

The warden was tall, wiry built, strong, and spent most of his waking time doing his job. We occasionally found him right where we were about to be. That's not to say we had anything to really hide, but those edges of legality were pretty close.

There was the time the Ole Man sent the registration in for His boat to the state capitol for the validation stamp and bow stickers. It was sent in plenty early to get the paper stamped and have it returned to Him, but the ice went out of West Grand Lake a few days earlier than predicted. The registration was not in the mailbox yet. So, being a good fisherman, but a lousy bureaucrat, the Ole Man went fishing. I ought to know; I was right there with Him.

The logic was unbeatable: "They got my money a few days ago. It's not my fault they're slow at returning it to me, just as it's not my fault the ice went out early. Obviously, it's time to go fishing when there's open water. The law says so. There it is, right in the title of the law book every year, *'Open Water Inland Fishing Regulations.'* See, I carry the book in my tackle box every time I go fishing."

The law book also carried a notation for those who mailed in their registration, that the registrations "will be processed and returned within two weeks." Time went by after He mailed it in; two weeks—I don't think so. Yet, West Grand was calling.

A lot of fishermen had the same idea. It was a spring ritual. Ice-out fishing is a much-anticipated event each year. Thousands flocked to waters not flowing freely since sometime last fall. There was still some ice in the coves, and there was the occasional block of ice, even an ice pan or two. Boating meant careful avoidance of the ice. Still, West Grand attracted many anglers every year. On the day in question, there were perhaps seven or eight boats at The Narrows, one of the more-popular fishing spots.

Warden Clements was there, too. Checking licenses and boat registrations. Our time came. "Hi, boys! How's the fishing?" Warden Clements was always friendly, professional. We used a few "sirs" to show respect for The Law and showed him our licenses and fish. He said they were real beauties, and was ready to pull away when he noticed the boat-licensing stickers were out-of-date. There was supposed to be one on each side of the bow; they come with the annual validated registration. "Hey, Ole Man, aren't you a little late getting the boat registered?" Friendly. No edge. He just expected an explanation, or you just knew you were going to get a summons to court. That's his job. Part of the boat registration paid the warden's salary and allowed him to carry out a lot of other work the Ole Man would agree with.

The Ole Man was caught unawares, or so it seemed. He sat without voice, completely forgetting His clear logic as expressed to me before we left. He mumbled. He stumbled. Warden Clements was the one who got Him out of trouble by asking, "Have you sent in to the capitol yet for the registration and stickers?" Finally, He knew what to say. "Yes, yes I did, I mean, I have—yes, it's their fault. The State—I mean, the State screwed it up. They're late . . . real late."

Warden Clements scratched his chin, allowed as how slow the mails were, and promised to check in a week or so to see the boat registration stickers himself. That way, he'd be doing his job and the State would have its money. He wished us continued good luck. As he pushed away I was thinking what a truly nice guy the warden was. He showed great judgment by allowing the Ole Man time to get the stickers and registration. He checked us out quite often over the years, so he knew we always paid the necessary fees. By letting the Ole Man go without a ticket, he was showing his trust that the truth was being told.

As soon as the warden pulled away the Ole Man was mad at the world.

"Crazy thing, The Law is. Shouldn't have the right to question my word. No way. I told him I paid the money. That should be the end of it. Wardens! They're always sneakin' around. Doing people in for nothin' and still botherin' the average guy. Now, he's comin' back. He said so. He's going to check to see if I was lyin'. He's got no right, I tell ya. No right at all. He's sneaky."

I thought the warden *was* right, and professional, so I just kept my thoughts to myself.

"Reminds me of those legal mooseburgers we were cooking at the duck hunt last fall, right there at Home Base. They were nearly legal, and he had the gall to ask where the moose meat came from. When I told him I thought it probably came from a moose, or something pretty close to a moose, he blew a gasket. Remember? He was totally out of line, a wack job, gonzo, psycho warden. I know fully well the State now has a moose season every fall; why couldn't someone who shot a legal moose give me meat? I mean, that could happen. Wacko warden is just lookin' to find me guilty of a serious violation. Now, ain't he?"

I must have missed the boat. Why was the warden out of line asking where the moose meat came from to make mooseburgers? The Ole Man was not being fair, and I said exactly that to Himself. He jumped back as though I'd just sold Him a cheap imported double twelve-gauge side-by-side and promised it was really a Purdey.

"You're getting more like Herself all the damned time. You certainly are. Can't you see the plain, unvarnished truth when it's as clear as I just told ya? That moose meat was nearly legal. It wasn't no poached moose."

I acknowledged the moose was "nearly legal," but pressed Him on the point of legality. "If the moose meat is legal, why not tell Warden Clements how you came by the meat? It's as simple as that. I don't even know where it came from; you just brought it with you and said it was 'nearly legal,' and I thought you knew what 'nearly legal' meant."

The Ole Man never answered directly; instead He said, "You're getting more like Herself, I tell ya. There's no need of Herself, or you, getting too involved with worry about me being illegal. You're just as big a thorn in the butt as Herself. Oh, all right, it's none of your business, but I'll tell ya the story, the whole story, and then you'll see it's nearly legal, just like I said."

With Warden Clements he wound up asking him for proof it was illegal, and the warden just got frustrated and walked away. Now, hopefully, I was going to get the truth—or at least His version of the truth. The Ole Man said, "It started with a note from Jake, asking to meet me at Logan Brook with a good sharp knife. He left the note in my locker at work, and stated when I should show up. So I went. And, there was this big bull moose and Jake. The former was dead. The latter was alive. Now surely you can see I had nothing to do with killing a moose, right?"

I agreed, but asked Him to flesh it out.

"Well, now, it seemed strange to me to see Jake bent over this woodland giant. He was using a nice hunting knife to whack away at the meat. Jake urged me to do the same, saying he would tell me what happened later because right now he was too busy. I dug right in but kinda kept an eye peeled for Warden Clements. I was nervous, not knowing what happened. Still, I like moose meat, and wasn't about to let it spoil. After a while we got the meat chunked up and put it in the back of Jake's pickup. Then, we covered it up with a nice big tarp. No one could tell after we threw a couple of bales of dog bedding straw on the tarp. I knew Herself would never approve of having moose meat in the freezer, so we unloaded it at Jake's as soon as it got dark.

"After checking to be sure no one was looking, we got the meat inside Jake's place. We got it cleaned, cut to meal sizes and in his huge freezer, without saying much. 'Course we kept the shades closed and the lights low. Just a normal evening at home. Now, you see? It's pretty clear what happened, ain't it?"

I wanted to ask something simple, like if it was so legal, why were they sneaking around like true poachers? But, knowing a storm would erupt, I compromised and apologized by asking, "I guess I'm rock-solid between the ears. I don't understand yet."

He looked disgusted. "Jake sort of found the moose. He
was on his way home from his brother's place after a long
day of cutting long logs in the woods. It seems his brother
was having back trouble and needed help in getting the
long logs to the mill to pay the hospital bills and to feed
the kids. Without his logging job, there was no money
coming into the house. With the last load on the truck, Jake
was hauling about twelve cords of green rock maple, in tree
length, to the mill in Sherman. At Logan Brook he came
upon a big bull moose standing in the road. Neither one of
them moved fast enough, and Jake hit the moose a
100,000-pound glancing blow.

"The moose was dead, but Jake was able to see the meat was perfect. The truck bumper, the big industrial kind, barely showed any impact marks, except for moose hair and blood. The moose was off the road perhaps fifty feet from the logging road. Now, Jake is a law-abiding citizen who knows the meat will go to a needy family after the warden has processed it as a motor vehicle–wildlife accident. He knows the warden will probably take some to three or four families he knows will use the meat and whose income is near poverty level. His brother's family would not necessarily qualify, because the back trouble is recent, and they normally have enough money for food. Dilemma for Jake? He wants his brother to get most of the meat, after Jake gets some.

"Jake knew how Warden Clements hated paperwork, so he decided to save him the trouble of filling out a moose–truck collision report, and chose his brother's family to get the meat, but he needed help. A moose is a big critter to carve up; a big bull is even more work. So he got me to help. We kept maybe two hundred pounds of meat, as a fee for our labor. See how it's nearly legal? Regular accident, no paperwork, most of the meat goes to a family what needs it. Legal, I'd say. When the warden asked about our moose-burgers, it was none of his business. See? I told ya."

I shook my head and walked over to the bar to get a sip of Old Stump Blower.

13

Farmin' Togue

MOST PEOPLE THINK OF FARMS as places with cows, corn, or horses. There has to be some kind of crop or end product related to animal husbandry. New agricultural projects have produced aqua farms for catfish, salmon Alaskan style, or even some shellfish; we know the traditional farm doesn't plow up a row of brook trout or togue. However, the Ole Man was positive there was farming to be done in the outdoors, most especially in the watery wild lands.

When the Ole Man said He was "Goin' out to the farm," He meant He was going fishing. If it was "togue farmin'," you're likely to think of togue fishing at a lake, called West Grand or other substitutes. There was a "togue farm" in the Allagash on Eagle Lake, an island He actually called the Togue Farm (Farm Island). It's a long story, but you get the gist. For the Ole Man, fishing for lake trout is an ersatz name for togue farming.

His farm operations do have a product—fish for the freezer—but they are never profit-making American entrepreneurial centers of commerce. They eat cash for things related to fishing, such as boats, outboards, gas, fishing

necessaries, and special things to keep baitfish cool or fillets frozen. And that's just getting started. To make it a "working farm," as the Ole Man calls it, there are many extras "necessary" for those who take fishing seriously.

Direct logic is one of His best conversational justifications for weird ideas. He says things clearly in a cloud: "Togue are good to eat. Farms have edible products. Therefore, we need to change the image of our products. The fillets only come after working hard. We are selective and throw many potential products back in the water, so I guess we're better referred to as *gourmet farmers*. Right?"

Well, I stammered around the idea of fishermen being called gourmet anything. I failed to see what fancy labels had to with the price of eggs, anyway. You simply went fishing for lake trout or togue or lakers. To go beyond those choices was folly, and I said so.

"You are a simpleton, aren't you?" He was clearly irritated by my brashness. He then gave me what I think is the finale of simple direct logical thinking: "A farmer is proud of his farmland, and I believe most fishermen I know are serious about their togue-farmin' acres, too. Pretty simple, isn't it?

We're togue farmers just as much as the Pattersons are potato farmers. It just makes good sense. I can't see how you can deny it."

One step further out there: He thinks the best boats, finest rods, highest-order camping gear, and so forth are all— and I hesitate to tell you this—he thinks those things are *fertilizer*.

"You might call them farm equipment, but you have to admit, the best baitfish for togue is to be totally equipped to put out your best effort with an eye to the future—a kinda farmin' fertilizer for fish. A good farmer gets loans and such to go plant a crop or for the harvest expenses. We do the same exact thing, don't we? That's farmin'. That's fishin'. They're one and the same thing, professionally."

When I stood there, dumbfounded, He added, "Why this idea has never caught on, I really don't understand. The facts are crystal clear. If you are putting in a decent garden, you have to work hard, keep checkin' on the seeds and seedlings to get a good crop. Checkin' out the togue crop is needed, too. Herself gets all unjointed about it, but the crop has to be given close watch, so I have to go to West Grand, Matagamon, Eagle, or wherever the crop is near harvesting. Wives are just too suspicious of hunters, and, particularly, at least in my experience, fishermen."

I never asked to go togue farmin'. I got told, "There's work to be done, and we need to do our duty." How can I disagree with that logic? What patriotic person could refuse to work on a conservation project? I enjoy the work. I mean, this is not an effort-free afternoon of snoozing in the backyard sun.

The cool breezes coming across West Grand Lake on a hot July afternoon create a relaxed atmosphere while farming togue, but it can be very busy. The Ole Man says of these days: "We're out doing fieldwork, research, to get a better product. We have a responsibility to the next generation to hand down a farm capable of even more productivity. It's as simple as that, I'm sure you agree. We're really farmers who do a lot of basic and even advanced research on a glorious part of the outdoor world. Kinda like the folks who read *Scientific American*. Our journal of advanced study is *Field and Stream* or *Outdoor Life* or maybe *Sports Afield*. Science people always have their professional journals."

There are some pastrami sandwiches in the top shelf of our upright cooler (refrigerator with ice) where we also store our beer. It helps the nerves while doing research to pause for a break. We have to ply the waters with our poles for hours on end, so the break is a necessity for our continued good health. The small specimens we catch are noted and returned to the water for additional growth time on the farm. The ones we catch that are ready for harvest—we'll probably take some samples home to the freezer for more study. It helps shrink the family food budget, something most families want to do.

We go ashore to check out the woodlots near the farm, too. The trees need evaluation for cooking up a shore lunch on some trips, or for good, seasoned camp wood when we stay there doing research for a week at a time.

There even comes a day when the youth in town may get to spend some time on the togue farm. They don't seem to see it as a bad omen of hard work, and seem to be genuinely fooled into thinking this is an actual farm with domestic animals, albeit scale-laden, subsurface creatures not subject to easy access for inspection. They actually have fun while trying to do an inventory of available stock in the watery corral. To do this, the only tools you need are a fishing pole, some live bait, a boat, an outboard, and some time to do the work. Youngsters find the hours pretty much fly by as they catch enough fish to make them smile. Some even take the fish home to do more research there. Science needs young people with an interest and skill in the various applications.

Jimmy Prouty's daughter was the most successful youth project we ever undertook. Sarah was about twelve years old, a middle-school girl whose father had died in a tragic plane crash. Jane, her mother, called the Ole Man one day and said, "Sarah's been missing her father greatly; you know how he used to take her fishing for lake trout at Matagamon Lake. She loved going. Well, I was wondering if you could include her on a trip this summer. It would mean a lot to her."

With that kind of entry it was arranged to take Sarah with us on a three-day trip, with the campouts to be had at Louse Island. "It will be a good history lesson, too," said the Ole Man, "what with the Thoreau guy, the East Branch of the Penobscot River, the old loggers, the CCC road builders. There's a bunch of history. We can tell her about togue farmin', show her how to do it."

The farmin' trip went well. Nearly too well. Sarah caught several fish more than the Ole Man, getting the largest laker, too. She was a pleasure to have along. I thought the

Ole Man might make girl or woman jokes, but He didn't. He was on His best behavior, actually enjoying teaching her skills. Her father would have been proud.

At lunch on the third day she said, "I'm going to be a full-time fish farmer when I grow up. I decided to major in the science of fishery management in college. I can double-major by adding business courses to the list."

We noticed how she handled and cleaned the fish, how she baited the hooks with sewn-on live bait, helped run the camp, and did everything necessary to be a good team member. When she wasn't around, she went for daily walks around the lakeshore, looking for interesting fossils.

The Ole Man said, "You know, Sarah's an amazing young lady. She makes sense when she talks. She knows practical skills, too, like cleaning or cooking fish. I think she just might do it all."

A decade later Sarah graduated from college as an aqua business manager with a degree in fisheries. She married a cattle rancher from the Gulf Coast of Florida, where her husband worked in the family beef business, and she raised catfish on her own pond ranch, using in-law land. A year or so later she was actually expanding her business, and the in-laws were happy to reduce the size of their cattle herd to give her more catfish land.

When the Ole Man found out, He jumped all around, saying, "Holy cow! I mean, Sarah is a farmer, a REAL FARMER! She is farmin' catfish because we taught her how to farm fish. I think I'm goin' to ask the IRS idiots again about my business deductions, because now, what with

Sarah and all, I have perfect proof: Togue farmin' leads to the other species, like catfish down south." He was convinced. His search for a way to convince government, federal or state, of His farmin' business expenses was ongoing . . . and not successful.

While cruising around the farm we often find others who are visiting, so we stop to chat about farming. The Ole Man says, "Talkin' shop with the other serious farmers is worth a great deal, because sometimes there's plenty to learn. It's a kinda businessman's lunch. The government won't allow us to deduct these expenses from our income tax, though. The government's plain stupid. No other way to say it. They won't even allow deductions for depreciation when an outboard needs replacement; can't deduct fishing gear, either. They won't allow us to be called a nonprofit for IRS purposes—nothing. They're a pretty bad bunch, I tell ya."

One day when we were checking on the farm at West Grand Lake, the Ole Man told me, "Secrecy is the only way to manage the farm. The secret is necessary, because too many other people would want to horn in if they knew we possessed so many acres of prime, crop-producing terrain. Sarah's got a whole different deal. They allow her to deduct things. Maybe by keepin' it quiet we're better off in the long run. No tax breaks, no herd of fellow businessmen. Just a few amateurs like you, me, and Jake Goodwin."

The next day, at work, I realized that this is probably all a sham. My wife thinks that togue farming is "an infection you and the Ole Man concocted to escape reality and family life. It's not even a white lie. It's a varnished tale of foolishness. You know it."

I think I've been hanging around the Ole Man too much. It makes sense to me. I want to retire to togue farming at Eagle or Matagamon or West Grand. I've already got my bag packed.

14

The Snowshoe Web

WHEN WINTER COMES, it isn't hard on the Ole Man. He doesn't withdraw to a cocoon to wait for spring. Some people have trouble with seasonal affective disorder, but the Ole Man has two seasonal addictions to keep Him busy all winter. "What with rabbit hunting and ice-fishing, I ain't got time to get the blues all winter." He didn't mention it, but bobcat hunting with the hounds was a third alternative when the urge for variety settled in.

Idle winter months are a mental problem for those without a winter of dreams. Following the Ole Man around all these many winters, I can say that to enjoy winter, all you need is some warm clothes. And maybe a beagle or two, some ice-fishing traps, a good shotgun, a pair of snowshoes, an ice auger, a small mound of shells, an ice chisel, some dog food, an ice strainer to keep the holes clear of ice, a leash, a dog whistle, a snowmobile . . . Ah, I guess it takes more than warm clothes.

Rabbit hunting is my number-one winter sport. There's something about the beagles, the snow, the snowshoeing to get the ghost of the woods, the camaraderie, the beauty of the winter woods. It gets surging around in your blood as the seasons change.

The onset of winter makes the beagles restless, too. Queenie, the Ole Man's hound, has many seasons of experience. She's quite the dog: smart, hardy, loves to hunt. She possesses a great cold-weather nose and is always ready to go hunting. Rattle her chain leash and she is jumping around, intensely eager to get outside to begin the hunt. She even seems to know when the weather changes. It would not be long before rabbit hunting starts. She greets every day with renewed excitement.

Queenie is a different dog all summer. She snoozes in the sun, hardly lifting her head when you walk by her dog run. But, on a crisp fall day, especially late in the waning days of November's deer hunt, Queenie knows it is getting close to the time she will be spending her days in the woods. She keeps a close eye on our daily routines. If there is an early snow, all hell breaks loose because the level of excitement has been maxed out. Snow is a definite connection to rabbit hunting.

We never hunt rabbits without a dog. Some days others join in with their hounds. Queenie gets along well with them as long as she can dominate. She hates lazy dogs, and treats them with disdain. When other dogs are there, she has to lead the chase. It's in her nature. She leads nearly every chase. Hunting without dogs? Never. The Ole Man and I are pretty poor at finding and sniffing out fresh snowshoe hare tracks in the dense covers.

As if it isn't enough to put up with overanxious hounds, I
have to endure the antics of the Ole Man, too. He likes to
hunt snowshoe rabbits even more than His dog. He studies
the hounding aspects of each and every choice in the chase
as though He was inside the pack of beagles. I often hear
Him holler out, "Now why did they leave the alder run for
the edge along the field? They should have stayed in the
alders all the way to those jack firs." The dogs undoubtedly
thought otherwise. The trail went where the scent trail varied—toward the edge of the field. Where the Ole Man
thought the rabbit should run wasn't always where it went.

If you visit the Ole Man's house in late November you're
likely to find Himself putting a final coat of shellac on his
snowshoes. He likes to give them about thirteen coats every
winter, or so it seems. He claims the extra weight of the
shellac is not too hard to carry around because it saves the
snowshoes for hard use, year after year. "A pair of snowshoes
is like a fine pair of well-fitted gloves or a good pair of hunting boots, all broken in from other seasons. Same with
women. It's easier to keep them maintained than to have to
start all over again with a new crop. Makes sense to me."

I think He's attached to his snowshoes in a sentimental
way, but you're not going to get Him to admit that. Most
serious outdoorsmen get attached to things they associate
with fine trips afield, especially in their favorite sports.

When I see Him with shellac, allowing Queenie to
snooze by the fire, I know rabbit gunning is close at hand.
Since the Ole Man often shoots a deer early in the season,
He begins to anticipate hounding fairly early in November

some years, getting ready to go out as soon as the whitetail seekers have put away their rifles. After deer, He fiddles with late-season waterfowl, but the focus is on a winter of rabbit gunning. We have half a dozen coverts we hunt every year. We don't have the time to go there between seasons, so it is more or less than a half-year since we have last seen these forest mixtures, or have visited rabbit-hunting companions.

Take the Jake Goodwin Camp cover, for instance. It is a paradise of old tangled pines mixed with Christmas tree stock all the way to the edge of a wild apple orchard—or rather, an orchard allowed to turn wild after the farmer went on to other crops. Abandoned farm acres sure make good hunting places. This was one of the very best in our neck of the woods. It still galls the Ole Man that "a cover that good would have to be partially owned, maybe even legally, by a useless, good-for-nothin', cantankerous, crooked, stinkin', no-account of a guy like Jake Goodwin. It defies all logic."

Off and on, mostly off, the two of them have acted like friends. They are both good outdoorsmen. They come from the same common history. Jake may not be married, but over the years, there have been a whole host of women who have taken him on as a project. None successfully, as of yet. Just last spring the widow Sally Bartlett chased Jake for weeks with home-cooked meals, cleaning up the house. She called it the "spring cleaning of the last decade or two." Jake isn't overly neat about the house. Yet, no marriage partners for him. If Herself wasn't a saint with wings sprouted, the Ole Man would certainly live alone, too.

Jealousy over outdoor achievements has been a hallmark of the pair for all the years I have known them. These scuffles resemble two teenage suitors of the same pretty cheerleader. They get strictly focused on beating the other. Bragging rights.

Take the time right there on Jake's Camp cover during rabbit season a few years ago.

The Ole Man had some guests from "the outside" who loved rabbit hunting. He knew exactly where to take them. Since they were from a distant part of Herself's family, the Ole Man wanted to impress them with His hunting skills and His great wealth. "I want them to go back to Pittsburgh and say what a great hunt they enjoyed, and, family rumors to the contrary, what a great guy I am and how much land I own. Hundreds of acres."

His idea of wealth was to "hire a guide." He thought and thought and Jake was at the top of the list. He looked like a guide, could hunt like a guide, and if pinned down, he could answer like a guide. The Ole Man would hire Jake, but there was more to it. The Ole Man thought that the prominent spending of money on his guests, his obtuse talks about "my acres of woodlands," were sure ways to impress city people.

On the big day the guests arrived and were duly impressed with the Ole Man's obvious wealth, although I think they may have wondered why one man needed so many fishing rods, or why the need seemed to be there for racks of fine guns. It took piles of money to buy those things, that's for sure. They were too polite to ask silly questions.

Next morning Jake, the new hire, arrived in full guide regalia. His well-worn red-and-black-checked mackinaw with green wool pants, nor'easter cap, and L.L. Bean boots with trigger-style mittens, complete with holes worn through the woven fingers—a guide for sure, and one who lived in the woods. Jake looked the part.

I think the Ole Man was impressed. He wanted to play lord and master, the local success story. Even Herself—who normally can't stand Jake because he's "shiftless; never even settled down at his age, well, just imagine"—today, she was polite, courteous to Jake with the relatives present. She offered to make a lunch for them to take afield, but Jake quickly said, "I've taken care of everything. No need." It was part of his profession to make the lunch for clients. He was ready.

The guests were middle-aged, old Pennsylvania settler stock, upright and straitlaced, used to civilized, urban lives. It quickly became clear they were not of the outdoor bent. Too much dignity for that. He was a banker, she taught high school English. Both were well dressed for the hunt ahead. Surprisingly, in good spirits. I say "surprisingly" because they spent an entire evening talking with the Ole Man, enough to wear anyone down.

Everything went well on the hunt. I was fully taken by the way the Ole Man catered to them. Warm, friendly, courteous, telling jokes, helping them with difficult passages in the woodlands. They seemed to be enjoying the music of the hounds. Jake brought his dog, along with Queenie; together they made a chorus of sounds. I was glad

I had come along. This was a side of the Ole Man I'd never been privileged to see before. He was even gracious to Jake, allowing our guide to lead the hunt. He even asked Jake questions as though Jake was the local expert.

The guests left happy. They were impressed with the Ole Man's forestlands, his command over His "employee," Jake. The hospitality was impressively carried out, as if this was the daily routine. They said over and over again how the rabbit hunt was the highlight of their visit to "the gentle wilderness of the Northeast." They loved the primitive life. Maybe not the highest of compliments, but it wasn't the worst scenario either. They could have seen the Ole Man while He was in sideshow mode. Not pretty.

After they left town Jake Goodwin started pounding on my door. Only ten minutes since their departure. "Got to tell you the real story," Jake said as he came charging through the door. I glanced at the oak door to be sure he hadn't cracked the glass panes. Jake pounded it hard enough for me to be concerned about my door's state of health. No damage done.

"It was this way! Last week the Ole Man drank too much Old Stump Blower, went over to Dakin's Sporting Goods and ordered a full dozen of the top graphite high-tech rods to fish this coming spring at Swift Brook. In His stupor He thought the model was twelve and the quantity was one, but He filled in the wrong order blanks. When the clerk asked Him about the quantity He was faced with a dilemma: Did He want twelve rods of the model number one, or did he want one rod of the model twelve? The Ole Man was so angry with the clerk questioning His order, He simply went with the flow of alcohol in His bloodstream and ordered twelve rods."

Turns out the Ole Man was having this flushing of Old Stump Blower with good reason. Herself was "hassling" Him about the amount of money He was spending from the family budget on outdoor "extravagances," to the point where they were short of money to pay monthly expenses. She claimed he was spending 71.1 percent of the take-home pay on hunting, fishing, and camping. The Ole Man claimed this was a "mite high." She claimed they were down to using circulars for toilet paper.

After the slip at Dakin's store, He was in a mess. He could go back down to the snippy clerk and admit that He'd made a mistake or He could try to save face at home. Well, He knew Herself's relatives were coming soon. She would want Him to cooperate and be on His best behavior. Points to be gained—big points, if He could put on a good front while they were here.

So, He went home and made a deal with Herself. He would be on His absolute best social behavior while they were here. In exchange, she would call a halt to complaining about what He spent for a full sixty days. He was nice as pie and all went super well.

So that's why Jake was hired, why the Ole Man seemed to love having her relatives go hunting with Him. Jake's pay was a full dozen decoys from a collection hand-carved in 1898. The Ole Man hated to see them go, but He needed to make an impression, and Jake, knowing what was going on, said, "I wouldn't have missed it for the world. This was a fun way to spend a day. Really fun, guiding the Ole Man, just so He could impress some relatives with His wealth. Watching Him tell them about all the land He owned . . . I tell you, it was a hoot. I wish Him luck paying for twelve of those rods . . . maybe, just maybe, we might be able to make a deal." Jake had a time of great glory at the Ole Man's expense.

15

Leavin' Home for Good

ALL OF US LOVE OUR HOME GROUNDS. The center of our life nourishes us through thick and thin, through happy or sad events. When the sun goes down, home, or what we call home, is where we unwind and prepare to join the world again with the renewal of the sun.

Travel is also a part of our life. Satisfied with home, we still look forward to journeys far away. Call it wanderlust. Call it "The grass is always greener." For many outdoorsmen, the idea of faraway travel means Alaska, Africa, Terra Nova, Quebec, the Yukon, or maybe a wing shoot on doves in Argentina. Dreams of the exotic. We read the back pages in the outdoor magazines and fill our minds with adventure—some possible, some only good for cold winter nights. Huge trout, trophy brown bears, an impala, or perhaps a nice antelope fill the reading dream with a sense of variety. Home is still home, but the distant outdoor life is pulling at your consciousness.

Whether for adventure or for fun or for experimentation, we all seem to want to see the other side of the far hill. Even the Ole Man had thoughts like that.

One recent fall He gave in and flew to Alaska.

"I want a really big bull moose, not a tiny feller such as we have around these parts. You know, move up from the minor league to a place where giants still roam the woods." He had a dreamy look in His eyes—faraway places, with a life neither of us knew much about.

The Ole Man was a local expert on Alaska after nearly two years of library books, scads of magazine articles, and lots of letters to outfitters and governmental agencies. His mail carried dozens of Alaska postmarks, incoming as well as outgoing.

The place He chose was in the heart of the Yukon River. He carefully planned every step, throwing out Alaskan landmark names as though they were located just ten miles away. His research was thorough. Some people at work thought He must have been there before because of the way He spoke about the smallest details of life in the Alaskan Yukon River country. While home life went on, the remote Alaskan interior was starting to occupy every thought in His day. Mr. Keegan, His boss, told the foreman, "I'll be glad when the Ole Man gets Alaska out of His system. Right now I try to avoid Him. Tired of His stories about a place He hasn't even visited."

We all wished Him well. When the plane left for New York with a nonstop flight from JFK to Fairbanks, we knew we would be hearing about the adventure.

The trip was too costly for me. I went back to life at home, but often thought about the Ole Man's trip to a dream hunt. It was enough for me.

About three days after He got home, I stopped in to ask about Alaska. I was a little surprised He hadn't called me earlier. I chalked it up to jet lag. He said He wanted me to hear it "from start to finish, all at one time." The fire was stoked in the den's fireplace, glasses of Old Stump Blower were poured; the tale was now to be told.

"I liked the flying better than I thought I would," He began with a look of mystery. "I wish you or Jake could have been there. It would have made it even more real. But, that's all in the past now. The die has been cast. I can tell you right off, it's one of the few times outdoors where I had a great time without friends being there. My guide became my friend. He is a great outdoorsman." He was speaking almost as though still caught in a dream.

He swished His drink around the rim of the glass and looked off in space, saying, "We got up early the first morning. I say 'got up,' but actually I was awake for hours because of the constantly howling malamute sled dogs. They yap incessantly. Every bush village I visited was packed with dogs; in some there were more dogs than people. I wish Herself could have seen the hundreds of dogs; she thinks I have too many with a measly half-dozen.

"I'll tell ya later about all the wonderful bird hunting, but first let me tell ya about the moose hunt. It's the one big-game animal I always feel uncomfortable around, even the moose back home. My father shot one of the last legal ones, the massive bull head we have over the fireplace at Home Base. After 1935 we went all the way to 1980 without the modern, annual moose hunt we have today. 'Course, the moose hunt of 1981 didn't come about . . . politics. I guess I'm drifting away from my story. But moose are the giants of the forests, around here, or in Alaska.

"I wanted an Alaskan moose as big as my father's Home Base trophy. Or maybe that's what I told myself. I just wanted to walk on Alaskan soil after decades of reading about the state. Getting the bull moose would be a bonus. The thrill of the land, the wildness, the differences with being back east. There is an aura in those thousands of square miles. The generous sweep of the land with mountains, a dominant wash in the Yukon River—a river with majesty, depth, power, history—a real presence. The natives still use it as a highway, no pavement, but a really intense highway nonetheless.

"Oh, I almost forgot. I did see a fish wheel while I was there. They were trying for dog salmon, getting plenty, too. They split them and hang them on dozens of sapling racks. They're used to feed the dogs all winter. Just like a freezer provided by nature. Grab a few salmon off the rack, throw them to the dogs. Presto, the dogs are fed, no need for supermarket dog feed transported way back in the woods by supply boat or charter plane. Cheap food.

"When the other species of salmon come in the wheels, they help feed the villages along the Yukon River. The water current carries the fish as they get caught in a huge scoop of clear screening. As it goes up in the air, it tilts, spilling the fish into a holding box in the center of the wheel. Pretty slick . . . twenty-four-hour fishing machine.

They check the box every day or so and take home the fish. Slick work, I tell ya. It's almost like a farming operation."

I had never seen the Ole Man like this. He was spellbound, with a dozen side tracks going at any given time. The thoughts were damned near spiritual, philosophical, the dogma of a convert. He'd never been a close observer of the local social life, yet in Alaska He was a full-time student. Take a good outdoorsman from New England and transport Him thousands of miles away to the broad river plain, and the love of everything wild comes out in the contrasts between home and the reality of Alaska.

The Ole Man talked for hours while we drank only two drinks. I was fascinated by the tale He was telling. The feelings, sights, sounds, and textures of the place. The topics were varied: the people, the distant mountains, the animal life, northern lights, stars in the sky different from ours, and the smells, especially of dogs and fish. He was painting a picture in the air. I expected at any time He would finally break into the yarns with a blow-by-blow of His moose hunt. If not the moose, than at least the ptarmigan He must have shot by walking the backwater sloughs.

The evening wore on. I wasn't aware of how many hours passed until the grandfather clock in the den struck a single chime. It was getting to be the early-morning hours, and yet I wanted to stay for more. He got out some cheese and crackers while I poured us a tall, but weak, drink with ice, Old Stump Blower and water.

He took a day trip to visit an old mining camp in the outback. There was a day exploring a great feeder river near Nulato, where Jack London stayed and wrote a couple of his best short stories. There were three days spent in the twisting, turning wild, slow-moving waters of the Kaiyuh Slough, where the wetlands breed millions of ducks and geese. He spent two days on a riverboat loaded with school supplies for the dozens of villages scattered over more than a thousand miles of the mighty American side of the Yukon River. It was an annual trip for the boat. It was once in a lifetime for Him.

Finally, I could stand it no more. I had to know. I asked, "How was the Alaskan hunting?" Everyone who has never been there wants to know the answer to the question. Everyone who has been there just says, "It was great." The Ole Man looked up from His rocker by the fireplace, yawned, stretched, threw another log in the fire, and said, "Got another match for my pipe?"

Once He had the pipe stoked up again, without waiting for me to re-ask the question He said, "It was good. I got me a moose and I shot some birds." After hours of tales, detailed descriptions, mixed liberally with emotions, He was content to let the actual hunting be answered by a single sentence or two.

When I left the house an hour later, I was still mystified by the evening. The Ole Man was transporting both of us to a place where time stood still, the rarefied air was pure, the land, undefiled by man, the population of wildlife, dozens of times larger than the human count. Why was He so interested in the diversified Alaskan life of both man and animal?

As I rounded the corner of Main Street on my way home, I found my answer. There was a brilliant display of northern lights right here in northern New England. Even in my preoccupation I paused to admire the lighting dance of ions in the sky, a mystery that had been entrancing mankind for thousands of years. I have often heard southerners visiting the northern areas of the country and encountering the northern lights for the first time. They say, "I could spend the whole night watching those displays, and you people hardly seem to notice." True, familiarity does breed a kind of shrug in the shoulders, but they are still spectacular displays.

These visitors are fascinated by the lobstermen, the loggers in the dense commercial forests, or the people living a few miles back on a dirt road. The style of life shocks their sense of normal, average, daily life. The visitors notice things like the widely scattered white quartz rock, the almost tropical growth of lichens on some spruce trees, or the babble of brooks heading steeply down a ridge. All come to us, but not to them.

The Ole Man traveled on a trip like that. He was giving me lessons on Alaska, its land, the people, the feel. The actual hunting was totally outshone by the milieu. The "out-of-stater" is a figment of the imagination. There is no such thing as a division. Janice Joplin said, "It's all the same day, we're on the same train . . ." She was right. There's one world we all spin around on every day.

You might say that the one who learned the most from the Ole Man's Alaskan trip was me. He already knew the obvious: "The huntin' in Alaska was good."

16

Vagrancy Law Disproved

MY WIFE HAS A HABIT, one she repeats frequently, of saying that I have a close association with vagrants. According to her, they are shiftless characters who hunt far too much, spend too much time looking for scrawny trout, miss church services for Sunday turkey shoots, are always buying expensive shotguns when they already own a small armory, grow hunting dogs the way most people raise radishes, buy part ownerships in crazy things like power ice augers, rarely are home for holidays, and are never excited about their professional, moneymaking careers so vital to keeping things running at home.

They are hunters, fishermen, campers, trapshooters; there are some trappers, snowmobilers, all-terrain vehicle drivers (ATVers) . . . but not one is a vagrant.

According to me.

When she gets in one of these moods after I've just purchased another case of express loads for duck hunting, I find the only thing I can do is remind her she has plenty of company in our small town. This can turn out to be a mistake if she gangs up with Herself and some other wives to rein in our outdoor lifestyle. What one wife forgets to use to stir the brew gets thrown in by the others, until they have a laundry list of complaints.

Take the last woodcock season.

The Ole Man took a few "personal days" from work. His reason was sound, clear, right? After all, woodcock southern migration routes are often erratic and short-lived. A cold snap with frozen ground, and the woodcock disappear hereabouts until the next spring's flight north for breeding. In the last season we saw "native" timberdoodles hang around, but the migrants were still north of us. A low-pressure system was headed our way. Cold weather. The Ole Man was logical. If He didn't get time off from work, He would clearly miss the bulk of the action opportunities—for a whole year. No one could argue with these facts.

I approached my wife about calling Mr. Keegan, the boss, to say the Ole Man and I were victims of the same flu bug, "or whatever you want to say. It would kill two birds at one time." With that she started to haul me over the coals because of all the things around the house I left undone during the summer and early fall. According to her there were "a thousand things, at least." There was a leaky faucet in the upstairs bathroom. The leaves hadn't been raked since 1969, the year of the Woodstock concert. And that was the year I disappeared on a caribou hunt to the George River country in Ungava, Quebec. There was firewood to split and stack for the stove and fireplace. Or the faulty light socket in the bedroom closet; kept blowing fuses. It needed to be replaced. This was all according to her. She's a good woman, but sometimes her logic goes completely astray.

After a hastily called conference with the Ole Man, it was decided not to say too much about the upcoming trip until the first frosty morning. Then, the woodcock to the north of us in Canada would need to start their trip south because heavy frosts take away their insect and worm feed from the surface. No feed, time to move south. When this happens the "visitors"—migratory birds—stop over in our covers and give us great shooting. Timing for the hunter is everything. A cover can be empty one day and filled with visitors twenty-four hours later.

For about a week I listened to a faintly received Canadian radio station for the nightly weather forecasts. Since I rarely listen to news on any radio or TV station, my wife thought it was "nice to see you broadening your educational horizons by listening to the Canadian news, sports, and weather. It might give you a better balance about important world affairs." At least I was out of the doghouse once in a while. She didn't know I was waiting through all the other junk broadcast just to hear the local weather in the Canadian province nearby.

One night I heard what I wanted to hear: There was going to be a heavy "killing" frost for several nights upcoming. We would soon be up to our elbows in Canadian timberdoodles. By figuring the frosts to the north and looking at the calendar, I saw that the best hunting was going to be during the work week. Isn't that the way it goes? When the best hunting or fishing weather is there, so, too, is working for a living?

I called the Ole Man to tell Him the good news. It was time for action. Whether Mr. Keegan thought the Ole Man and I calling in for personal leave within five minutes of each other was unusual or not, he never said. Our wives saw through the ruse immediately, as though we were two degenerates sitting on a sidewalk swigging from a gallon jug of cheap wine. It's a good thing we weren't connected to pretty eighteen-year-olds, because there was a domestic war without adding any complications. There was the fully disgusted contingent who thought their husbands were childish, irresponsible, inconsiderate vagrants if they went, and there was the other side who thought their lives would be ruined without some quality R & R provided by a woodcock hunt.

We left at dawn on Monday. The equipment taken was whatever we could gather without making it look as though a safari was under way. The Ole Man took His Parker double out to the Jeep in two bagged loads mixed with garbage He was taking to the town dump. A full case of number-eights He wheeled out to the Jeep in a wheelbarrow, covered by old clothes (prime hunting apparel).

I made the same diversionary moves at home. We wanted everyone to think we were going to work, except for the boss, Mr. Keegan, who already knew we would be missing our wives. "Personal leave" was supposed to be used for serious business like "signing the mortgage for a house, meeting with a lawyer to settle an inherited estate, going to court, or other such occasions." It was part of our contract.

It is doubtful Mr. Keegan would call migrating wood-cock a serious personal business affair. First, he'd have to catch us.

Some things were naturally purchased the previous week to have on hand for the woodcock emergencies. Separately we made investments at the local liquor store in a half-gallon of Old Stump Blower, because, as the Ole Man said, "We will need it to ward off serious infections caused by combat fatigue brought on by dawn-to-sunset workdays at Home Base, or locations reachable from there."

The rusty, sloppy old Jeep was ten miles down the road before the Ole Man remembered that He'd forgotten to bring His special supply of wild rice to be used with the evening meals. "Woodcock require wild rice. Now, danged if I ain't gone off and forgot our gourmet wild rice I get from Minnesota. Well, can't go back; it'd look worse than it already does. We'll have to make do by finding better-tasting birds."

The first cover was a setting where I would like to spend all of my autumn days for the rest of my life. There's a long abandoned farm where the many apple trees are surrounded by alders, white birch, occasional spruce, fir mixed with a few fledgling maple. The hayfields are now growing up to wild sapling trees mixed with wild apple, thorn plum, high-bush cranberry, and scattered raspberries. The wildlife call it home.

None of the trees are gone beyond the stage where they no longer assist wildlife. No mature trees for logging. These trees are teenagers and sprouting out the gospel of growth. It's the kind of place where you can almost dream about a rabbit setting up short, or where a visiting woodcock, looking down from above, would want to settle in for a day or two of rest. The deer and bear feed on the apples, as do the partridge. As we got out of the Jeep, the Ole Man said, "This place is the Park Avenue of habitats. Even a dumb, clueless critter could earn a livin' here."

136

The first three shots to come up in front of Lady, the wonderful hunting Brittany, favored the Ole Man. He was pleased to get two of the three shots, but not happy about missing an unencumbered left to right. "Shoulda busted that one. I need more practice," He said.

I wanted to tell Him that all three were easy shots, but knew it would lengthen the week considerably. The one He missed, I think He was too quick, too anxious with the trigger, but we all miss some easy ones. It's part of the sport. I miss those myself.

I blew shot number one. I nearly always do that, and have been known to continue the streak longer than I ever thought possible. I need more practice, too.

The woodcock is a hard target to get on. They jump straight up, level off, zigzag at any time, look easy to shoot, but hide behind an alder as they depart. Even in the clear their flight is gamey, deceptive whirls of dip and do.

When the bird surprises me I often blurt out one shot from my over/under and then settle in for my last shot. The bird, knowing he got a free pass on the first one, adds zest to my shooting score by zigging right when I was hoping for a zag. Expert shooters tell you to wait until the bird is at full height, in the process of leveling off, to touch the trigger. I know that. But year after year I fail to adjust my style, even with the massive amount of trapshooting I do to prepare. The woodcock simply give me free shooting lessons. When I'm just about getting good, having expended hundreds of rounds at blank air, the season is over. In twelve months I forget and begin at ground zero again.

The weather was bright fall blue. Every step taken was from one Currier & Ives scene to another. The only touch nature added was a sling full of glorious color. Even Lady didn't need instructions to tell her this was prime-time hunting. Every muscle, every sinew, quivered with alertness. I can close my eyes now and see the woodcock fly, the color of the fall foliage, see Lady freeze with a lifted front paw, nose stretched out, see the Ole Man shoot. It was bliss. The workaday world was gone. Therapy.

I can't honestly say how many woodcock came to the bag over the next week. I can recall one I missed when a partridge tried to flap my hat off and a woodcock chose the same moment to get up some air speed. I can even remember a perfectly retrieved bird Lady brought back from a tangle of wild raspberries.

When the week was over I was sad to leave such great days for another year. The migration was passing and the birds were headed south. Sure, we would get a few hours here, a day there, but nothing beats devoting your full time and focus to the chores at hand.

On the way home the Ole Man brooded about losing the few days of hunting that may have awaited us. He was otherwise pretty quiet in the old Jeep until we passed the boundary for our town. Immersed in deep thought. Then, He leaned over and nearly whispered, "Funny, but I don't feel like a vagrant, and we made out just fine without the wild rice."

I just nodded my agreement.

17

A Lady from Big John

WHY A GROWN MAN GETS SO EXCITED over a plain, average, maybe even homely dog is a mystery to those who don't hunt. They can't understand why a man would smile for days at the mere prospect of a new puppy coming home.

The puppy will require basic training, weaned away from chewing on the furniture, stopped from cutting through dangling electrical cords, chased off the divan in the parlor, need several trips to the vet stretching the credit cards even more than the cash for their purchase; still, to the hunting fraternity, the gun dog is an investment in future outdoor trips. Good ones. Great ones. Unforgettable hunting days, when the dog is the star ingredient in the hunt.

The Ole Man, or I, or probably you, will find lots of excuses to loaf extra days every year with every pup that comes our way. "Oh, honey, the dog needs to be trained for the fall hunt." Or, "Honey, I need to get the dog outdoors more so he will be in shape for serious hunting soon. His breed requires a lot of time afield to be worth the investment we're making. It's a hard job for me, but in the long run, it'll be best."

Sometimes it works. Sometimes they still want the lawn mowed.

I am not destined to win the argument with the wife. She is not going to believe I need a dog, need to train a dog, need to add another dog (hunting other species, or to replace an aging warrior), or need to spend those hours—it must total in the hundreds each year—to get a prime, ready-to-roll, hunting dog. When a hunting dog is in his prime, the animal can be a real beauty to behold. The instincts run deep and the ability is a developed natural skill with a strong reinforcement of many practice sessions.

My wife, however, doesn't see the beauty. She only sees the money being spent.

So it was that the Ole Man needed another Brittany pup to train for the fall upland season. She was born January 29, one of six. Both parents were veteran field dogs, good at the game. It was hoped that this pup would continue the heritage. A hunter has to believe.

Along toward the last part of March, Big John called the Ole Man. He was calling long distance, so naturally, the Ole Man had to talk loud to be heard over the wire. Herself was away in the kitchen when He took the call in the den. She heard every word, of course.

"THAT PUP IS ALL READY TO GO, HUH? WELL, I'LL BE DOWN TO PICK HER UP TOMORROW. MILD-MANNERED, ACTS LIKE A LADY. NOT TOO BIG. SOUNDS LIKE IT'S JUST WHAT I WANT. OKAY, I'LL BE IN BRADLEY BY TEN A.M. WITH THE SEVEN HUNDRED IN CASH."

Boy, oh boy, was the Ole Man in for trouble. Not only had He not mentioned the fact that He was acquiring a new dog, but He slipped and mentioned the price. Usually, the prices on outdoor purchases shrink by half when the opposite sex is around.

This time, however, He spelled it right out. Herself was through the door before He'd even put the phone back in place.

"You need a few more loose screws, Ole Man. I don't want any more dogs. Between guns, dogs, and fishing tackle, you have every room in the house looking like a sporting goods store. I'm glad they don't have dogs for trout!" She was burned. But she was also the first one to offer the dog a delectable goody from the kitchen, too. When it was cold outside during the winter she worried about warm, clean bedding. When they got sick, she flew to the vet. When they passed on, she cried more than most people do for their kin.

So it was that the bright, sparkly little pup from Big John arrived home at the Ole Man's place, the very next day. Since it was decided she was a true lady, the Ole Man allowed as she needed no other name. From now on, it would simply be Lady.

The trip home was a pleasure. Expectations, dreams of time spent together in the future, all to unfold in the months and years ahead. The eight-week-old pup stayed in my lap for the entire trip home in the rattling, rusty Jeep. The first of many rides. One couldn't help but wonder if this would be a great dog, a good dog, or one someone would need to adopt as a pet. No hunter likes to think of the latter option. We all hope and believe in the best, getting the best breed, from the best hunting stock, paying out the big cash amounts. We want—and deserve—the best. But, even with the training, it will be up to her; either she has hunting instincts and talents coupled with a great desire to hunt, or she is a lap dog forever.

The fact she was bright was clear right from the beginning. After only a single day in the house she established in her mind that the dish on the kitchen floor was hers to be

fed from. The water supply was right there, too. The Ole Man called it Lady's "wear and tear center," because after a busy day exploring her universe, she always managed to recover from her adventures by getting water and seeing what was in her food bowl. Extra table fare was eaten first.

If the dish was empty, she carried it around the house to announce it was time for a refill. If you filled her dish with dog fare, she would regularly wait until the people ate supper, washed the dishes, and moved to the living room or den before she would ever touch the dog food. She was especially fond of the times when the Ole Man was left in the kitchen alone, because then her dish always got liberal helpings of people food. Bite-size venison steak was one of her favorites.

The Ole Man kept a woodcock wing in each slipper in His bedroom closet. He loved to holler "Fetch!" She would charge upstairs and bring each of the slippers tenderly down to drop at His feet. Herself was not so crazy about the new scratches on the hardwood floors brought about as Lady tried desperately to gain traction for a faster run to get a slipper. It was a game with a price to be paid. After she grew to maturity she would carry both slippers at one time to the Ole Man soon after He got home from work. "Wish I could have trained Herself to do that," He said quite often. (Herself is a tolerant woman, but . . .)

For Lady it was always the outdoors she liked best. All sections of the lawn required a brief sniffing inspection before passing on to other areas. An unsuspecting robin was the first bird she ever "pointed." I think she knew right off this wasn't a target game bird, because she always acted ashamed or sneaky if she messed with lawn birds.

Before the season opened we tried her in the field on every day we could get away from work. The Ole Man said, "She's not perfect, but neither's your shootin' as far as I remember." He missed birds, too. But I noticed mine were called "clean misses," while He rarely referred to His own as anything but "real close shave for that bird, wasn't it?" Or, He said, "It's a shame that bird will have to live through a real cold winter when he had an easy chance to fold his wings the right way. It serves him right. I hope it is cold this winter."

The dog was able to point woodcock, but only in a general way. You knew the bird was somewhere close, because she acted gamey and half-froze into a point several times. Sometimes the timberdoodle acted up by jumping for the sky when we were too far away. The dog needed gun experience and more time with the game-bird scents to figure out all the details.

The experience with gunfire the Ole Man provided first with a few blank .22's fired when food was placed in her dish. She quickly grew to love the sound of gunfire, and associated it with good eating.

On opening day we were up a full two hours before dawn's first light. Bacon sizzled in the frying pan, bread was in the toaster, coffee was brewing, eggs at the ready when I walked through the door. We ate quickly while Lady looked on. The Ole Man was still finishing a piece of toast when He got up to open the gun cabinet to get out the old Parker double.

Lady knew something was up. This was a big day. With the gun and now a smell-saturated hunting jacket brought to the kitchen, she simply went wild with puppy excitement. Breakfast was something only fat people would be interested in. She raced upstairs and brought back both woodcock wings, minus the slippers. The Ole Man got out the dog whistle and bell.

"Damn! That dog knows this is the main event already, and she ain't even had a single bird shot over her yet. Now, if I could get her to remember to bring me extra shells for opening day, she would be about fully trained, I'd say." He was excited, too.

All the days and years ahead were to be filled with everlasting memories of the good times in the upland. But today was the first, and it was something a dedicated hunter always looks forward to—new dog companion, new season. It was long anticipated.

"Kinda like women," the Ole Man said. "It's not the actual gettin' that counts. It's just all the figurin', all the workin', all the preparation for the fun to come. It was the same for me when I was a young hound."

18

Sweat Forms on the Ice

THE DUCK-HUNTING CAMP we all called Home Base was not always used for rest and for recreation only during the month of November. The Ole Man was sometimes known to use the escape for such things as setting out "a batch of corsets." To Him, this was ice-fishing for salmon, with tilt springs from a women's corset used in place of the normal spring steel everyone else uses. "Corset stays are stronger, don't bend like cheap steel; they are more traditional, just better ice-fishing trap springs than steel." It was His law.

There would be little variances in the kind of day that ushered Him away from a warm rock-maple fire in the fire-place at home. The wind would howl, the temperature would slip downward, and the fire in His veins would immediately call to set out some corset-spring traps on Ragged Pond.

I was sitting in His den one Friday night on the eve of the opening of ice-fishing. He wanted everyone to know this winter was especially cold, and "it's froze solid all around. Plenty of ice. Now, we need to get things ready, no matter how hard the blow." Outside the wind was gusting over thirty miles per hour. I noticed that snow seeped under the doors in my car on the way over here; it would be even colder in the morning. The windshield held a heavy coating of ice, too. Not to mention a foot of fresh, blowing snow and subzero temperatures. Yeah, it was the kind of weather forecast the Ole Man always chose to go ice-fishing.

He was rubbing His hands together—not from a need for warmth, but in anticipation of the ice-fishing tomorrow. "Where are your corsets? Tomorrow we need to get an early start on the season at Ragged. Of course, we *could* miss the opening and stay home if you think it's too cold for sissies like you and me."

Staying home would be worse than enduring the extreme weather we were sure to get. Never hear the end of it.

The Ole Man was crowding me a little. What He actually wanted was a day or two at Home Base. He told me once, in a rather serious, stern manner, "Buildings get lonely, too, you know. They need to see someone loves them." He was the one who missed the refuge of Home Base and the fantastic days of duck gunning at Black Hole or just simply seeing the smoke curl up from the chimney on a cold morning's dawn.

Even the Jeep needed tire chains the next morning to get us to Home Base on Ragged Pond. Even then, we bounced, slid, twisted, and turned our way through heavy ruts to get there. This was a day that would certainly duplicate the weather of the previous evening, except perhaps the wind had picked up a bit more.

A small brown toolbox in the rear held the tackle we needed, or thought we needed, to get the job done. It always went out neat, clean, and tidy. Every piece of green line, every hook, every sounding sinker and leader was in its proper place. On the return trip the box was wet, half filled with snow and ice, or at the very least carried tackle in helter-skelter fashion. Ice-fishing's cold fingers did not allow much patience with the neatness of a tackle box. You are satisfied to get all the gear back in the box. Super neatness comes in the leisure of the home. Often, by the time the box was reloaded, your fingers were already turning white because gloves are impossible to wear when handling things like hooks. Too clumsy. Add ice-cold water to the mix and it's easy to see why ice-fishing takes desire, courage, tradition, and stubbornness to carry off year after year.

The wicker basket occupied the place of honor. It was hand-woven by a Native American tribal member who lived on the reservation, making his living by weaving local woods into pieces of art. This basket was made specifically for the Ole Man. The order was placed by telling the artist the basket was needed for ice-fishing. Right from the time the Ole Man picked it up He felt proud of the results. It was sturdy ash, split carefully, woven skillfully, with a balanced handle to allow a hefty load. It looked good and proved to be useful immediately.

Over the years, the basket's use was enlarged from just carrying fish home from ice-fishing to being used on night trout-fishing expeditions. It also held fresh fiddleheads, and sometimes was even used as a lunch basket. Pieces of outdoor gear take on a life and importance all their own.

With constant use these baskets do wear out. Any retired ash wicker basket the Ole Man has worn out gets a lifetime pass as a container for things like decoy storage or organizers for small fly boxes. The fact they are worn by contact with ice or streamside rocks, or bouncing around in the Jeep, does not mean they cease to be treasures for the Ole Man. He thinks of them as friends, with a lot of outdoor memories tied to their worn and frazzled look.

Next to the wicker basket would come allegiance to the set of snowshoes. They were used on balmy days, like the opening day of ice-fishing. They also saw service throughout the winter for rabbit hunting, occasional bobcat trips, or for snowmobile survival gear. Often, they were a key part of the day outdoors when snow covered the ground at great depths. Snowshoes give you access to the wild, unplowed outdoors.

The "webs" were not put away in the spring until they were repaired, shellac-covered, and examined closely for anything amiss. Your enjoyment afield needed to be guarded with a little TLC. It would pay dividends the following winter. With winter trips behind them, they were left standing quietly in the corner of the attached shed. To look at them there no one would imagine they had much value to the owner. As you entered the house I doubt you even saw them on most days. And yet, the Ole Man looked on them with fond smiles, no matter what the season.

When Herself moved them to the cellar one day when she was cleaning out the shed, so people could get through to the house, He blew a gasket. "Where in hell's name are my snowshoes, woman?" He asked upon coming home after work. Herself answered, "I needed to clean out some of

your junk so the rest of the world can get into the house without stumbling over a heap of debris. I moved them, and they're going to stay there."

After a back-and-forth marital skirmish, the snowshoes went back to the shed. However, a lot of other stuff was relocated to other storage areas. He still felt Herself was out of line.

We didn't get to Home Base until nine a.m. on opening day. Treacherous travel was the reason. It was hard going. The roads were not really safe to travel. Even the Jeep's twenty miles per hour seemed a bit high. Wind was sweeping clouds of blowing snow over the road at a rate that was difficult to believe. Take one look at the accumulation and you see the effects of snow driven by wind. One spot was bare. One was covered with four feet of the white stuff.

Ragged Pond was just over the knoll behind the camp. It was not a particularly good landlocked salmon water, but we fished there for three or four days every winter because our retreat, our home away from home, our bachelor headquarters—Home Base—was so close by. Convenience fishing. Campfires, camaraderie, plates of hot, steaming, homemade, stovetop foods. Man food.

I got elected to "go out and get some holes cut while I get the fire goin' in the camp." I stopped for a few moments as I watched the Ole Man swing His webs toward the back door of the camp. I was faced with carrying the tackle box, traps, ax, bait bucket, and power auger up a rather steep hill. The Ole Man was wiser than I gave Him credit for.

Since I forgot to bring a broom or shovel from camp, I was forced to cut a spruce branch to sweep snow off the ice. The wind was making even breathing a chore. The blown ice crystals stung when they impacted the face. The snow was about three feet on the ice, but fortunately, it was lightweight and responded to the spruce ice broom. In five minutes I had cleared enough space for two good holes.

The power ice auger roared, faltered, and died. I took out the plug, froze my fingers, checked to see it was getting gas, froze again. Nothing. I would have to take it to Home Base to see if we could get it going. Back home it started on the first pull. So, I used the ax to cut through two feet of ice. With the ax work I felt a trickle of sweat running down the back of my neck, despite the extreme cold.

I decided to get more traps set. By the time I'd completed hole number three I was ready for a break. The warmth of honest hard work was spreading throughout my entire body. I was in the mood for a good pipe. I got out the tobacco from a pouch and tamped down the weed. It tasted better than in my living room. I was here in the wild, with the cold winds and the low temperatures, but the feeling of success was in the winds of my mind. Inside my body it was comfortable. All was right with the world. If I was home I would be looking out the window, hoping the weather would improve. Out here, it was perfectly all right the way it was.

Anyone passing by would have thought me a lunatic. Three fishing traps set. Standing there puffing on my pipe while the arctic winds rearranged the landscape. A flag broke my dream. It was a nice fat salmon I decided to keep. Out on the ice it froze almost instantly. I put it in the wicker basket, thinking aloud, "Fish number one." I stuck my hands under my sweater to warm them up. I needed to put another minnow on the hook and reset the trap.

About the time I was finished with the reset the Ole Man came along. "Hey, I see you got lunch ready for us already. Ain't it just like goin' shopping out here? I mean, the salmon are down there in the refrigerator and we're up in the freezer compartment, and all we have to do is open the door and they just volunteer to join us. Just like leprechauns, magic, and ah, whatever you call that psychology blabber. Life the way it ought to be. Enough yakking; let's get the rest of the traps set and retreat to a warm Home Base for a fresh salmon bake."

19

You Should Have Been Here Yesterday

EVERY TIME YOU TURN AROUND IT HAPPENS. Someone caught a whole mess of lunkers here last Thursday. The parson shot a limit of grouse in the morning before two weddings and a funeral. A young kid collected an albino buck in your favorite deer cover while you were off visiting the in-laws. Jake got a fifteen-pound lake trout on the first pass while you were replacing the shear pin on your outboard after hitting a log floating just under the surface. The Ole Man said He used to catch five-pound brookies in Swift Brook every time He went there.

Reminds me of the way I look back at my youth. Seems how every young lass in the county was waiting for me to call for a date. Could it be my memory has forgotten the rough edges? There was, after all, the time Sarah London . . . ah, well, that's a whole different thought. I'll get back to that another time.

Today and tomorrow I can guarantee a full-blown hurricane-force wind will be blowing every time I step up to our trap's number-three station. I can also flatly guarantee the Leonard fly rod someone got for ten bucks at a yard sale will find its way back to my rod rack at a very inflated price. There's a universal law here somewhere to make me wonder why I get stuck on the outer edge every time.

However, there does come the day when it's my time to say to the other guy, "You should have been here yesterday. Wow! Was it ever great."

It happened just last fall. The Ole Man was supposed to join me for opening day at Black Hole near Home Base. Jake was coming along, too. Three times in the days leading up to the departure time our trio met to lay out the plot. Jake Goodwin was going to take the sculling boat to an area we called The-Other-Side-of-Black-Hole. His duty was to get the ducks moving and to block the retreat. The Ole Man and I would hunker down in the blind on the sand spit. The ducks were going to have a rough day of it. The plan was infallible.

It was to be a monumental day in my outdoor life. I was being placed second only to the Ole Man in the sporting hierarchy. I was located in the blind with Him, while Jake was demoted to bush league, out there paddling around, scaring up the ducks—a kid's job.

And then things started to fall apart. Jake got a bad cold and backed out of the whole hunt. The Ole Man was forced to work the day shift at the personal invitation of Mr. Keegan. It seems there were too many people calling in sick and He was needed absolutely. The Ole Man was sad about missing opening day, but he vowed revenge. "I'll get my pound of meat out of this. You'll see. Yes, sir, I will." I think Mr. Keegan knew where the Ole Man would be if he didn't give the order before He got a chance to be "sick."

Missing opening day was a big deal for the Ole Man after so many years spent at Black Hole. I was feeling sad for Him. I even thought of offering my services to Mr. Keegan in His place, but I gave up on that line of thinking because I figured if Mr. Keegan wanted the Ole Man that badly, there was little I could do. Herself was not overly happy with the work assignment, and I couldn't understand why. Maybe she really didn't mind all those days He spent outdoors. After all, we did bring home a pile of good table fare.

I was going to Home Base alone. I wouldn't want the old place to be lonely on opening day. I got all my decoys packed with my other gunnery duffel. I even decided to stop and visit with Jake.

He was in the bedroom, cuddled up with a good book, Kortright's *The Ducks, Geese, and Swans of North America*. The fire was blazing, a glass of Old Stump Blower freshly drawn, sitting on the nightstand. There was also a mixture of medicines, enough to cure a bout of cancer, heart trouble, and perhaps a gastric upset, all in one dose.

Jake was sad, too. Just like the Ole Man. With no wife to weigh him down, there was no chance he was ever going to miss an opening day. He didn't count on the sudden, severe illness, he said. He also added, "If Mr. Keegan asked me—ordered me—to work on the opening day of duck season, I would just quit my job." He was plain enough about that.

I left Jake's in a strange mood. I wanted to go duck hunting, but I wanted my friends to be there, too. It wouldn't be the same without the Ole Man being there to throw the blocks out at the hint of dawn. If Jake could have been there, too, he would have been the icing on the cake.

As I swung the wheel of the car into the final road leading to Home Base, I was in need of a warm fire, a single nightcap, maybe a few pages in a book. I planned to go to bed early. I was hoping my mood would change. Opening day of waterfowling was usually a big deal.

I went to bed early with hardly a note of pleasure in my closing thoughts. The boat was moored at the dock. The decoy box was sitting outside on the porch, with an extra two gallons of gas in case I needed motor power to chase down a cripple in the marsh. I placed the biggest anchor in the bow to add weight so the boat would ride more normally in the water. I usually occupy the bow while the Ole Man operates the outboard.

The day pack I would load with sandwiches, there was a ready thermos to fill with hot coffee, and my twelve-gauge over/under shotgun with a huge pile of shells stayed at the ready. I planned on action. My hunting coat was draped over the chair, my boots ready to slip on.

As a last tour of readiness duty, before bed, I wound the alarm clock fully, setting the alarm for two full hours before daylight.

At the roar of the alarm clock I bolted out of bed. I was psyched. The gloom of the previous night had vaporized. I was excited about the hunt, even being alone.

Breakfast was done, coffee made. All I needed was to motor on down to the Black Hole. It was a great day to be alive. I could feel the excitement building; outside there was a hint of light on the eastern horizon, and I could even hear the whistle of wings overhead. All was perfect. The motor roared to life with ease, and the waters were smooth traveling.

The decoys took more time to set out alone, but I was ready in plenty of time. I even had a full dozen spare decoys in a box in the bow. While I waited for the legal time, I thought about Jake still at home, while the Ole Man slaved away at work. The wind began to pick up, and I knew this would make the ducks restless to move on. Perfect.

Shortly after true light the ducks started to move. They trickled in. A pair of woods settled only ten yards beyond the decoys. A whole wedge of blue-winged teal passed within mere feet of the end of my gun barrel. They quickly flew to the edge of the marsh. Four blacks dropped their wings to land just out of my line of sight, behind the beaver house.

And, finally, it was legal time. A lone black came in at tree-top level and dipped to investigate my decoy set. A charge of Winchester 540 powder was behind the full charge of steel sixes that made him drop like a load of bricks. Great start!

At the echo of my shot the swamp was alive with newly located ducks. They were moving. The air was rich with our lively national treasure. As if there was a last echo of my first shot, there was a three-shot volley from Ragged Pond, our winter ice-fishing hole. No one ever hunted Ragged Pond, at least not in my memory, but things were getting more crowded every year. People love duck hunting.

I missed my next two chances. A fat little blue-wing
came in from a very low angle over the decoys. That's one
of the hardest shots for me to make, as the bird is a low-
level target coming in from the horizon. I shoot over, too
high, or more often, too low, missing by a mile. This one I
missed cleanly with both barrels. First barrel, modified
choke. The second one was full choke. I still missed.

My fresh loads were barely back in the barrels when a
pair of misplaced pins came in from on high. They were
winging by at twelve o'clock when my steel sixes passed
several feet behind them. I often miss shots at that angle,
too. Oh, well, practice will make perfect.

A volley from over the ridge at Ragged Pond told me the
stragglers were still moving around. The terrain at Ragged
Pond is not even passable duck cover. The steep shores, deep
water lacking duck weeds or wild rice, the open shoreline—
just not a duck-hunting paradise. Somebody was getting
lucky or maybe just firing at the sky. What we all used to call
"skybusters." Anyway, I was in the best place at Black Hole.

The next flight was some time in coming, so I decided to
leave the gun broken open while I retrieved the downed
black. You guessed it: A whole gang of blacks suddenly
came within inches of tipping my hat off my head. They
were close. I snapped the gun shut, too slowly. Ah, heck,
there will be others. I grabbed the black and admired his
size as I swung him aboard. Good eating ahead.

The Ragged Pond hunter, or hunters, blasted away again.
They sure were seeing action. Maybe I was wrong about it
being a poor cover. Occasionally, I could hear distant

booms and thuds as hunters in the far reaches of the swamp were emptying their shells. They weren't close, just background noises.

Back in the blind again I poured some coffee as my eyes swept the horizon. Too bad Jake and the Ole Man had missed out on this great duck day. It was a glorious fall day—windy, but since I was dressed for duck hunting, it was really quite pleasant. Winter would not ambush us; we had puffy clouds and winds today, but there was definitely a strong hint of winter settling all around me. Fair warning.

I know nonhunters think all hunting is just killing animals, but that is far from the truth. The really nice parts are the moments of reflection, the outdoors, being there when wildlife is passing, the adventure, the action, the traditions, the fun of feeling alive and taking part in life. An example would be a pipe of fine tobacco, cup of hot coffee, leaning with my back against a fir tree on the back edge of the blind, looking for ducks, but enjoying the moment. The sound of webbed feet splashing down close by brought me fully awake.

They were blacks, three of them, sitting right in my decoys. Worse, they were swimming away. I'd need to wait for a better chance. I cashed in on two high-flying blacks, or would have connected on one if the blind had allowed my swing-through to be effective. Instead, there were two belches from my gun, a dull thud as the barrels struck some blind supports; it totally shook up my recovery schedule. Birds were flying everywhere by the time I got new shells in place. A band of scaup whistled by my shoulders and a wood duck crossed in a bank—all at the same time. I fired at the

lone woodie. This time I connected as if it was an automatic reaction. Hard shot, good shooting. Maybe, lucky shot.

It was a beautiful drake wood duck. Some of the feathers would make good flies, either for us or for others we exchanged feathers with in a postal exchange for duck hunters. Woodie feathers were valued. I like the meat, too. Sandwiches came out of the bag. The coffee was cool enough now to drink. After lunch I collected two bonus birds and, one short of a limit, I decided to go back to Home Base to relax. There would be plenty of time later in the afternoon to limit out.

As I approached Home Base I saw a column of freshly charged smoke curling from the chimney. Not the kind of lazy, firing, burning-low kind of smoke that should be coming from there. I immediately thought Jake must have recovered from his illness or another friend of the Ole Man might have dropped in, decided to wait to see how we made out. Maybe Mr. Keegan let the Ole Man off easy with a half-day of work. I was curious.

I gave the outboard another notch. Maybe the Ole Man would still have time to have a chance of limiting out. He'd definitely want to get hunting. He would be fuming while He waited for me to get back, so I opened the outboard throttle all the way.

At the dock I made a quick half-hitch on the mooring lines and ran up the slope to the camp. The Ole Man's Jeep was sitting in the yard with His canoe on top. Over near the back door, on top of the woodpile, there were clearly duck feathers sticking up over the top edge. Curious, very curious. A closer look, and I saw the ducks made a full two-man daily limit. Two hunters cleaned up in the morning hunt. The crowning touch was a pair of Canadian geese hanging from a nail on the shed door.

My curiosity was near the bubbling-over stage. What in hell was going on?

Jake was there by the fire with his socks hanging over the edge of the mantel. He carried a glass of Old Stump Blower in his hand. I knew instinctively it was my bottle because a quick glance revealed that the amount in my bottle on the nightstand had shrunk considerably from last night. The Ole Man came out of the bedroom, seemingly half-awake after a nap. I felt my sense of humor slipping away. I shuddered, stumbled, stuttered, and found myself unable to ask a coherent question. I was bamboozled. I just knew it.

Now I could see. I was the third wheel in this plot. It was a hoax: sickness, working overtime. Baloney. These two ageless rowdies had planned and executed a seamless scheme. They were at Ragged Pond to stir things up while they got the cream of the shooting over there. How? Ragged was not a great cover; not even a good one.

The Ole Man's grin was overbearing. "I didn't have any fear you wouldn't shoot enough to scare them up. I just knew the low flyers would escape your efforts. You never could hit those shots. I also knew a bunch of geese have been hanging around Ragged for most of the summer and fall. Ready to be plucked, I thought. There just wasn't enough space for three gunners. Still, we needed someone at Black Hole. You were the best one we could think of, my boy. Glad you kept the opening day at Black Hole tradition open for us, too, I am. I even enjoy your whiskey. It's the right brand—Old Stump Blower. It's too bad we didn't think to bring any of our own."

They both thought it was a whale of a deal, great setup— an even greater enactment, as they got geese as a bonus.

I would hear the story retold hundreds of times over the years, especially as a new fall season approached. It was a memorable opening day.

I did go back out to pick up my daily limit that day, but I still wanted to get out of the minor leagues someday soon. I wanted to be there when "you should have been here yesterday" was actually happening. Come to think of it, I *was* there. I just needed to give it a few years to find that it has now become a local legendary hunt, and I was a key character in the success.

I guess I can swallow that. I already swallowed my pride.

20

One Less than a Brace

SPLINTER WAS THE NEW DOG AROUND. She was a direct descendant of the great, great brood mare, Queenie, whose own exploits hunting rabbits are so legendary, you probably already know her by name and reputation. The old beagle bitch was top-flight, right from her earliest tramps in the woods. A natural hunter, through and through. She never wavered in her pursuit of any rabbit lying in wait for her.

As with all things mortal there comes a time when the life span of a dog, or of a human being, seems to be far shorter than was imagined in a youthful glance. It isn't pleasant to realize with each passing day that we get one step closer to the grave, but with short-lived canines, the time passes even more telescopically. A typical man will outlive several generations of hounds, pointers, or retrievers. The facts of life.

And so it was with the Ole Man and Queenie. For several years He said, "I think we can stretch her hunting years by at least one more." One spring, after several lasting injuries, the vet advised against future hunting with Queenie. "All worn out from aging," he said. And so it was. The vet said we might hunt her a time or two in the early fall when there was no snow to wade through, but as a front-line hunting hound, her career was over.

The Ole Man had been through this before, many times. He was practical about the whole replacement process. He had bred Queenie in years past and possessed a real up-and-comer in Splinter. She was all the snowshoe rabbit hunter could ask for in a young dog, a chip off the old block. Her father was a good field hunter, too. Splinter would become front-line hound. Her performance on the rabbit trail was nothing to snicker at.

Still, although necessary, the Ole Man didn't think she was quite a finished product yet. The fifteen-year-old Queenie was still number one in His mind. Old habits are hard to cancel with a visit to the vet. Queenie didn't want to be replaced with any upstart pup, even her own, if at all possible. When she slept by the fireplace her legs moved constantly, her nose twitched expectantly, her tail wagged. She was dreaming of the hunting season ahead.

So, when the Ole Man told His hunting cronies that He still hunted with a *brace* of hounds, He was telling a slight exaggeration at best; in truth, it was a bald-faced lie. I was a little uneasy. Telling a tale like that with the sporting crowd often leads to a challenge from the gang.

No challenges would ever be made. Queenie didn't last through the deer season. It was only a couple of weeks shy of the rabbit-season opening when she quietly breathed her last, in her sleep, in front of the den fireplace.

Nothing could console the Ole Man. It was a trying time. He didn't even bother to finish the deer-hunting season. He moped around the den, not giving much thought to his passion for deer hunting. It was a deep mourning.

The first week of the rabbit season passed and all he did was get out the photos of Queenie hunting, Queenie on the trail, Queenie posed with several rabbits, happy hunters, and other hounds. He possessed slide trays full of Queenie hunting. He brought out albums of Queenie in print form. He talked about Jake's Cover, the covers on the Winding Hill Road, or the alder runs of Swift Brook.

By Thursday of the following week, things changed. I went over to His den, half expecting another morbid session of rehashing the past. It wasn't to be that way at all.

When I walked into the den, I knew the spirit was returned. Splinter was flattened by the fireplace, opening one eye to check me out as I walked through the doorway. The Ole Man offered a glass of Old Stump Blower and motioned toward the snowshoes leaning against a bookcase. They were ready for a weekend hunt. It was a return to the good times; the mourning was over, a new life beginning. Except for a few lapses when He referred to the pup as Queenie, it was a good night of planning the new adventure.

Friday it snowed—much more than the weatherman had predicted. The wind blew, the temperature dropped, and it looked as though the hunt might have to be postponed for a few days. But a postponement would have signaled that the Ole Man was less than fully confident in the new dog.

"Not going is a poor way to start Splinter's career," the Ole Man said on the phone, "so you better get your stuff ready to leave as we planned."

We went on time. Saturday was a winter's day with all the trimmings. Cold, snow blowing, hard snowshoeing, with the puffy white stuff blowing all over. It was even harder on the dog. We should never have gone, was my thought. It was miserable hunting. At least, I saw it that way after an hour of fruitless effort on the part of all three of us.

Sure there was sign—old sign, by the apple tree edge and by the waist-high young pines. Evidently the sign

wasn't fresh enough for the beagle, because she was only able to stay on the scent for a few feet before losing the trail. It was quiet in the woods except for the gusty wind.

Suddenly, the Ole Man bellowed. He was snowshoeing a parallel trail about fifty yards from my traveling lane. We were trying to help the hound find a fresh track. The next holler told me to bring the dog over to His location. I did not have Splinter. She was hunting, too.

When I appeared over on His trail, He gave me a questioning look, saying, "Queenie would have had one going by now. There's plenty of old sign here, and the rabbits ain't moved to Chicago, now, have they?" He saw one rabbit when He first shouted to me. Then He saw a second rabbit ghosting through a thick tangle of jack firs.

"Saw two of them, dead to right. Damn. Face it: That dog isn't up to the job yet. Queenie would have started them; strays would have been pouring out of their holes in the dense cover. It would have been a war out here. What have we got? Nothing. Absolutely nothing. We might as well pack up and go home. She's not ready to hunt, and I'm not either."

I was unable to think of anything to say. In a way, He was right. Queenie probably would have started rabbits by now. I could tell Him Queenie *was* the better dog. I could tell Him Splinter was young and held great promise; her day would come. I believed that. So I took the least-noxious stance: I kept my mouth shut.

All of a sudden there was an extremely loud bellow directly behind us. Splinter shot by, nose to the ground, tail wagging vigorously. She was at work! The bawling sound veered left into the thick, black hole. It was just as though we weren't even there. She knew fresh rabbit tracks when she smelled them, and this was a fresh one to her nose.

Her barnyard commotion caused a bunny to squirt right between the Ole Man and me as we watched. Neither of us had a gun ready or could have fired anyway, but it was certainly an encouraging turn of events.

I made my way around the edge where the small firs run up against the pines. The Ole Man, drawn back to reality, webbed downhill, to try and get lucky. The hound was still bellowing ahead of us. His parting blurb to me was, "Got to get that rabbit on the first pass, because Splinter doesn't have the experience to hold the scent on this lousy-weather day."

I thought about it as I slogged forward.

Three times around Splinter held the trail. The rabbit bobbed while we zigged or zagged. Her sound faded and got closer. The hunter waits, the hound works and reports. We just never saw the snowshoe flying by. Not times three. Splinter's run was letter-perfect. Queenie would have done no better at her peak; I knew that. I hoped the Ole Man did, too.

The heavy snow produced snow bubbles on the lower limbs of the evergreens, giving the rabbit a free—unseen—pass around the loop. It is very difficult to see the white-on-white rabbit under these conditions. Snowshoe rabbits, wearing white all winter, are hard to see on freshly fallen snow. Throw in the noise of the wind, and it's hard.

Bang. Bang. About a thirty-second pause and two more shots. I stayed where I was until the Ole Man, grinning from ear to ear, came up close.

"Hell, I've got a limit! I could have shot two more. It was exciting!"

About that time Splinter started bawling and I took off. She had run rabbits all around the Ole Man. Only one of the four He shot was a stray. The other three, Splinter was right on their butts, chasing them in heavy cover, through the cold and wind.

I got two in the next half-hour while the Ole Man snowshoed around, taking the rabbits back to the Jeep and dropping off His gun. The next time I saw Him, He was smoking a pipe and still grinning. The fact that I'd just shot my fourth, making both our limits for the day, wasn't lost on Him.

Splinter was getting ready to go again when He snapped on the leash, ending the hunt.

"I guess I need to apologize to Splinter. I had doubts. She has skills. Seems she knows her business better than I thought. Much better. I mean, she was perfect; Queenie sure passed on the heritage to her. She'll get a hundred percent hamburger tonight—her favorite."

He was bursting to talk. Excited, loosely joined thoughts. "Guess I've been lucky. Two terrific dogs in a row. I haven't completely lost Queenie; she's still right here in the woods with us. By God she is. I still have a brace of rabbit hounds. Yes, I do."

What could I say? In a way He did. Mother and carbon copy daughter. A brace of rabbit hounds.

21

Before You Bust a Cap

LATE AUGUST UNTIL THE MIDDLE OF SEPTEMBER is a dead zone outdoors. The salmon craze is beyond the summer peak and into the fall fishing season. Hunting has not yet started, and the trapshooting days are still ahead. Dead time.

People like you and me are not tied to the back lawn or the navy surplus hammock slung between two trees. We want to leave the concrete, the backyard, the neighborhood behind. Out there no one will call, no children will demand attention, no one will tell us the garbage needs tending or the faucet in the bathroom is leaking.

Out there, the Ole Man calls these times "the best time there is for a guts-in, wandering, need to prove nothing to nobody, scoutin' trip. That's how you get ahead. Scout out the terrain. Become aware. Find, see, explore a new huntin' place. Get it all worked out in your head before it is needed."

He handles it at home by starting out the day impressing Herself with the suggestion that He needs to make a list of work projects on the to-do list. He looks pensive. When the time is right, He will say it's a good day to help out the environmentalists by cleaning up some outdoor garbage careless people have left in a place He's noticed. Herself is suitably interested in His newfound public volunteering spirit. Possibly something good will take place today. He will ask for additional garbage bags and head for the Jeep.

"I'll be back when I get the good deed done," He says as He leaves home. It all looks mysterious, but interesting. Herself is satisfied and happy to see her husband out to do good.

He gathers up two bags of roadside trash in fifteen minutes. The rest of the day He is free to explore. The good deed is done. The excuse for roaming around is secure. He will bring the two bags of litter home to be put out with His own weekly trash.

We don't need any guns, rods, or duffel. He has a pail of tea makings always ready behind the driver's Jeep seat. I pick up a can of stew at the corner store while waiting for Him to arrive. I am off "visiting a bunch of friends I haven't seen in quite a while."

As planned, we head back to the deer country behind the duck camp, Home Base.

We can get in a day of checking Black Hole, looking at moose near the Swift Brook Meadows, or even see if the lies about the clutches of partridge are right. The liars are always saying they saw birds on the road's edge coming out from Stump Pond. Now, in all my years in the woods, I never saw sixty-four partridge roadside, not even on my best day. Today we saw a mere thirty-one birds along the road coming out by Stump. So, we knew the liars were just practicing their art.

We stopped by a trickle not even on the map and decided to explore the acreage. This is the kind of day where treasures can be found. A plan without a plan. There were a bunch of woodcock in this lowland of slight wetness. No trout, but a small beaver flowage where ducks would settle out in the open. "This is a feeder ground for Black Hole," said the Ole Man. "Sort of a holdin' tank for our extra duck supply. We increased our knowledge of the local wilds. Useful stuff; much more interesting than community service work or volunteering."

We worked our way out to Home Base near Merrymeeting Bay. It smells somewhat salty around the marsh. The freshwater smell of Ragged Pond blended to allow us a glimpse of the contrasts. We walked up a ridge we never explored before and found a good place to shoot passing

ducks. The birds circling to land at any of several dozen local potholes or open waterways would need to bank and adjust their incoming flights near here. By watching for a half-hour we saw several flights skim close to bushtop heights right near us. With a gun in our hand we would have shot several. Another useful tidbit for scouting day. New ideas, new approaches. Hard, but pleasant work.

The old duck camp seemed to long for our presence. Out the back door I saw a family of young black ducks making their way through the lush green of a late-summer cove edge. Water barely visible with all the growth. The mother duck was no longer concerned about keeping them all together. They were dispersing and feeding on their own, much like teenagers getting ready to leave home. They stayed visible for a long time.

An American bittern was the next guest to register. He was picking insects as he walked through the edge weeds and riffles. It wasn't a big pond, but wildlife was teeming if you considered all of the insects, birds, minnows, raccoons, fox, moose, deer, bear, beaver, muskrat, mink, otter, pine marten, deer, and many others who used this as a resourceful place to dine. A waterhole is very important to animal life.

When I tried to get too close to the bittern, he struck his classic fear stance. Head held high, he dared me to take notice, to advance, to shake his confidence. Of course, standing there in a sparsely covered pond, he looked a bit foolish, but often his stance blends easily where there is a mixture of dead trees, broken limbs, or tall reeds. The perfect cover. At those times, in those covers, you can get within inches of them without realizing a bittern is standing there—hiding, frozen, a statue resembling a dri-ki limb or dead sapling. If he moves at the very last second, it scares the hell out of you. A sense of shock at the sudden movement to flight with something so close, so wild.

We ate our lunch and headed for the Jeep. It would be an afternoon on Swift Brook. Some of our days are spent there in trout season, but this would be different. Our quarry was the moose, just to see how they were doing, how many were around. This is strictly informational field research. I might shoot a few photos, but NEVER bust any caps. Moose are the giants of the North, biggest land critters. By far.

Often, while fishing for trout, we see moose, sometimes close enough to get caught in a backcast. I never have my camera with me during the trout wading. Today, camera in hand, I hope to get some good shots. My wife thinks this is "a lot of work to get a photo you could get in summer or, even better, on the Internet on a wildlife site." I don't think she understands. I want my own photos. I want to concentrate on trout fishing when I'm there earlier. Now, I want *my photos*. My memories, not those of a professional photographer who probably doesn't even know where Swift Brook is.

The Jeep slid to a stop in a mud puddle at the edge of the brook. We were five miles away from regular roads. The four-wheel-drive bounced us up and over rocks, blowdowns, and tree stumps to get us this close to the waterway.

When we stopped I had a puddle to jump over as I stepped from the vehicle. The Ole Man felt only hard, dry dirt on His side. As He watched me scramble He was grinning from ear to ear. When you go with Him, you get used to these little "jokes" or setups. In some perverse way He gets a thrill out of each incident. I always fight back by not acknowledging the event. Nothing happened, according to me.

There was a whole series of lazy sloughs in this area of the brook. Each water-filled arm or slough possessed different characteristics. Some were nearly stagnant water. Some were deep enough and held enough spring-fed oxygenated water to be decent fishing waters. Moose like the slow-moving waters often covered by lily pads by midsummer. It's a feeding place, a chance to ward off blackflies and mosquitoes while standing chest-high in the waters. Classic photo country.

There were millions of flies here today. I generously sloshed on the fly dope. We made our way along a cedar edge, close to the waters. Glance either way and there were feed beds for moose. The muddy bottoms would act like quicksand for you or me, but to the splay-footed moose the enlarged brook waters were home, sweet home.

I snuck over three-quarters of the way across the cedar point when a rushing flow of water reminded me of what I was looking for. A mature cow moose, equipped with a spring-born calf, stood up suddenly about a hundred yards away. She knew something was up, but her poor eyesight needed help. She twitched her nose.

My scent was drifting in the opposite direction. My telephoto lens got a few decent images, as the moose was wary but unwilling to stop feeding. By edging a little closer my shots got better. After a full twenty minutes of ignoring us being there she decided there was something not quite right even if she detected nothing with her nose. She moved away with the smaller moose following her every footstep.

The next hour was dry moose hunting. We saw a few mergansers (American, not hooded); we also saw a family group of blacks. A crow called, a red squirrel was watching us with vocal disapproval, a deer crossed in front of us, probably a doe, too hidden to get a good view. No camera shots here. Besides, I really wanted moose.

Dark was fast approaching. Time sure does fly when you're having fun, and this day was a lot of fun. At the second-to-last slough we found a young bull watching our approach. The hair on the back of his neck was raised. He glowered at us as if to say "My slough. Stay out." He posed no real danger, but the stance was thought-provoking. The lighting wasn't bad. Where he stood in the water were a few rays of sundown light at its brightest. Good photos. I was happy. He was gone. The light was fast fading.

The Ole Man arrived home to much "praise" from Herself for being so valiant at getting the roadside litter cleaned up. Supper was a little burned. He told a little fib in saying "We got most of the stuff hauled down to the dump; just brought home the last couple of bags." I called home to say I was having a great time with my old friends and we were just getting ready to go coon hunting. The Ole Man and I settled in the den for a period of relaxation. That eco-work cleaning up the environment is hard labor, with long days.

22

Smell of Fried Fish

WHEN YOU STOP TO THINK ABOUT IT, there are very few things that use the free air space around us as a method of transportation. Birds use the air. Planes, rockets, bullets, arrows, and the rest are ways mankind uses the air. We all breathe air to get life-sustaining oxygen. We can get diseases transmitted through the air.

Pollen from hundreds of thousands of flowers is carried on the currents of the air. The trees of the forests reseed themselves largely by free aerial distribution. In freak storms these seeds can be aerially transported for miles.

Of course, rain, sleet, snow, and hail are carried by the air. Without the transportational factor, gravity, we would have rain falling up or snow falling up, down, maybe even sideways. Or would we? In any case, the air above our heads is often filled with some form of precipitation on its way down.

Since mankind came around there has been artificial air pollution caused by our daily activities. Air lifts. Air settles. Today, with all of our industrial air pollution, we even have "air-quality alerts," when the air gets dangerously overloaded.

Heavy smog, millions of kinds of chemicals riding the free transportation of the air around us. In the era before man there were aromas carried from a victim to the hunter species. Mountains blew their tops, creating another natural pollution with varying effects. Also, we have to mention the occasional asteroid. Ask the dinosaurs.

Speaking of aromas, scents, and nature's hunters (we were speaking about that, weren't we?), the smells carried in the air today are some of the finest since air was first used for transportation. I guess I better retract my opening line and say it's quite plain that thousands of things are transported by air every second of every day. The air around us is full of things, both wanted and unwanted. I'll bet you could even start a business cleaning the air. Modern. Up-to-date.

Smells. For example, I can remember my mother cooking fresh apple pies when apples first matured every year on the neighborhood trees. She would say, "They are just right for cooking, but not yet ready to eat off the tree." She would get some from the old tree in the backyard and, within an hour, the smell of apples would fill the air inside the house.

I can still remember how long the time spent waiting for the pie to cook was for me. My mother used to say, "Go weed the garden or do something useful for a change." So, I'd sit downwind of the open window in the kitchen. Or, I'd dig worms around the edge of the garden. In either case I was adding to my collection of ten thousand garden worms for selling roadside, for fishing purposes, or just enjoying thinking about the smells emanating through the air around home. Aromas stick in your mind. Freshly dug garden worms. Fresh apple pie. In a boy's mind they are closely related pleasures stored in the depths of memory.

All the residents of Boston rushing to get ready for a summer's fishing trip wouldn't exhaust our supply of worms. But, an apple pie, fresh out of the oven, could be eaten in minutes—if my mother allowed. She never said, "Share with the family."

I could identify all kinds of good whiffs. There was the time I smelled trout frying over the fire from nearly a mile down a mountain stream (actually, I figured the Ole Man sent me in the wrong direction and was already enjoying the newly caught fish, but I'll get back to that later). On some occasions my sense of smell got me in all kinds of hot water. I almost flunked my first annual physical at work because I smelled too many great foods—up close. Ate them, and possessed more than "love handles." I lost the weight to satisfy the doctor, but more to stay employed.

I also got married from having too good a sense of smell. My wife-to-be cooked up a large plate of delicious venison steak I thoughtfully brought along on a date-cum-picnic back when we were talking about getting married. When I found she could cook fantastic biscuits and both white and oatmeal bread, I signed her on for life. As I remember it, I ate sixteen of her freshly baked biscuits at our engagement party. They were good. Still are. I knew she was making biscuits because I could smell them from her brother's house, nearly a mile away. I swear I could. I remember her saying she "might" make some biscuits when we were talking on the phone, but I still believe I could smell them from a great distance.

So, these smells carried in the air are just a part of my daily life. I think this is why I like to swing on ducks, hunt woodcock, or blast away at a fast-disappearing partridge. It gives me a chance to blast away at these aerial phenomena best seen, heard, or smelled while airborne.

My story about smelling the Ole Man cooking fish in the Big Spring Brook country has a lot to do with my account of acute smelling powers. It shows how valuable a great sense of smell can be.

We were fishing trout during the May fly hatch. That's usually about the first week of June, maybe a week or so either way. All winter we tied some neat imitations on cold, stormy wintery days. We were waiting for a day like this to use them. Our imitations were always tied to match the local hatch. There are some tiny variations from one locale to another. Every spring we made our scientific observations and our scientific work would come to fruition. To add to our knowledge of science, we needed to work hard to see how effective our observations were on the local trout. The trout acted as a judge of our science studies. Did we tie flies almost perfectly matched to the local mayfly specimens? I guess we did. The trout—the judges of the Supreme Court—thought they were dining on the real thing.

The water level was just about perfect. We made our way up the old logging road, just to the east of the babbling waters. Sometimes we could look through the trees and see the holes we would be fishing on the way back down the brook. We fish down, not up. There are exceptions, but the rule is to fish downstream. These glimpses of perfect trout waters were just a tease. Something to think about as we traipsed up the trail the loggers used to get trees out of the woods.

It was hard walking. Hard to do scientific work on mayflies, trout, water conditions, and natural habitat, but we did it every year.

The air was filled with the smells of late spring—maybe even early summer. A mix of dandelions, fiddlehead ferns at maturity, and musty spring decay of last summer's plant growth was stirred in with a few extras, like wet cedar or coming cattails. An exotic aroma. Alluring.

I would have gone deeper into the headwaters of the stream, but the Ole Man was huffing and puffing just to get this far. I decided to stop and ask Him if He wanted to rest.

I was surprised when He said, "I sure would. I certainly do need to stop." He even made excuses like "I'm getting along in years," "I'm gaining too much weight right now," and "I don't seem to be sleeping well these days." I was really beginning to think I should have stopped earlier. The Ole Man was getting old.

I gave Him the day pack with the frying pan, butter, bread crumbs, salt and pepper, and the small nest of eating dishes. A pretty light pack for backcountry cooking. I watched Him trudge off toward Dead Stump Pool and turned to go a mile upstream. The brook is not wide enough for two fishermen at the same hole. Dead Stump is probably the best hole in Big Spring Brook.

Since He was aging, I would give Him the best hole. I would fish from above and then be fishing behind Him heading downstream to the Jeep. It was the fair way to do it.

As I fished down the large brook, I wondered how the Ole Man was doing, and if His shortness of breath was a sign of things to come. Serious aging. I hurried through some of the holes. When I went by Dead Stump Pool, I caught a two-pounder on the first try. That was hard to believe. The Ole Man missing an easy taker? On the second cast I got one of nearly the same size. My creel was crowded by the two easy takers. No one leaves brook trout of that size behind. I lingered. I was also thinking, How could He have missed the two best fish in the brook? It was then that I smelled frying fish—not cooked yet, just getting brown. I could tell from the aroma.

That no-good faker! I had been had—again. He wasn't getting all feebled up. Now I remembered. He hadn't been all choked up chopping firewood yesterday. Or last week, when we dragged His canoe over three miles to get it to Lost Pond. He was playacting today, with me as the audience. The only reason it took me two hours to find this out was because I was fishing waters He had not covered because He was supposed to start at Dead Stump. The two-pounders and the smell of frying fish was a dead giveaway.

One thing was for sure: If he left the terrific fishing for wild brook trout at Dead Stump Pool, or maybe even Big Spring Brook, the fishing wherever He was must be some terrific. I looked for signs He might have left in the mud. I tried looking for broken ferns. I was hunting. What I was looking for was one cagey, crooked, blasted, old man. What I was finding was nothing. I needed to think harder about where the brook-trout fishing was better than here. I was stumped.

I finally decided to just fish down the stream until I came to the Jeep. I would enjoy myself along the way. Getting another fish or two was still ahead. It was still a wonderful brook to fish on, even if He was playing a game with me. You probably think I'm a game hog. I caught two wonderful trout, plus another above Dead Stump I haven't even told you about. With three nice trout in the creel, I headed downstream.

It's just that I would like to outfox the Ole Man, just once. I'd like to catch Him at His game and somehow twist it in my favor. I'd like to come back to camp with a nice fork-horned buck without Him saying He needed help getting a ten-pointer out of the woods. Or, perhaps a day when I got the hardest shot on a duck and He missed an easy one. Biggest fish, heaviest trap score, most rabbits . . . something.

As I got close to the Jeep I smelled fried trout, fiddleheads cooking, butter mixed in; across the air it sure smelled wonderful. As I came into sight He said, "Thought I might cook up some fish while you were dragging your feet coming down through." A three-pounder was filling up the oversize frying pan, even though He'd cut the huge trout in two pieces.

He motioned to the cooking fish and added, "These small ones are a real nuisance. Would have thrown this one

back, but the hook was lodged in his gills. Would have died anyway. Shame to waste these minnows. Ah, sure is."

I checked his creel and found two others, both larger than the one in the frying pan. I measured the largest. It was nearly twenty-two inches. Heavy girth. BIG BROOK TROUT. Very big. He was a winner locally for sure. I was also sure there was more to it. I could smell it in the air. I glanced back to see the Ole Man with pipe in mouth, hat pulled down over His ears, and a wild smile that said *I'm glad to have you witness this.*

"Caught them in Lost Pond. Got to thinking about how just over that little hill right there is the pond, and so I asked myself, why not give it a try. No time like the present, I thought. The other day when we dragged the canoe in there I knew the mayflies weren't quite ready, but would be with every passing day. I was right. You see?" He motioned to the three pieces of evidence. "I figured I could be generous and give you Big Spring Brook all to yourself; that way you wouldn't be just trailing me. You'd get better fishing."

The other news He kind of dropped slowly was, "By the way, Lost Pond is just about a hundred and fifty yards over the first little ridge. Guess there's no need to drag the canoe three miles after all."

The grin was let loose with a full pipeful of smoke as He laughed Himself silly.

The next time I smelled fried fish, I vowed I was going to be the one doing the cooking. Yes, I will. Someday.

23

Pass the Worms, Please

EVER HEAR OF MAKING YOUR OWN trout regulations? Some guys I know do exactly that. They extend the regulations for every brook, river, pond, or lake where they fish. The lands around these waters are not theirs. They do not own the water, either.

Year in and year out these anglers are seen to conform to a very special set of sporting laws. A single violation is enough, from their viewpoint, to void all future invitations to fish with them. Permanently barred. It is that serious.

The exact dimensions of the Rules for Fishin' are usually determined by an early spring meeting. It is an annual event always held at the Ole Man's place. Those in attendance are given the privilege of making laws by virtue of their serious devotion to fishing, a sincere interest, demonstrated by logging thousands of hours each year to the pursuit. They must also, of course, be known to have abided by the Rules for Fishin' during the previous year.

Jake Goodwin will be there, even though the Ole Man often feels Jake bends the Rules too often at certain points in every season. Like the trips when Jake goes with the Ole

Man and outfishes Him. Yet, for all His trying, He has never caught Jake in direct violation of the Rules for that year.

Roger "The Gentleman" Thurlow, Loren Ritchie, Warden Clements, Barry "Flash" McLaughlin, Bob "No Deer" Dyer, Mike "Trees" Eash, Yale "Canoe" Stevens—they will all be there to join a flock of others who file through the door. It's an exclusive club, but democratically inclusive. With all the regulars the Ole Man's den will be packed, a lot more than Reverend Duster's Easter Sunrise Service on a hill overlooking Mount Katahdin. Everyone is serious about this business; Old Stump Blower is kept put away at a distance. Except, that is, when Jake gets to filibustering. No one can stand that for too long.

The session always opens with a few words from the Ole Man: "You all know why we are here. Ain't no use in tellin' no lies about the size of the fish. In case you forget, one of us was probably along with you on the trip and can tell the difference between five pounds and the truth of two pounds, seven ounces. Remember, we use all state laws as the MINIMUM LAW. We abide by every regulation the state issues. The Rules for Fishin' only add some things to them. All right, I'll open the floor for discussion."

If no one quickly jumped in, the Ole Man was liable to begin reading a page or two from *The Compleat Angler*, which wasn't too bad, except He sounded as though He just graduated from the William Jennings Bryan School (second grade, maybe). Nearly as bad as Jake's filibusters.

This year Flash McLaughlin jumped in. "I want to say I think we should make a rule that no one under the sun can fish Duke Brackett's farm pond. Last year, the same idiots who sit here today were known to have kept *three* trout from his pond. It's supposed to be catch 'n' release, you know."

Jake was on his feet in a second. "I didn't either catch any fish in there for keeps. I was having fun with the Ole Man, and just used Duke's pond for a holding pool. Told the Ole Man I caught the fish there, but they actually came from Swift Brook. Flash, you're just jealous because you and Him lost a bet I couldn't catch three trout over two pounds from there in five minutes. I won, too."

McLaughlin took his seat while the gathered crowd roared. Loren Ritchie made a motion to bar Flash from fishing in Brackett's farm pond for one year, and the motion passed, with an amendment stating that members were in agreement that betting about fish amounts and weights on *any water* was unsporting. Of course, there were about a million exceptions, and it all ended, without regulation, as a giant laugh.

Several routine motions to make certain waters "fly-fishing-only" were made and passed without much debate. Two motions were made to make other waters "fishing-for-fun-only." The hope was that youngsters would get first crack at these popular waters as they were left by the State under the general fishing laws. Too much pressure causes a decline in the fishery. Whether you call it "catch-and-release" or "fishing-for-fun," the idea is to keep the fish in the water while still allowing an angler the opportunity to try his luck. Let the kids keep the fish if they want to.

All of this was routine work. The big order of the day was to set the Rules for the BIGGEST FISH OF THE YEAR

CAUGHT UNDER THE RULES FOR FISHIN' REGULA-
TIONS. This was the prestige award of the year and meant
a free Orvis fly rod, bragging rights, power in the sporting
community, and a real nice wall plaque. The Ole Man dis-
played three such plaques in His den. Jake had four. Getting the "free" rod of your choosing meant you got to fish
with equipment purchased by the other members. Think
about it. Every member who doesn't win is assessed a portion of the bill for the rod and the wall plaque, which, by
the way, has a brass fish depicted with a fly in its mouth,
with all the engraving block-printed in big letters, with the
year of the award and the angler's name. The losers pay to
honor the one winner.

Not every trout water was open for the competition. You
couldn't count any fish taken on a trip to Alaska. None from
Labrador or Nova Scotia or Quebec or Newfoundland. Fish
from the Broadback or Rupert River drainage were outlawed, too. In fact, by long-standing tradition, the number
of waters open for this competition was limited to in-state
freshwater waters open to the public. And even then there
were additional rules made to clarify which waters qualified.

For instance, the section of Swift Brook below the old
lumber mill was off limits. None could be entered from the
upper part of Big Eagle Lake. In Minister Pond there was a
restriction to shoreline only, and any caught using the raft
stored there were strictly outlawed. It was deemed unsporting to use a raft in a small trout pond.

The list of Rules, whether old, new, or passed, rejected,
revised, or under discussion, dragged on and on. Canoe

Stevens got to his feet to argue at length about making dry flies the only legal equipment allowed in the capture of a fish for the competition. "It only stands to reason that anyone can catch a fish with drowned worms or sinking wet flies or using old beer-can tabs equipped with treble hooks. I think it's time we made a pitch for the good and the pure."

The Ole Man flew to his feet, aided by two glasses of Old Stump Blower poured while Jake was giving a long dissertation about something or other. "I believe I agree with Canoe. We ought to vote for the good and the pure. In fact, I think dry flies only would be a great Rule we could all support with vigor. Please remember, all the Rules for Fishin' need to be made tonight. No second chances until next year. We voted on having just one meeting night because having three or four nights of meetings to set the Rules would be just like the state legislature—and we all know how ridiculous politicians are. Let's not waste fishin' time. Let's vote for good and pure—dry flies only."

His voice was rising with every sentence. By the end of His rambling words His voice sounded like rolling thunder. The Ole Man completed His speech and returned to His seat to await a motion from the gathered experts. An affirmation.

Flash McLaughlin, who had downed five Old Stump Blower drinks during Jake's dissertation, roared out his motion: "I'd like to see the new Rule go into effect with just one amendment. No women, wives especially, will be permitted on the trophy waters, and violations where you fished with women would mean a five-year exclusion from the competition."

The words were not finished echoing across the crowded den before Herself came busting through the door. She ran over to the Ole Man, grabbed His gavel, and threw it in the fire. Then, with a vengeance, she grabbed the remaining half-empty bottles of Old Stump Blower, opened a window, and proceeded to pour the contents out on the grass.

Her eyes were spitting fire. Her body, which was considerable in size, quivered with anger. "This meeting is hereby called to a halt. You husbands see very little of your wives as it is, from April until October. If you barred women, the results would be disastrous for family life. Now, I want a motion from the floor to adjourn without considering this other foolishness." She was mesmerizing—simply awesome in the way her speech caught the attention of the men. She wasn't backing down.

The Ole Man, white-faced and sad, made the motion she asked for. It was a unanimous vote. It was the first year worms were legal in the competition.

I might add, when the next year rolled around, and every year since, the meeting for Rules for Fishin' has been held at Jake Goodwin's. Since Jake never has live-in help and has never married, the meeting is held without any interruptions. We like it that way.

24

Why Try Brand X?

"SO, YOU'RE TRYING TO BE LIKE HERSELF—just a bit of downright cussedness running through to the core?" He was ugly, disturbed, striking out at whatever or whoever was at hand. I suppose, looking back on it now, He did have the right to think I was selling Him down the drain. It wasn't that I made a practice of it, you understand, but this was to be something special for years to come.

The Ole Man held His guns as sacrosanct. There was real emotion there for these pieces of wood and steel. The L. C. Smith, the Parker, a nice Purdey, to name just a few. He owned a couple of special Winchesters, a Weatherby, two Brownings, a European drilling from 1910. Oh, I guess He was obsessed with fine firearms, like the three-barrel European drilling—two shotgun barrels and a single rifle barrel—which gives the hunter access to rabbit firepower or a single big game choice from the rifle barrel . . . instantly. Each of His other guns was used for special purposes also, some real, some imaginary, some planned, as in the .458 Winchester He bought to use in Africa for "an

upcoming safari big-game hunt. I've got it all sighted in."
Africa? I guess it's still possible; certainly not likely.

I could remember mornings when He got up early just to
make sure the gun was totally ready for the day's hunt. It
was a "modified and full" day on some decoying ducks, or it
could be an "open-bore and modified" day in the heavily
foliaged upland. He seemed to take as much pride in His
guns as most people did in their family photo albums. Not a
day of the open season or the preseason passed without a
remark or thought about the "need to upgrade my collection of gunning tools."

When a gun got dunked in salty water or got sprayed by
a trip through a freshwater swamp, He invariably treated it
as an emergency. "Blood is needed," He would say. That's
His name for Hoppe's No. 9. A safe room in the Holiday
Inn (His gun cabinet) was needed as an immediate treat-
ment. In a few days He would disassemble the gun for a
second time to be sure "no infection had set in."

It got to be a fanatical association of man and gun. He
was incapable of being neutral about certain guns in His
collection—or guns in general, for that matter. He hated
automatics, semiautomatics, military weapons, or any gun
poorly made or not engineered properly. "Get one of those
sloppily made guns, shoot poorly, go home to a pigpen. No
need for a man to own or use anything but the best. Lasts a
whole lifetime, too. Probably several generations. Never
need to buy another Purdey, unless you want it for a second
purpose. Parker did good work, too; balances perfectly,
comes up right on target. Every time. I think my favorite is

the L. C. Smith with perfect twenty-six-inch barrels, at least in the open upland." He could talk about guns for hours. He knew His stuff, and He did own many fine guns.

I remember a day in the late fall, when most bird hunters had long ago set aside their guns to get ready for the upcoming deer season. They were home resting this fall dawn. We were deep into the Qualey Place. It was located about a mile off the last four-wheel-drive foothold. No one hunted there, because access was strictly by foot, and the first stretch was a swampy tangle of mostly sodden hummock grasses, mixed with little islands of alder tangles. Not friendly.

At the Qualey homestead, abandoned perhaps a hundred years ago, the apple orchard grew up many times wild. The trees were about three feet apart, and getting an open shot was impossible. Still, partridge and woodcock worked the fringes of what used to be a 160-acre farmland.

The Ole Man knew enough to know hunting here meant no competition. The leaves were long gone; although many of the woodcock passed through long ago, there were still strays. The ruffed grouse were the main target of today's hunt. Lady, His able veteran Brittany, was up to the job.

The gun the Ole Man chose today was the L. C. Smith 20 side-by-side. Good in heavy tangles where open shots were hindered by a mass of branches. As we approached the first good stand of wild apples, we heard red squirrels announce our arrival. Overhead we heard and saw flocks of Canadian geese winging their way south.

My thoughts were broken by the bark of the Smith as the Ole Man fired at a grouse rising near a strip of alders and apples. When He missed a bird, I could often hear Him ring out with "honest, reasonable, hearty cussing." Since I heard nothing I knew He was successful. It isn't that He minds missing the shots as much as He feels He has let the gun down. "Great guns deserve the best shot in the bunch. If you can't shoot well, you shouldn't have a decent gun. No way."

He was a good shot, but the best shooters still miss birds. It isn't the gun's fault. A fine tool from a great gun maker is still just a work of steel-and-wood art, ready for the job at hand. In addition to gun and man, there is the other element of hunting conditions. Trees, tall grasses, limbs, wild structures of all possible combinations mean getting a free shot, such as you would get in an open field, is not in the cards while you are hunting. The partridge knows full well how to use these tree limbs to make good an escape. It's all part of the allure of upland hunting.

There were "honest misses" the Ole Man seemed pleased with. If you missed five birds in a row when the "hunting was too good to last," this was excusable. An expert marksman would be finished hunting for the day in just a few minutes. Limiting out early meant a pretty boring day if you needed to wait around for your companions to get their limits.

The Qualey Place blew hot and cold. The hunting was always good, but because it was so remote and untramped by most hunters, the Ole Man always felt especially peaceful here. "This place is like our own hunting preserve the kings would have owned centuries ago. No other hunters allowed, because they won't make the effort. Plenty of game left at the end of the season. An ideal place for you and me."

The hunt went well. We got partridge, the dog worked the cover exceptionally well, and we filled the pockets of our hunting jackets with good-tasting wild apples. All should have been calm. But, as I thought of the big dustup the Ole Man had had with Herself, the one I started to tell you about earlier, I realized I was actually involved in setting the stage.

Herself wanted to buy something nice for His upcoming birthday, and asked me for gift suggestions. I remembered the Qualey Place the previous year and how the Ole Man had said, "I need a new gun to handle briars—one that's open-bore, would not cost an arm and a leg, and is still very well made." I thought I knew just the gun. It fit the bill for covers like the Qualey Place. In fact, it was still being made, so availability was not a question. I told Herself about it without thinking about the Ole Man's strict rule. "I never want a piece of currently produced junk. I want the old Winchesters, Smiths, Parkers, Ithacas. The guns they make today will wear out long before the classically made guns even need a minor repair. They don't make them . . ."

The cardinal error was mine.

I told Herself there were a number of over/unders, and I told her the gauge, the chokes, the expected price, the manufacturers, the place to get the best price. When she got around to buying the gun, she called me and asked if I thought Brand X was well made. I said it was perfect, and I meant it.

Down went the cash, home came the gun. The Ole Man's birthday was on Saturday, and she knew He would want to try out the gun at the Qualey Place.

On Friday night we all gathered to honor the Ole Man's birthday. Cake made, friends invited, gift gun at hand, all wrapped by Herself. I gave Him an L.L. Bean shirt, the chamois kind. He owned about a dozen of them. Jake gave Him a pair of new felt boot liners. There was a case of clay pigeons from the gang at the plant. At the very last moment the box with the Brand X shotgun was brought out.

He was polite about it, but quite obviously disturbed about the last gift. His expression of gratitude was nearly perfect, but there was a sound of near disappointment in His voice. I couldn't understand why He was so quiet in His acceptance, why He was not rejoicing. The Ole Man's emotions were worn on His sleeve.

He said He was pleased. He said it was the right thing to get. He said it was badly needed. The more He talked, the more I began to think I was misreading the whole situation. Maybe He *was* pleased with Brand X.

The next day when He got out of the Jeep with the Smith, I knew the whole score. The explosion took place the night before, and He blamed me and Herself for getting the gun He wanted but not made by the right maker. Finally, the whole story was coming out as the hunt progressed.

The new Brand X gun was at home, a "cheap imitation." The Smith was "okay; barely." The truth was, he'd ordered a gun from a dealer specializing in classical weapons. They sold Him an old gun He wanted modified slightly, with custom work. Now, He was "stuck with two Qualey Place guns. The one I ordered is not quite ready, and the one you bought with Herself is not going to be used by me."

So the Smith was today's gun. I thought I could save the day. I thought I had the perfect solution. Hide the new Brand X gun; use the new classic He was having modified. With a collection as big as His, the gun could easily get lost. But the row had already taken place, and He was not about to back down, not even for the sake of domestic tranquility. After a little more thought, however, and a little more effort traveling around the hinterland of the Qualey Place, He backed off.

"I guess I could use the Smith now; the classic won't be ready in time for this season, anyway, and I'll tell Herself I'll use the Brand X for a while and still have a new gun by next fall. I'll use the Brand X as payment for the work I'm having done. See?"

I thought it might be a smart way out for all of us. Herself would be praised for the expensive gift. I would be off the hook. The Ole Man would eventually have a gun for the Qualey Place. The Brand X gun would get a new home. There would be peace in the valley.

25

Clark Settlement Doodles

A HUNDRED AND FIFTY YEARS AGO the pioneers broke ground on the quarter-section farms north of the town of Patten. They cut down the best pine to mill for lumber to build home, barn, and sheds. They were families from Western European countries who were looking to start a new life in America. Many of the new immigrants were related groups of two or three nuclear families desiring to establish a homestead in the wilderness. Very few singles came to the Clark Settlement, as the new hamlet came to be known.

Their horses toiled for years to haul firewood, but mostly to clear trees away to create farmlands. The first year the trees were cut, or girdled, or fired, or whatever was necessary to get crops planted between stumps. Gradually the virgin forest became open to the farm fields we know today. Each farm kept a good-size woodlot for their needs. Some of the homesteads failed from the very beginning. Not everyone is cut out to be a farmer. The land was fertile, but compared to the Midwest, where soil was deep and trees were few and rocks were nonexistent, the acres of New England required a lot of effort to simply get started.

The rock walls are left around every cleared field. Millions upon millions of rocks removed from croplands by man and horse or oxen. In many of the Clark Settlement homesteads the only remaining signs of previous occupation by mankind is the rock walls, the abandoned apple orchards, an occasional dug well, a flower bed of daylilies, a cellar hole or a slab of poured cement floor. Everything else has returned to tree growth. A hunter's paradise.

The first settlers would have been getting along in life by the time the family finally had cleared the trees, shrubs, and, most importantly, the roots and rocks from the fields. It would be up to the following generations to develop organized farms with clear borders on every field. The work of getting a dug well rocked up to deliver clear, settled water for man and beast must have been a lot of handwork. They still could function today to supply water, but the hunter fears them because they can become traps for luckless gun dogs who fall into one.

One rock foundation has huge slabs hauled in place by horses. The buildings are long gone, but we sit there to eat lunch every upland season. It is now a full mile from even a hint of a road, but there are at least three other foundations within a half-mile of this place, so at one time, this would have been a four-house series of farms. No longer. We hunt woodcock and partridge there in the fall and rabbits in the winter.

There were at least three Mr. and Mrs. Clarks, according to county records. Undoubtedly, the whole group of farms in the township was for them. Which one is lost to history.

Now, only two farms survive out of nearly one hundred. The population in 1876 was officially 389. Today, it is two households, with a total of 7 people. The rest is gone, returned to trees. Not virgins, but they don't know it.

When we are hunting the Ole Man and I often pause to wonder: Did they move to Nebraska or Ohio? Did they move to find better soil? Was there a single son, and he chose to be a Boston banker? The only local clue is a small graveyard with perhaps seventy-five marked graves; few have readable names, and those that do are the same last names as residents of other scattered, still-surviving towns. Maybe they just moved locally. We still wonder.

The Ole Man stalks the Clark Farms as though they were hallowed grounds. He sincerely believes He is giving honor to the settlers by continuing to use what they created, and to continue their hunting practices. "I even have a gun they might have owned if the timing was right. That's why I like old guns: They act as guides. They've been on many hunting trips before I ever bought them." Could be, could be.

When He goes to the Clark Settlement Road He never cusses—not even when He misses an easy shot. Never raises His voice, either. It's sort of like being in church. He loves to go there, but acts as though the Clarks and their neighbors were still there to watch over our hunt. We found one old barn beam with two hand-hewn blocks still attached. The Ole Man thinks they were used to hoist up moose, bear, caribou, deer, cow, or horse to be aged and cut up for family meat. The huge beam is now reduced to about a three-foot surviving section. It measures a square ten inches on each side.

"Big tree and a lot of work by this guy to get this beam ready to hoist up as an anchoring piece of the frame of his barn. He worked hard. I hope he enjoyed his life. I bet he used these blocks with wooden pulleys and heavy ropes to hoist up many a moose or deer, or maybe a migrating caribou."

Now, it was our turn.

The Ole Man has the section of beam and the blocks in His den. When He found a wooden pulley, partially decayed, lying on a rock line nearby, He acted as though He'd found the Holy Grail.

As additional evidence the Clarks were hunters, the Ole Man sees all kinds of things the rest of us fail to see. He swears He sees old hunter tracks. No, not actual footprints, but things like square pegs in a decaying shed, "where he

hung up a brace of partridge, or maybe he was a trapper and stored his traps here." Another person might say he used the pegs in a shed to store farm implements on the wall. But not the Ole Man.

The remains of the root cellar have a small area near the surface blocked up with rocks to let in the outside air. It was carefully done to keep out critters but allow in air. It was simply an old freeze box common to many rural farms of the era. It was used to store large quantities of meat during the winter. This one would store about 150 pounds of deboned, cured meat. "About right for leftover moose or deer, I'd say. Right?" He was sure.

But whether any of the Clarks were truly hunters or owned side-by-side Damascus-hammered shotguns of the late 1800s, we will never know. The answers are buried with the lives of the people who lived there. It was not, as far as we now know, ever recorded. Most early settlers were part-time hunters, because they had to be. They left behind evidence of a life filled with hard work, family, crops, trees cut and cleared. When a timberdoodle skyrockets near a decaying barn, it is probably repeating, for the millionth time, what woodcock have been doing there ever since the forests were first cleared. We have enjoyed many great hunts on these lands.

Even as we hunt these covers they change. Some of the best apple trees have died out, often replaced by spruce, white northern pine, or rock maple. When the trees get too big, they no longer provide food for partridge or small popple; places where woodcock used to dig for worms every

October are replaced by more mature trees and heavy cover not liked by the doodles. So, the woodcock stop coming there and find other places to eat.

The adjustment to this fact of life is hard for the Ole Man to swallow.

"You'd think it would last longer. You really do. Some of these Clark acres were just perfect growth for upland hunting when I first hunted here, and now they ain't worth the powder to . . ." He never finishes this sentence.

I used to tell Him, "We don't stay in kindergarten forever, do we?"

He just mutters and mumbles about my lack of respect. But I think he understands. We are all part of a passing scene. Nothing alive stays the same. Every new sun sees some life depart and other life just beginning. That's the way of it.

The woodcock are out there at the Clark Settlement Road today, when the season is right. Tomorrow, they may be gone.

26

He Handles Thieves

DUCK SEASON WAS DUE TO OPEN the next morning. We were late getting out of work and slightly tired when we got to Home Base, the Ole Man's hunting cabin in the backwaters of Merrymeeting Bay. It was great to be back there. For an outdoorsman, it's a little bit of heaven,

Something was wrong: The door was open, the lock smashed. The old Jeep was barely stopped before the driver's door was opened with a strain on the canvas hinges they were not designed to handle. This was not the way we dreamed of relaxing at the duck camp.

The Ole Man was inside in a flash. I was coming through the door when he roared, "I knew it! I knew it! The apes stole my kitchen stove! I hope it smokes every time they light it, or better yet, blows up or burns their place down." It was one of his favorite possessions, one rivaling the L. C. Smith, the Jeep, or His Leonard fly rod.

There were few things the Ole Man hated so much as thieves. Vandals who shot out electric company insulators on transmission lines while calling themselves deer hunters were on His list. Those who used a road sign for target practice made the list, too. Guys who shot deer while using a night light, and those who filled a pack basket with a hundred trout—they were on the list for sure.

We never did catch the vandals who broke into His camp, but there's one kind of thief we did catch. On the opening day of duck season that year I heard about it again and again. The guy we caught was carrying 101 brook trout. To the Ole Man he was a "perfect jerk who should have lived back in the day when getting the rope was a civilized thing to carry out justice. He wouldn't be a repeat offender, I'll guarantee you that much."

It was similar to the break-in at Home Base. We were just starting our usual trip to Swift Brook when Warden Clements stopped in for a visit. We were half packed, but we welcomed him just the same. He looked like he needed a drink of something strong. Usually he was the vision of a Boy Scout, with uniform and skin scrubbed clean. Even though he often worked at night, he always seemed rested. Tonight he looked tired and the uniform looked "lived in," such as you might imagine after a hard day in the woods had worn you down.

He refused the drink offer and slumped into the waiting den chair. It was the Ole Man's favorite chair in the den, meaning Warden Clements was really tired. No one ever sat in His chair, not even Warren Page, who stopped on his way back from an Atlantic salmon trip to the rivers of New Brunswick. Even as a virtual stranger who knew the Ole Man simply by reputation, he instinctively knew enough to avoid *the* chair.

Clements summed up his problem day: "Those trout thieves are at it again. I know for a fact those guys are taking out way over their limit, but I can't prove it. One of the thieves has been giving out free trout to people all over town. Yet I know he doesn't even go fishing except once or twice a season. He can't possibly be getting his fish legally. There's a law violation there somewhere. But every time I check him out, he has exactly his legal limit. No more. No less.

"I just came back from following this crew for two days and they never violated the law one time, at least not where I could see a violation. Not even the litter law. In fact, they stayed in camp for most of the day, only throwing a worm in Mallory's Pool once or twice in twenty-four hours. I can't even figure out how they get their limits. Lights out by nine p.m. They seem to be living the quiet life—much too quiet. I hung close, even sleeping with the blackflies just a hundred feet from their campsite."

The warden told a sad tale. I listened, but I was unable to help with anything except sympathy. The Ole Man was all ears, and kept asking questions about who, where, when, and what was the possibility of another approach. The warden said normally he wasn't able to divulge details to the general public, but with this case, he felt the public was getting ripped off, and he clearly needed our help to get this problem quickly resolved.

By the time the warden left it was too late to go to Swift Brook that day, and so we rescheduled for the next day, our day off. The Ole Man was in a foul mood as He said, "I'll see you *first thing*. Don't be late."

Herself met me at the door a long time before dawn the next morning. She was up early to make coffee and get breakfast. Her coffee is ten times better than His, but I don't tell Him that. I was further surprised when she said, "I've got coffee, breakfast, but no Ole Man. He left a while ago. Said for you to eat up and wait. By the way, He left with that gang of rowdies the warden was talking about last night. They went to Swift Brook."

I was flabbergasted. Even for the Ole Man, this was pretty weird. I pressed Herself for details, but all she said was, "You know Him. He just asked you to wait here and eat up. I don't even know how long He'll be gone, or why He went with them in the middle of the night. His comings and goings are odd."

I ate breakfast, drank three cups of coffee, and fumed. I went to the den to thumb through the latest outdoor magazines. An hour passed. I waited. I was hurt. I thought I was a partner. What the hell was going on? I waited for an hour and then headed home. I thought I was going to Swift Brook fishing with the Ole Man. Instead, I went home, took a nap, and got up to mow the lawn. Still, no word.

I needed to visit the dump (transfer station, if you like). I got rid of my household stuff and stopped at Jake Goodwin's on the way home. He couldn't help me any; I guess I just wanted somebody to talk to. Even the sight of Jake's new partner, a beautiful young Lab, did not shake my depression. Jake was full-of-dog. He'd traveled to New York to get the dog, and he was justifiably excited with the potential. But I wanted to concentrate on my problem. I headed home again.

My wife wouldn't tolerate my mood, so, with nowhere else I wanted to go, I went to the Ole Man's house again. It was nearly dark and He still had not returned home. After a restless half-hour and getting more angry than moody, I walked over to Loren Ritchie's. He had a beer taproom in his house he called The Rath Cellar. It was there I found him. The place smelled of beer and popcorn.

Loren poured me a draft and together with Flash McLaughlin, who was there talking about an upcoming camping trip they were planning, we talked about the Ole Man. Without naming names, just as I had done at Jake's, I told them about the warden's dilemma. They were wowed. The mystery with the Ole Man interested them, too.

Loren said, "That old coot is always, always up to something. Your guess of what's going on is as good as anyone's, but, if He's wasting His day off on this project, you can bet the result will be a doozy."

We talked of fishing, dogs, guns, work, women, wives, laws, local gossip, and got out the Old Stump Blower. It was getting to be a full-blown session of male testosterone gone wild as the hours passed. I had a good time.

When the subject returned to Warden Clements, we all felt the same way. He was a real professional and he was fair, but tough as nails. If there was a way to stop outdoor game hogs and thieves, he was the guy to enforce the laws.

Flash said, "I couldn't do his job. He misses opening day of deer season, fishing season, bird season, duck season. Everything. The warden works all the good parts of the year. His only real time off is in the off-seasons. For a guy who loves hunting and fishing like Warden Clements, that means a big sacrifice. I guess law enforcement means more to him than it would to me."

After a couple of Old Stump Blowers I said my good-byes and walked home. I walked by the Ole Man's house, fully expecting He would be home by now. No Jeep. No lights. No Ole Man. It was approaching twenty-four hours of His being on the road. I continued walking home.

I hit the sack. I tossed and turned. My wife told me to lie still. "You thrash around like an elephant whale breeching." I got up to slip downstairs to sit alone in the dark. I was still trying to work it all out. The next day—this day—was a workday.

I went to work with a total lack of sleep. I had an attitude. I wanted to poke someone in the mouth. The Ole Man was supposed to be there, too. He wasn't. He had not called in, either. Mr. Keegan wasn't happy. He came to see me. I obviously wasn't able to help him. He was unhappy and needed to call in a substitute. I was unhappy with everything. Life in general.

After work I drove straight to the Ole Man's house. No one was home. Damn! This was getting to be a real nuisance. To say the least. My mind would not focus on any other topic. I needed an answer as to what was really going on. It just wasn't like the Ole Man to miss work, to not at least call in, and it certainly wasn't like Him to miss a fishing trip with a buddy. He was usually fifteen minutes ready before any buddy arrived for a trip. Even if He set the time, He still expected everyone to be on time, ready to roll.

Nothing was left to willy-nilly arrivals and departures on outdoor trips.

I remember times, often really, when, if we were picking Him up to go fishing or hunting or camping, He would have all His dunnage piled by the street's edge when we arrived. There was no getting ahead of Him. If the Ole Man said, "We'll leave at five a.m. sharp," you wanted to be there at 4:45 with all the bells and whistles in place, or suffer a day's worth of berating.

On the next pass by the Ole Man's house, the Jeep was there. So was Warden Clements's pickup. I almost missed the driveway from staring too hard. Although I usually knock before entering, this time I made an exception and weaved to the right of the house to enter the den directly.

There was a celebration going on, and they were so engrossed in it that they hardly noticed my presence. Old Stump Blower was flowing freely when the Ole Man finally glanced my way. He simply said, "Pour your own." The warden did not have his uniform on. I don't recall ever seeing him out of uniform. He wore jeans and a chamois shirt with a baseball cap. He looked rested and very, very happy. The Ole Man looked as tired as the warden did two nights before.

It was time now for me to hear the story. It would all come out, I thought. But all I got were little blurbs, snippets, followed by belly laughs and backslapping. What was this about a railroad flare? The dark of night? The 101 fish in a four-man party? The Ole Man was "guilty"? Of what?

Finally, without fanfare, the Ole Man turned to me and apologized for His behavior. Yes, He actually made an attempt to say He should have called me to cancel our trip. But, He said, "laying out the trap to catch the thieving poachers was just far more important. Sorry, though."

I remember saying, "Catch the poachers? What are you talking about?"

He began, "I called up the ringleader. I told him I knew where some really big brook trout were hangin' around, and made up a story about lookin' around for new fishin' buddies. He swallowed it whole. I told Him to bring along some friends if he wanted. So, at dawn we met at Swift Brook. I stayed away from the Dead Stump Pool section, but we fished some pretty good holes. It almost turned out to be a flop, because the first day we only caught mediocre trout, and even the poachers threw them all back in the brook.

"I was getting worried, but dreamed up the scheme to camp there overnight. I was surprised when all five agreed to stay. I went back to town to get a tent, some grub and stuff. What they didn't know was that I contacted Warden Clements and told him to be on standby. I would use a railroad aerial flare if it was at night, or three quick shots repeated three times if I had them dead to rights during the daylight. Then, he could make the pinch. The thieves got back to Swift Brook just about the time I got camp set up. I was leery about the outcome."

Warden Clements was nearly speechless. He had not heard all the details, either, so for two of us, the story was spellbinding, and the Ole Man loved it that way.

The Ole Man was a good storyteller. He could be animated or fling His hands around or simply look perturbed. This time, as He continued, He was serious.

"I got them talking about fishing, but they were close-mouthed about details, at first. When the second day came, I planned to show them better waters. But for now, story time around the campfire, I wanted to hear some of their news. Finally, they owned up to how they got so many trout all the time. Sometimes, they dynamited a small beaver flowage or pond with some waterproof stuff a friend of theirs in the navy had stolen from a base supply. Sometimes they drained the water down at night and walked around picking up the keepers and lunkers as they found them in small pools. They were craftier than they looked."

Things were just getting good; the Ole Man began to flap His arms, and His voice was getting higher.

"The damned predator poachers, the thieves, use explosives pumps and all kinds of illegal stuff against the trout. I made up my mind to hang in no matter how long it took. The ringleader even thought I was an outlaw like them. He told me they blocked the outlet by the mill and ran the big-wheeled navy pump the guy stole for them to pump out the mill's pond, then took every single trout left flopping around. And, it was all done after dark. Never in the day.

"Well, they wanted to get to work right away. No waiting for dawn. So, they set explosive charges in about five places where a wide pool houses lots of fish. Then, another trick. The explosives they use to stun the fish, or kill them outright, are *silent* explosives—something the military has

been developing for years. I heard it. When it goes off there is a great big *whoosh*. No big bang. Anyway, it was very effective. There were fish everywhere. So I told them I had a big flare in the Jeep that would light up the whole area so they could load up on brook trout while they were stunned by the explosives. Hundreds of brook trout on the surface, dead or stunned. The ringleader told me to go ahead. So I signaled Warden Clements here by setting off the aerial flare. After I lit it, I made like I was getting more garbage bags to load trout. I tell you, those trout were flopping around everywhere. Never saw anything like it. Some dead, but most just stunned, lying on the water's surface, like they'd fainted."

Warden Clements and I still needed more.

"Well, the warden here, he arrived in overdrive time. There were the five crooks and me. He said the flare was visible all the way to the meadows. He made his arrests right off and called for a backup unit. The sheriff's department sent one. He sure was slick."

There were a hundred questions in my mind. How did the thieves get the trout back to town without the warden catching them?

Warden Clements said, "That's a story I can tell. They were 'fishing' at night and getting all the fish home, cleaned, and in the freezer by dawn. Then, they went fishing during the day and caught a legal limit, all for show. I can't search a home freezer without a court order, and to get one, I need probable cause, something I didn't have. It was all very frustrating. But now we really have them on a whole list of charges. The number of dead trout that night alone was 589. These guys are going to jail for this. All five of them, thanks to my star witness here." He was pointing at the all-grins Ole Man.

When I asked about the navy's pump, I got that story, too. They stored it under a hillside barn and put bales of straw in front so it wouldn't be found. The old couple that owned the barn kept an alcohol still in the woodlot, four pit bulls roaming the farmyard, and were selling booze cheap to the poachers. The story was wild. A local crime organization.

The State now had a witness, the warden got his poachers, and the missed fishing trip I was sore about was long forgotten. We were having a party. I still could not reconcile my thoughts completely. Why did the Ole Man get involved in the first place? A do-gooder he ain't.

"I can't stand the waste of wildlife or fish," He said, adding, "How I got started? Ah, glad you asked. I thought Warden Clements here needed an inside man. I thought this lack of activity in the daytime was a large hint for an after-nightfall scenario. You know, fishin' at night, or doing something illegal but offbeat. I even thought about those quiet explosives, 'cause I'd read about crooks using them to break into warehouses and banks. A brook is just like a bank; the assets are liquid, ain't they? The only way I was going to get them was to go with 'em. Sure enough, it only took a short time. I'll get it squared away with Mr. Keegan, too."

This was to be a classic story to be told again and again. It would be told in trout times. It would be told while duck hunting or in deer camp. The stolen stove could be replaced with a new one, but the dead fish were gone forever. Breaking up a poachers' ring helps us all.

The Ole Man did Himself proud.

27

Double FF on Black Bear

AT THE TAIL END OF SUMMER last year, the fishing slowed down to an all-time low. It was muggy, sticky, miserable— the doldrums. Not a breath of air.

The water in the brooks and rivers was low enough to cause concern for the safety of the trout population. On some portions of Swift Brook the water stopped flowing entirely, leaving only pools of shallow water, except for the deepest holes. In the stretches where the water ceased to flow, the barren rocks were exposed, and some were developing a green scum where stagnant water was left in ever-smaller pools. Only in the spring-fed areas did the trout seem to survive at all. Fortunately, the trout species possessed good sense and quickly sought out these safe havens before being isolated in a stagnant pool. Survivors.

Fishermen in the area, real fishermen, ceased all fishing, because it was the only sporting thing to do. They sought other pursuits. Some were seen more often at the watering hole. Others even considered taking up golf or tennis. I thought perhaps this was the moment to "go full-time at trapshooting." I could certainly use the practice. Maybe my efforts would increase the value of Remington stocks.

The Ole Man, on the other hand, was not about to take up golf. "It reminds me of a farmer trying to get the rocks off his cropland. Pickin' rocks is not one of my favorite chores, and golfing looks like a sport where you throw rocks all over a mowed field and then try to hide them in a woodchuck hole. Can't see how a grown man can get very excited about it."

He *was* getting ready to do something. I saw a lot of new catalogs dealing with primitive weapons and black-powder muzzleloaders. Drinking a glass of Old Stump Blower and studying catalogs until late in the night, He became an expert on muzzleloading weapons qualifying for the primitive weapons hunting seasons. There were choices of newer types of powder, smokeless, neat loads not requiring constant cleaning of the gun. Many, many models were on the market, but the Ole Man chose the traditional black-powder guns from a hundred years ago. These guns fired a percussion cap to ignite the F, FF, or FFF black powder, just as it was graded centuries ago.

Black powder is explosive to handle and leaves a residue requiring soap-and-water scouring after each shooting session, but it's highly appealing to traditionalists. The Ole Man is the poster boy for conservative traditionalism. The more conservative, the better.

He learned about spit-patches and oil-lubricated patches. He learned about patch and ball materials, because the differences in material affected the accuracy of the ball. He learned about the advantages and disadvantages of choosing either a ball or a cast bullet. There was the matter of caliber of the bore, accessories to carry in the field, ways of keeping the powder dry. Lots of details in the black-powder hunt. He was planning to be ready by early September.

That seemed to be the magic date: early September. Several more clues came forth when He brought out a new .54 Renegade from Thompson Center. He was mysterious about His new project. A muzzleloading, black-powder gun, but not the old gun from the last centuries. I was surprised—not that He chose the ancient black powder, but that He had purchased a new gun. In everything else He wanted old guns, not just old technology. But I have learned not to try and outguess Him. Besides, He told me, "Renegade styling's more suited to my desires right now. I'll learn about old muzzleloaders later and buy a good one. This gun will get me started."

It wasn't a squirrel rifle or a gun for crows. Deer season was months away. How would He use this gun? Practically, there were better choices for varmints, and Wimbledon competitions were not His style.

Black bear! That was it, black bear hunting. September was the best month in the year to hunt bears feeding on natural crops maturing right then. Apples, oats, corn, all either wild, as in the case of apples, or planted by the farmers. The idea of hunting over parts of a dead cow or sitting at the dump was not in the cards for Him. The choice was to hunt the black bear in his natural autumn haunts.

When I asked the Ole Man about it, He finally told me about His plans. He, of course, enjoyed keeping me in the dark until He brought out the gun. The Sherlock and Dr. Watson bit is an essential part of our relationship. I think He carries it too far, sometimes, but this time He told me He was going to hunt McAvoy's oat fields. They were secluded, vast in acreage, and always inspired black bear raids. Ideal for a new sport. Ideal for the Ole Man. I wished He had included me in the planning. It sounded like something I would enjoy, too.

This remote set of fields should be productive gunning. They are surrounded by woods on all four sides, sort of an open invitation to a dinner visit from the local bruins.

On one occasion, several years ago, we were on our way to Davidson Pond for late-season brook trout, around the first week of September, when we were startled to see nine bears feeding in one McAvoy field. The oats were golden in hue and the bears really stood out with their deep bluish-black fur. It was a sight to behold. Big bears, little bears, female adults and male adults. A town meeting at one of McAvoy's oat fields. Bears do considerable damage to oat fields, but the farmers all say they figure it in as one of the fixed costs.

We trudged on to continue with our fishing venture, but the memory is still clear. If the Ole Man wanted to hunt bear, this would be a good cover to try. Both oats and apples get a little bit of fermentation if left out too long in the season. Farmers watch the oats carefully as they turn from green to golden yellow. When they are ready the farmers bring in the combines to mow them down. Both offer great hunting opportunities.

Sometimes rainy weather makes the oat crop difficult to harvest. If the oats get too old, too mature, they can get a little fermented, and the bears sure know it. It's a funny sight to see bears a bit under the influence. They frolic around, lie down, roll over, and generally act a little stupid. I guess I've been known to behave a bit crazy, too, if I've tasted too much fermentation.

I joined in on the hunt. I opted for a muzzleloader made by a local gunsmith sometime around the Civil War era. "J. J. Waverly" was punch-stamped by hand on the .50 caliber rifled bore. The wood was rough but, with a lot of my time and very little money, it was presentable. I shot and cleaned the gun almost daily. My wife said, "You either smell like soap or black powder. I don't know which."

For a couple of weeks we were either firing up the lead furnace, scrounging for lead, buying lead, casting maxi balls or conical bullets, or cleaning our guns. Waverly and Thompson were ready to go hunting. Traditional black-powder muzzleloader loads with a coarse muslin patch and a rammed-down ball or bullet. The Ole Man used 90 grains of FF Dupont. I used 80 grains of FFF or FF. They were accurate and mean when we used one of our home-cast lead concoctions.

We were now a full-fledged expedition. The slow trout season and the drought were forgotten. It was getting to be bear season. Our supply of powder and caps flexed up and

down depending on work, target time, and the opening day
on September 1.

To get to the McAvoy oat field we chose, we got the Jeep
within half a mile and then snuck along a trail to stay
upwind of the bears. Black bears have terrible eyesight, but
are talented with their noses. The early fall dew was on the
grass, close to frost temperature in the air as we made our
way to the edge of the field. We moved slowly, almost as if
we were still-hunting. I can't help the urge to hunt on mornings like this. Sunrise was just ahead as I stopped at one
good site and the Ole Man grabbed a place to stand along
the field's easterly edge, a couple hundred yards from me.

The Ole Man's stand was carefully chosen. Mine was
more a good viewing opportunity I chose on approach. I
saw an ocean of standing golden oats. He saw the oats, but
also overlooked a clump of about a dozen wild apple trees. I
could smell the apples from clear across the field. Earlier He
told me, "There should be a bear or two there to eat a free
apple and fill up on the oats. I've been checking it out."

I wanted just oats, because I believed they were ripe; the
apples still needed a frost or two to soften them up. Our first
morning was uneventful, except for the huge white-tailed
buck feeding along the edge of the field. He wandered
around the clover growing wild on the edge country. He
stopped every few minutes to check the air and look around.
His big ears were focused and alert. Satisfied there were no
threats here, the buck returned to a leisurely breakfast. The
rack was a perfect ten points. The deer was a large, prime
specimen. After an hour of my watching him he just flicked

his ears in my direction, took three quick bounds, and faded into the woods. Vaporized.

The Ole Man saw a cub without a mama, not unusual, as the first summer gives the cubs more confidence and a desire to wander around. This is a vulnerable time for them, a time they can get in trouble. This one was just a black butterball wandering in the oats.

Bears are leery about showing themselves in broad daylight. The mama bear was probably not far. Other adults, maybe, too. We would try another time. The workaday world went by slowly for the next few days. At coffee breaks we talked bears, guns, and the McAvoy oat fields. About four days into the bear season we went back to hunt the late-afternoon shift. We moved carefully and again took our stands with a good view of the field.

A doe, a lamb, and a young buck all worked the edge where oats met grasses and clover. In my domain I could see all three. About a half-hour before dark I saw a red fox slip across the field to begin his nightly rounds. Other than these sightings I was forced to watch the empty golden oats waving in the wind. The cool breezes settled in and the woodcock started to wing in overhead. These would be native birds; not enough frosts or chill yet to bring in the migrants from the north. A lone crow sat in a pine stub, a group of grosbeaks flew by to settle in for the night. When the shooting light got dim I headed back to the Jeep.

The Ole Man was already there, but just by a few minutes. He greeted me with "I saw a medium-size bear, caught a glimpse of a much larger bear farther out in the oats.

Couldn't seem to get the right angle and distance to shoot. We only have the one shot to make hay. By the time we reload, the bear will be history. I also saw two young bucks feeding by the rock wall. A lot of potential. I think we ought to come back every evening this week to hunt. I just know we'll get lucky."

We did just that. Every night we saw a few game animals before the closing minutes. No shots yet. I saw a big bear in an adjoining field, but in the effort to get closer he scented me and skedaddled. The Ole Man saw a young male He could easily have shot, but He wanted a bigger one.

The following week we were feeling good about our chances. The oats were at their best and the bears would be getting used to a free meal, as large as they wanted, every evening. A good thing for us; not so good for the bears. It must be hard work for bears feeding on grubs in decaying trees. The oat field was like a diner with ready-made meals in unlimited supply. For this reason the bear consumes a lot of grain each night of the early fall. The farmer is happy to see you shoot a bear. They cost him a lot of potential money.

Wednesday dusk proved to be the right time. When we first arrived at our stands, there were bears everywhere, or so it seemed. My part of the field held a female bear with two cubs. Better yet, a good-size bear gave me occasional flashes of black out near the middle. I didn't know it then, but the Ole Man was looking over two large bears in his corner of the oats. Both were acceptable as trophies. They were feeding and rolling their way across half of the field.

The Ole Man made a little closer approach, keeping the light wind in His face. At just under a hundred yards, one of the two stopped, looked His way, lifted his forelegs above the oats to get a better view and scent.

"I checked my cap, steadied the rifle sight, and fired," the Ole Man recalled later. "The cloud of smoke kept me blind for a few moments. The hole on the forward shoulder proved about right; it broke both shoulders. The bear was down for good. I had my first muzzleloading black bear. Thanks to fate and no rain and no trout. Pretty good swap, I'd say. Better than taking up golf." He was happy.

Although I tried again every night that week, I found nothing of the right size. It was midweek again before I scored.

It was the first evening I'd found enough time to really hunt seriously. Work was busy and I was late getting started. I believe the bear I shot was about three ounces heavier than the Ole Man's, but you are never going to get Him to remember it that way. Never. He even said His bear tasted better and made a finer rug. I was happy with my muzzleloading black-powder J. J. Waverly bear.

The day I shot my bear was kind of a spiritual thing, bringing an end to the dry summer where fishing dimmed to a memory and this special kind of hunting enthralled me. Even though the Ole Man had already shot a bear, He went out every time I went. He wanted to be there when I got one. His gun was left at home, of course, as He continued to take His old stand to see what might be there. He simply enjoyed being out there, and my hunt gave him the excuse.

He told me, "I didn't want to abandon you in the middle of your hunt. 'Course, I ain't too happy about you gettin' a bear too soon, either. You could have at least waited until a day or so before upland birds get legal. Now, as it is, we'll have to wait, stalled, for nearly three whole weeks."

I knew what He meant.

28

And the Deep Snows Came

WE FISHED IN SWIFT BROOK until the very last day. Every day brought deer sign and more deer sign. A careful hunter takes note of incidents such as this because covers change, circumstances change, leaving open some doors while others are closing. Nothing is static in the eco-environment. The fishing that summer and fall was mediocre to terrible. But, we were seeing deer sign in new places, and the information was stored for possible future use. Normally, we hunt deer almost exclusively in the Alton Bog, more casually referred to as The Bog. But new hunting opportunities are always welcome.

From years past we knew Swift Brook was a place deer wintered over, but usually we saw few deer there in the spring, summer, or fall. The area was logged commercially about five years before, and this often brings about wildlife habitat changes, both good and bad. In this case, it looked good. The new growth was bringing in the deer. We have always thought the deer stayed away from Swift Brook except for wintering because the highland ridges beyond are lush with clover-laden fields, edged with wild raspberry, wild apples, young hardwood sapling growth, and everything a deer would want—except winter shelter in a cedar swamp.

I was surprised when the Ole Man took it a step further and said, "You know, I have a good feeling about this place. I think we ought to be here for opening day of deer season this year. A change would be good."

Hunting at Swift Brook would mean hunting from home and not using Home Base, the duck camp, as our hunting depot. When we hunted from Home Base we went to The Bog generally, with side trips to wherever we thought the whitetails might be that particular year.

Swift Brook it was. From opening day on, the mental commitment was to stick to this one area, for this one year, at least. We saw deer. We heard deer. The deer walked around us. They walked by us seeming to tease us. They were close, but no cigar. Try as we might, there were no open shots.

It started on opening day with three adult deer prancing around at precisely the right distance for us to not be able to see them clearly. The Ole Man caught a brief glimpse of two of them, and later I saw three tails, identified them as adults, but they were gone in an instant.

The day was the crispy fall type with low-lying fog until nine or so in the morning. With the lifting of the fog came a little warmth from the sun, and the hunter could move around without sounding like the little drummer boy of the Civil War era. There was very little wind, but a lot of what the Ole Man calls "thermal spirits."

I think the meteorologists would call them "valley thermals," but the Ole Man was sure they had a mind of their own, and certainly chose to tell the noses of all wildlife around that mankind was close by. On this day the thermal spirits were active all day. First it was as quiet as it could be, and then a light breeze seemed to come from nowhere, headed in no particular direction.

It's hard to hunt effectively with a fickle wind. About the time you have decided the thermals are coming from the east and want to hunt with them in your face, they switch to the west. You were going to bisect a certain ridge, but now the wind has changed your plan. You need a new one. It is frustrating for a man who wants to hunt in an organized fashion.

Opening day brought zip. Ditto for the following Saturday. We saw a young buck quickly take two bounds to disappear in young firs. Next day out was a blank for hunting success, but was a beautiful time to be in the woods. It was dead quiet; a shrew turning a leaf three hundred yards away would make enough noise to make you think a moose was surely on the way.

It became obvious we were unfamiliar with deer hunting at Swift Brook. The terrain was beating us. We did not know the habits of the local deer. A good deer hunter who hunts in the same cover year after year will get to know exactly where to get a deer, this season and in successive years. Certain underbrush where they often lie down, a favored tree for bucks to rub, a game trail near a small brook, or an alder run they use for escape. In your mind is a deer-hunting guide for a mile in all directions. Sounds trivial, but in real life, it's great information to possess.

When you are in new country, no matter how good your deer-hunting skills are, the deer have the upper hand dealt to them. Here, we knew the fish population well, but it doesn't help deer hunting. The deer were zigging, we were zagging. The sign was there. The deer were there. But not when we were.

So the days passed; we studied, we learned. The Swift Brook deer cover became better known to us. Finally, it came down to the last day.

The Ole Man grumbled, moaned, complained of various things He'd like to see come about, including a nice deep snow. "Snow helps deer hunting. You *see* where they were, how long ago, where they are heading, what they are eating, where they bed down; just about everything improves with snow."

On the night before the last day it started to snow lightly, then moderately, then in blizzard proportions. We were going to get one day of snow hunting.

At dawn we were in the Jeep. The Ole Man drove carefully out to Swift Brook country where He parked with the Jeep pointing downhill, in case we got an enormous snowfall while we hunted.

"We have about a foot of new snow now, but they are predicting heavy snow for most of the day. By parking carefully it will give us a good downhill logging road out to where they plow. The four-wheel-drive will help in case we get blasted today with a whole day snowing the way it is right now. I wanted snow—oh, wow, a little too much I'd say."

We both brought snowshoes. If the storm continued, the snow would be knee-deep. Not very easy going with the webs. The woods were dead silent as they always are when the snow is falling rapidly. Sounds are muffled and buffered by snow covering every limb, every tree, every square foot of the ground. Natural sound insulation.

We knew the deer would be lying down somewhere in heavy cover. We would need to find them to have a chance of last-day success. Needing to find them, we trudged away, fully aware this was a pig in a poke. Anyone who has ever hunted in a full blizzard knows what we faced. The snow got in the gun barrel, the sights, down our necks, dropped off limbs as we snowshoed by the trees. It was pretty, but required a lot of effort. The snowshoes worked just fine.

The woods swallowed every animal in the domain. No squirrel tracks. No deer tracks. No tracks at all. The animal life was burrowed away for the duration of the snowstorm. Any tracks laid down an hour before were now completely covered by shifting, falling, new snow. There was no sign of a letup.

We both carried emergency supplies. I checked mine with the tips of my left-hand fingers. I keep them in a small, zippered, nylon-covered flat pack. It fits inside my hunting jacket pocket. There are the usual waterproof matches, extra compass, rope, map, candy bars, granola bars, space blanket, spare mittens. Sounds large, but it's actually very small. It was going to be a hard day.

A high wind was sweeping my scent in all directions at once. The only way to hunt was pretty basic: Think like a deer and keep searching, as slowly as possible. There were no other hunters, only me, the Ole Man, the deer, the snow, the wind, the clock kept by the sun, the woods, and Lady Luck. If this didn't work, we would go deerless this season.

The Ole Man told me He was going to try the dense cedar run by the brook's edge. It was a place the deer often lived in winter. Checking the snow, drifting snow, snow on the ground, and howling wind, I thought to myself, This must be winter. Or a very good simulation of it.

I was headed toward the edge of a hardwood ridge where there are dense firs, pines, and hemlocks sprouting thickly in patches of an acre or two. By walking at a pretty good clip I reached the edge of the ridge in an hour. I was about fifty yards from where I'd planned to stop and wait awhile when a handsome buck suddenly stood up, just about thirty yards to my left.

The motion startled me. I wasn't yet thinking a deer would be around. The .308 Savage Model 99 lightweight came to my shoulder and was centered on the shoulder of the now-loping deer. *Bang. Bang.* It seemed automatic but, of course, it required a levering motion to chamber the second shot. The deer fell instantly, but just as quickly was back up on his feet. He was gone before I could chamber number three.

I'd committed a major hunting error. The deer had startled me, I wasn't ready, but I fired anyway. I stopped to rest a bit, looking around; I would move again when I had a plan in place. I knew he was hit, but I had no idea where. From previous hunts I knew my shots were usually a little too far forward, rather than back. I guess I lead them as I would a duck. This was a rifle. I should have aimed, not by point, swing, shoot. My error.

The snow was coming down even harder as I took up the trail. There was chest hair and bright red blood where the deer had been standing when I fired. Lung shot? Could be. The blood trail was easy to follow; I hardly needed to look down. Besides, there was only one deer track. The tracks were still running, but the blood soon looked fatty and dark. Gut shot? I hope not. I didn't know how many points he wore, but the rack was better than average. I knew that much.

The more he ran and walked, the deeper we went into dense woods. There was no plowed road in the direction we were going for seventy-five miles, at the border with Canada. If I caught up with him I would need to drag him out on snowshoes. A hard drag. A pattern was now developing, too. He ran a few jumps, stopped, probably looking back. Then, he walked away.

My eyes were glued to the left, the right, straight ahead. At ten a.m. I stopped to eat a sandwich but was unable to really enjoy it. I was thinking: You wait all season, the time comes, and you blow it. Damn.

I was standing looking at a small group of jack firs when I thought I could see a deer. I was sure it was a deer now. As I studied the outline I could clearly see a front leg turned at an odd angle. He stood there. I stood there. Minutes went by. Was it the same deer? Was he wounded? Why was he not moving? He was close, seventy-five feet at the most, but the blowing and falling snow made it seem a long way off.

I realized now: The deer was dead. Stone dead. He had walked into the vee of a crotched young maple and found himself temporarily lodged there. He either forgot to move or more likely died right there. He was shot just behind the forward shoulder, but high. A lung shot. The rack was huge.

The deer would dress well over two hundred pounds. It was the best deer I'd ever shot. The rack was massive, ten perfect points. I certainly had my work cut out. I was miles from the Jeep. It was to be a long, hard drag.

First things first.

My deer-dragging harness is a loop of heavy canvas about three inches wide. It is attached to strong rope about eight feet long, which allows you to adjust it for length. The harness allows you to drag the weight with your shoulders. It's still hard.

After the first hundred yards it seemed impossible. It was nearly noon, and I was still less than halfway back to the Jeep. There was a small road, unplowed, that led out to the plowed highway; at least, I presumed it was plowed by now. If I hurried, I could get there by dark. But it would mean not meeting with the Ole Man or the Jeep. When I got the deer to the plowed road, I'd have to play it by ear.

I wanted the deer out, today if possible. The storm was at its peak, and I watched for signs of overexertion. All seemed to be set for more dragging. Hard work in any weather. Harder with snowshoes on my feet. But the snow allowed the deer to slide a little easier, so it was a compromise. Drag, *puff, puff,* get my breath. Keep going. Stop and go . . . again and again and again.

When I finally hit the plowed highway, I left the deer and started walking toward the Jeep. I didn't know how far away it would be. Again, my lack of experience with memorizing all the land parts of the Swift Brook drainage was showing. I knew the waters; now I was learning the ins and outs of the land.

I wondered how the Ole Man was doing. There was no chance of Him hearing me shoot and no chance of my hearing Him shoot. We were hunting the same lands but in different acreage.

I lucked out when a passing state highway plow truck stopped to pick me up and dropped me down where the logging road led to the Jeep. It was almost pitch-black when I saw the snow-covered vehicle.

I was tuckered out. It took me a few minutes to realize the Ole Man wasn't here yet. Did He have a deer, too? Was He walking on snowshoes right now? I could do nothing but wait. In any case, the season had closed, and what remained was to get a deer, possibly two, and the hunters back to civilization.

The plow truck driver had told me what I already knew: "Not much traffic out here today. The storm has kept most people home." I could see why sane people had stayed home.

Looking out from the Jeep it suddenly dawned on me: There were *fresh Jeep tracks* back to the road and *fresh snowshoe tracks* heading *in* to the Swift Brook woods. I was pondering what I should have noticed when I'd walked in from the highway.

Suddenly, the Ole Man came back to the Jeep on snow-shoes, no gun. He was stone-cold sober-looking when He said, "As you can plainly see, I didn't need a gun on this trip out. I was looking for you; figured you must have a deer."

I told Him about mine and He listened quietly. I figured He must have shot a small one. Boy, was I in for a surprise.

After letting me ramble on He said, "I shot a deer right after dawn. In fact, I think it was about three hundred yards from the Jeep. I guess the snowstorm covered the sound of the shot. You say your deer weighs two hundred–plus pounds, dressed? Mine went two hundred and fourteen, and has nine big points. Can't see going to all that extra effort dragging for one point, can you?"

Mine had ten points and hadn't been weighed yet.

He continued, "Actually, I went home, got the deer registered, weighed, and hung up in the shed at home. Then I ate a good lunch, took a quick nap, and watched most of the Green Bay Packers game. It was quite a day."

Somehow He seemed to take the wind out of my victory sails. We both got a buck the last day of the deer season—two good ones. But the luster was off. He had done it better, easier, quicker. The straining at the harness for hours, the huffing and puffing; it was all just a memory now. I did beat Him by one point! Close enough.

We went to pick up my deer. The Ole Man said, "A real nice buck. I think they'll be twins, yours and mine. This deer looks a few pounds lighter than mine."

It weighed 212 pounds, dressed. I stressed the points on the rack. He talked about weight. Finally, with a big grin, He said, "You got one more point, but I got two more pounds of meat; I'll be happy to bring you over a pound of steak to even things out if you want."

And the deep snows came.

29

No Junk in This Mail

ANOTHER ORVIS CATALOG arrived the other day. I sat down in the den to read it from cover to cover, just the way I always do. Same goes for L.L. Bean, Eddie Bauer, Remington, Browning, Murray Spoon Co., Bass Pro, or any other outdoor equipment sales catalog I can get my hands on. They are dream books. Many adventure proposals come to mind with every page.

I have a habit, one I picked up from the Ole Man, of making up imaginary purchase orders on things I "simply must have." I even fill in the order forms, write in my address, add up the totals, and then lovingly set them aside. I spend ten annual salaries, every year. Of course, I never mail them. That would be nutty.

Or, perhaps I order a few snelled hooks with just the right turn and shape. Also, I have ordered a few new dry flies of the type most effective, I have read, in Brazil's Amazon River waters or in New Zealand or in Montana, just right in case I ever go there. I'll have something to look forward to coming in the mail. Boxed anticipation.

My orders go out in the first available mail, all for ten dollars or so. For a week or two, while at work, I'll think about the mail bringing me something other than monthly bills. When I ask my wife about the mail, she responds, "I don't think there is much except for an outdoor catalog, bills . . . and, oh, yes, a tiny box from Orvis." That's what I was waiting for, but she never seems to catch on, or maybe she has. I suppose I should tell her someday.

Opening every outdoor package is like opening a memory. Each thing ordered, each thing arriving is carefully cataloged for future use. A new lure, a hunting cap, or, heaven forbid, a new hunting jacket is something to cherish. It only gets better when you use it. Often. I have a Woolrich hunting coat of wool that I bought in 1972, or some such year. That coat has gone to Alaska with me. It has been to the McAvoy oat fields, too. Several times. I used it on trips to the Canadian Arctic, fishing, and on a Quebec moose hunt. Queenie, the well-known rabbit hound of a decade or two ago, used to sleep on that coat after a hard hunt; this was so the living-room carpet stayed good for company.

The coat was a bargain back then and remains one today, although at a much higher price. It shows no wear, after all these years, all these adventures. If ever I got divorced from being outdoors too often and the wife disapproved too much, I think I would use the jacket as my prime witness. Durability was a factor in my original decision to purchase the coat. Well designed, lot of pockets, a lined pouch in the rear to carry game taken, high collar with buttons to give protection from cold or winds, side pockets to warm the hands, Velcro ammo loops inside and out. Three layers of lightweight cotton and insulation topped with a heavy layer of virgin wool. Good investment.

Why so many pockets? Maps, compass, emergency kit, spare pair of gloves, lunch, and snacks. Why the high, buttoning collar? No hunter wants a hood when he's trying to listen for the big buck, but no hunter wants a dousing of heavy snow from the trees and limbs when he's rabbit-hunting on a cold February day, either. Collars with a lot of material, with buttons, allow you to warm up a frosted nose, or act as a wall against the cold wind or as a snow protector.

While we're on the subject of buttons, I want to convey another idea. I want no zippers on a hunting coat. Only a bunch of buttons will do it. They won't freeze in a duck blind and they won't pull apart just when you need them the most. My wife checks the buttons every fall and re-sews any that have worked a little loose during the year.

Length of the coat needs discussion, too. A good hunting coat need not drag at the knees like the Great Coat of the Czar's Russian Army, but it shouldn't be up under your elbows, either. I like it to be long enough to sit on. If you are going to use it to buffer your butt from a cold stump, it needs to be somewhat moisture-resistant.

That leaves the kind of material . . . wool. No, not an artificial wool, a substitute; you need real wool, straight from the sheep. The Ole Man got me going on wool. He says, "Wool is the real thing. When wet it stays warm. All the man-made attempts to equal it, all the 'miracles,' are just not up to the job of one hundred percent virgin wool."

Outdoor activities often mean getting wet. Wool is warm when wet. Buy wool.

When you buy the coat you should add a few extra pockets. My wife found room to put two on the outside and four inside. If you have a special need, like eyeglasses, a tailor will make a custom spot for you. A real custom-made coat. Mine has elastic bands on the wrists to keep wind and water out. There is also an interior waist-cinch cord to pull tight, or not. It's up to you. Woolrich did an excellent job on their hunting coats. I bought mine in red-and-black buffalo plaid with a reversible fluorescent orange to use for deer hunting. They carefully made the coat with no orange showing so it can be worn when duck-hunting, too. All this cost money to design and manufacture, but it's worth it. I have seen a dozen other manufacturers with excellent work, too.

Where did the coat come from? A catalog, of course. I searched a million pages of catalogs before finding just the right one. The whole process of finding one was just as much fun (well, almost) as actually wearing it on a hunting or fishing trip. I think this is probably why old-timer duck hunters hate to throw out used-up decoys or even many-times-reloaded shotgun shells when they have served so long. There are memories attached to each and every trip afield.

I now have three pairs of old waders I "use in the garden." My neighbors think I'm weird, but it's the only way my wife won't cart them off to the dump. When the temperature soars I look foolish out there, weeding the garden with waders on. I try to remember the cool days when the

trout or a two-foot-long Atlantic salmon struck my fly. It was cool then, and the waders stood by me, serving their function and keeping the cold water out. It was fun.

I've got to go to the mailbox by the road. The rural postal worker just dropped off my mail. I'm hoping my order from L.L. Bean is here today. I ordered a new Silva compass to replace my backup. I broke it last fall, deer-hunting. I fell asleep in a deer stand about eight feet aboveground. The sun was warm, I was a little sleepy, and bang, I was on the turf. It hurt my pride and broke the backup compass in my back pocket. I also ordered a new summer fishing hat, the type with breathing weaves to cool the top of the skull. My old one won't even strain gas anymore.

Author's Note: The more I associate with the Ole Man, the more I sound like Him. I just reread this piece and I can see a little twin-ism. My wife says, "It's like two hunting boots that have tramped around so long together that if one wore out, the other wouldn't be far behind." Speakin' about hunting boots . . .

30

Buyin' a Good Hat

JAKE GOODWIN ALWAYS WEARS A SIMPLE CAP. The sight of a baseball cap coming from Swift Brook or turning a corner on Main Street, when worn a certain way, is always a view of Jake. It's his trademark. He has his signature cap in green for fishing and bright orange for deer hunting. He also has them in camouflage. For all three variations he has a box of them. He orders them by the dozen. A family member gave him a brown hat for his birthday, but I saw him wear it just once, that day, and never again. Brown just isn't Jake Goodwin.

The subject of hats for the outdoors is something the Ole Man has plenty of ideas about, and he's always happy to instruct and share His complete knowledge with anyone who is in earshot. "You can always tell the cut of a man by the hat he wears. Take Jake Goodwin and his minor league baseball cap. About tells the whole story, don't it? He can't possibly know much about the outdoors. If he did, then he would have a proper hat, like mine."

With that He would reach up to touch the L.L. Bean felt hat He always wore.

Actually, the Ole Man's hats served several purposes. I've seen Him carry a week's supply of flies neatly attached by hook tip to the upper parts of His hat. On some days I have seen Him strain regular gas through His hat to use with the stove if He ran out of Coleman fuel or white gas. When He hurt His back, I saw Him use His hat to dip drinking water out of a brook because He couldn't quite bend over enough to reach the water.

Up, under the crown, He had Herself sew in a little compartment where He could store a waterproof Marble Emergency Match Canister. Besides this custom feature—I never heard of anyone else, except me, who does that—he also had a #10 Mickey Finn, a tiny Black Gnat on a #12 hook with turned-out eye, some four-pound monofilament, and three shells for his deer rifle. Smart old geezer.

It might seem strange to some why He'd use His hat as a storage compartment for essential supplies, but He always says, "The hat is the one thing I can't forget, because if I get a hundred feet from the house and I don't have it on, I feel the strain between my ears."

I only remember this happening twice.

We were over to Jake Goodwin's when he mentioned the brook trout were biting well-placed flies at Swift Brook. The Ole Man took His leave after a few lame excuses and headed for Cold Stream Pond. When I asked why He was going there and not to Swift Brook, where the fish were biting, He said, "Because Jake Goodwin never told the whole truth once in his whole life. If he said the fishin' was good in the brooks, then I guess it means the fishin' in the lakes and ponds must be gettin' pretty good. I figure Swift Brook is a hundred and eighty degrees from Cold Stream Pond. He'd see it as the truth." Simple Sherlocking, when you think about it.

In the rush to get to Cold Stream Pond He forgot His cap. As we returned to the house we met Jake and his truck wheeling it down the road to Cold Stream Pond. That meant he was going in a directly opposite direction for a trip to Swift Brook. His fly rods were attached to a specially made rack on top of his vehicle, and his canoe was on top, too. Dead giveaway.

When the Ole Man retrieved His hat, we made our way back to the "pond"—really, a lake—where we found Jake busy trolling a streamer fly; probably his modified, beloved Gray Ghost. He was cold to us, but resigned to the facts. We caught him in a little fisherman's fib. Where and how you fish is really a valuable secret. Jake blamed the Ole Man's forgotten hat.

The second time He forgot His hat, He swears it got Him the biggest buck He ever shot. I don't remember this particular event, but He swears it's true. Sometimes the Ole Man's word is not much better than Jake's, but here's the "true" version of the whole story: "I had fallen upon hard times. Hadn't even seen a good deer the whole season, and it was now after Thanksgiving. My mood around the house must have been pretty bad, because Herself *asked* me to go huntin' for somethin'. Mr. Keegan told me to take a few days off." He rubbed His chin with His hand as if to decide how to proceed.

"With them urging me on, I headed out for the back-country near Braley Brook. Carried a pack on my back with enough food for three days. Had everything I needed for comfort and slow, diligent, careful deer huntin'. I carefully planned out every hour of the next three days. Wanted to hunt seriously, without errors or misjudgments. I figured I would shoot a big buck, the last day of the season, just after dawn. I even knew where. The edge of the swamp along the logan there, on Braley Brook." He hitched up His pants, drew a deep breath, looked straight ahead, and said, "Well, I guess that sums it all up, doesn't it?"

I never tired of how He always thought the rest of the story was so damned obvious that "any fool can see how things turned out." When I spoke of the ending not being quite as obvious as He thought, the Ole Man made a face but said aloud, "I forgot my hat when I started out, and that put me fifteen minutes off schedule, so when I got to the edge of the bog three days later, the last day of the hunt, I was still fifteen minutes behind. The buck was late, too. We arrived at the edge of Braley Swamp at precisely the same time. I shot him— but fifteen minutes late. My forgotten hat . . . you see?"

The hunting hat was washed-out orange. The fishing one was a shaded solid green. Both were rumpled felt, the kind fishermen have worn for at least a hundred years. The Ole Man called His a "cap," or on other occasions, a "hat." I think calling it a cap is not accurate, but He says, "Both words are equal. A hat covers your dome. A cap covers the same dome. You've only got one head, sometimes less than one full head. In any case, it's a hat or cap. Take your choice."

When the faded orange hunting felt was hung on the back peg in the Ole Man's den, you could be sure the fishing-season time was getting ripe. The green hat would be in one of only two places: on the front peg of the rack, or on His head. In the fall, as the time of hunting approached, the orange hat appeared and the green one disappeared.

Jake once said, "It's the changing of the Ole Man's hats that causes the leaves to turn colors. It would sure be like Him to do it when none of us are ready. Surprised He ain't tried it on the Fourth of July, yet."

When I got ready to purchase a new hunting hat a couple of years ago, the Ole Man was just full of advice. "Just like gettin' a wife. You've got to be serious about it and train them right. If you don't start out on the same track, you will never be happy with the way it turns out."

Of course, I bought a felt hat from L.L. Bean, and for the first time, for me, I purchased one in orange and another in green, to be ready for the next spring. When they arrived the Ole Man came over for a first overall, thorough inspection. He picked each one up and looked closely at the cloth, the stitches, the feel of the whole hat. Then he said, " 'Course, they look all right, but they need a little mud rubbed in, a little bleach splashed drubbing in the sink, and a bit of wear before they'll be any good. But, overall, they will make good outdoor hats for the seasons ahead." With that He stepped outside, on my back steps, with my hats in His hand. Apparently, He was looking for something.

Or at least I thought He was.

Bear Brook runs through my property, and He took the hats there, threw them in the water, grabbed them again, wringing out the water as He stomped them, again and again, in the mud along the brook's edge. I was flabbergasted by His deliberate misuse of my brand-new hats. I paid good money for those hats. They were certainly not returnable now.

Inside, He took them to a sink, partially filled it with water, and threw the hats in as He poured a few splashes of bleach over them while keeping them in swirls of water, to which He added a handful of spruce gum He'd brought with Him. The whole process must have taken about fifteen minutes. He said, "You probably could wear them once they dry out, but I'd put them on the clothesline for a few weeks first. Even then, it will be years before they'll look like the hats of a real veteran sportsman."

He went on further to explain all the water, mud, spruce gum, and bleach, saying, "If you wore them before they looked lived-in, anyone with any sense would just know you were a dude. Of course, you *do* act like a dude sometimes, but you don't need to look like one. And don't throw them in the automatic washer, because they'd never smell good for years. Got to be dried outdoors and kept there as much as possible."

Since His inspection tour was over and He had nothing else to say, He tipped His well-worn hunting hat as He went to the door. As He got to the exit the Ole Man turned and said, "This doesn't mean your huntin' or fishin' luck is goin' to improve any, because your hats still have plenty of learnin' to do before they can guide you to the best spots."

And with that He was gone.

31

The Balance Sheet Says Zero

I COULD HEAR A LOT OF NOISE when I was still a considerable distance from the Ole Man's house. If the police were on the scene they would have called it a "domestic disturbance." I would never have known the cause of the row because I had already decided to turn away and go home, but the Ole Man saw me. He called, "Hey, get over here. I need a witness."

Herself said I was hardly impartial, and besides, "Every sane person around here knows the two of you are as crazy as loons."

He was not to be beaten here. "Whoever said loons was crazy birds? They can migrate thousands of miles every year even though they can barely get up enough speed to get off the water. And, you've got to admit, they add a lot of enjoyment to the summer season in ponds and lakes all across the north. Their lonesome song is the best-known wild sound around. And, the best-loved. In the water they are dignified, straitlaced, feed at the best fishing holes, and although they may look like poor flyers, they are actually strong once they get airborne. Crazy as a loon? My foot. I'd be glad to be called a loon."

"You're just avoiding the issue, like you always do when we finally get around to discussing finances." Herself was not going to be put off, even though I thought He made a good case for the loons. I wonder why anyone calls them "crazy loons" anyway?

"I am not avoiding the issue. You know perfectly well that any trade has specialized tools, and those tools are expensive. Hunting and fishing is no different than a plumber out plumbing or a carpenter out with his toolbox. Does a mechanic have only one wrench? I ask you, does he?"

I was getting the gist of the family feud. He'd overspent the family budget again. Herself was upset, and He was getting the third degree over the accounts. Even so, I thought His diversionary tactics were extremely well done. I never would have thought up the mechanic-and-one-wrench argument.

"Mechanics who work, and notice I said *work*"—and with this she raised her voice to the highest possible pitch without actually shattering glassware in the dining-room hutch—"with those tools earn money with them. If you were earning any money with the hunting and fishing 'tools,' we could all be spending the winters in Florida or in Europe. I could be buying my clothes in Paris, and our house would be used only for stopovers as we moved from the skiing property to the sun-filled life on our other property. Living with the seasons." Herself was really overstating her case; they probably couldn't afford a ski lodge. Besides, as far as I know, neither one of them even go skiing.

Normally I don't like to be around these domestic discussions or disturbances, especially if I am involved. This was an exception. I wanted to see how He was going to react, how I was going to be a witness, and why they were fighting over a few dollars.

He was getting a bit red-faced when He said, "Look, let's start at the beginning. I bought the over-and-under Winchester because I needed a gun to improve my cross swing on those blacks at forty yards, especially the ones that flare high comin' out of the turn. The Winchester suited my *needs* for this special purpose. It is a tool of the trade.

"Now, the Remington is a different story. I bought it because the front balancing is just perfect for those ducks jumping straight up from a reedy water where visibility is difficult. You need speed and balance. The Remington possesses perfect front-loaded balance. A rare and much-needed, special-purpose tool. A man needs tools. As you know, we love to jump-shoot ducks in saltwater marshes, and those fast-risin' ducks are a real problem, calling for a quick, accurate shot. A man needs tools."

The Ole Man looked like a boy with His hand in the cookie jar.

I was beginning to see Herself's side of the family discussion. Then again, He did have some real good points. Fast-flaring, high-jumping ducks in a saltwater marsh where the reeds grow tall *do* call for fast, accurate shooting. It does require tools. I testified right there that He missed too many shots in the marsh and needed a new gun, a new approach. They *both* frowned at me. Herself mumbled loudly, "One lies and the other one testifies to it." The Ole Man muttered, "I miss only a few—a very few. Never too many."

I guess I should not have offered testimony; this was a family debate.

Herself stood ramrod-straight, half-smile ready, set to begin her side of the story. Her lips suddenly froze solid as if she was formulating a serious response.

She began, "The Winchester was too much for our budget. All that fancy checkering and engraving don't make it shoot any better. I looked in the catalog, and there was a lesser grade in the same model. It lacked nothing in function, only in appearance. You could have made do with this gun if it was a tool you were looking for. Plumbers don't put engraving on pipe wrenches; neither do auto mechanics. And, I'll say right now, you don't *need* any more 'tools' to go in the woods. You already have more than the National Guard.

"Furthermore, the Remington is a ditto. The scrollwork on the side added hundreds to the price; totally unnecessary extras, totally unnecessary purchase."

The Ole Man said nothing. Herself was on a roll.

She added, "When you add up the bills, you forget to add a planned week's duck hunt in Maryland, and how you want to take the following week off from work because you just had to see if those two new guns worked on the geese in Merrymeeting Bay. No work, no pay, I might add. Where is all this money coming from? Nowhere, that's where. The bills are *not paid*. We are not even close to making ends meet. I want to ask your 'witness' a question. Mr. Witness, you've heard all the evidence; don't you think His spending is out of control?"

Boy, was I ever on the spot. I should have left before all the details came out. I knew about the upcoming duck hunting in Maryland; I knew about the week of goose hunting in

Merrymeeting Bay. I knew the guns were new. All I could think of was one of the Ole Man's favorite sayings, which I blurted out: "You can't take it with you, you know." I wanted to support Him, but didn't know what to say.

My foot twirling and poor response gave Him a final try. "All right, all right. Just to keep peace in the family, I'll cancel the Maryland hunt as soon as the travel agency opens in the morning. I haven't put a deposit down yet, anyway. I'm sure they won't mind too much."

Herself was taken aback. She didn't have a response, because she never thought He would back off. Her expression was still solemn but not quite as angry. Her tail feathers were pulled in; she wasn't accustomed to Him *ever* admitting anything He did was too much, or wrong. In the history of their long marriage, this was the first time He had ever given an inch on his actions or opinions.

After what seemed like a long intermission she backed away and said her head was aching. "I guess I'll go to bed to get some rest. I'm really sorry I made such a fuss." With that she went upstairs to retire for the evening.

The Ole Man invited me into the den to see His two new guns. When I asked about the Maryland trip, He smiled with a wolfish grin and said, "Never was a Maryland trip, but ain't that the slickest way you ever saw to get two new over/under shotguns in the house? And, Herself never even brought up the week at Home Base on Merrymeeting Bay; that was a real bonus bone I was prepared to drop. Now, I got two guns and a full week off to hunt those geese. You comin'?"

32

A Fireside Chat with Him

EVERY ONCE IN A WHILE we dig out the slides, photos, and Old Stump Blower. He builds a comfortable fire in the field-stone fireplace in the den and we sit down to an evening with two purposes. The first is to see where we have been, to retell stories brought up by the photographic evidence, even though we have seen and heard about these events many times. How many times can you tell the story of the Amazing Mets and the '69 World Series? The second part of the photo show and storytelling is to map out a future.

One Saturday evening last winter we gathered to do just that: plan ahead. Herself was going out to a church meeting accompanied by my wife. Perfect timing. With a cold, blustery winter evening ahead, we settled in for the main event. The four of us enjoyed a good evening meal together, and then the girls did their kitchen cleanup thing while the boys "adjourned to the den for an after-dinner drink and some serious work."

The women knew what we were up to and simply finished their chores and disappeared to their meeting. We never even heard them leave. By then we were on our second Old Stump Blower and were reliving some truly remarkable fishing we'd enjoyed the previous year. We even talked about the day the Ole Man had bought Lady, His terrific Brittany spaniel. I marveled about His catching the thieves, and we soared along Memory Lane.

All of a sudden He came to a screeching halt. His face brightened, he stood straighter, as though a load had been taken from His shoulders. I knew a trip was being formed when He asked a question: "Do you remember the time when we went over to Black Hole and Jake Goodwin tried callin' the ducks from the opposite shore, over by the pines?" He knew, of course, that I could remember every detail.

Jake is a pretty decent wing shot, especially on the bombers that fly directly over your head. The shot looks easy, but I've seen some good duck hunters miss almost every shot offered. The ducks come in five feet over the water and nearly take your head off as they pass by. Eyeball to eyeball. Jake figured he was just the man to be on the shore opposite from us, a flyway express straight from us to him.

He was even more pleased when he limited out before we did. The demonstration he made upon leaving his blind was worthy of an Academy Award. There were no two ways about it. His partner, Flash McLaughlin, a trickster in his own right, was busy taking pictures for a half-hour after they reached their duck-hunting bird limit.

Flash took pictures of Jake and the ducks, Jake and the duck boat, Jake and the big Lab, Jake and the tollers, Jake and the sun. I mean, it was unreal. They talked loudly, joked with each other, pointed at us, laughed some more, and finally, left. All of this took place in full sight of our blind, but we never let on that we even knew they were there. The regular duck route was to our left and they were hunting around the point to our right. We could ignore them and their celebration.

We never even fired a shot at two incoming teal. If we took both it would have finished out our limit, too. Fact is, we were too busy not paying any attention to them when the ducks flew by. We never even saw them coming. But, that's okay. Not seeing the incoming ducks made the Ole Man furious.

"Foolishness. Foolishness. To just sit here and let Jake put on a matinee while we don't keep a sharp eye for incoming ducks. The teal duo was an easy limit."

Jake probably knew we screwed up because while we thought they'd left, they must have been spying on us, because they reappeared with renewed vigor. The matinee was back on. Jake was tidying up the blind, gathering new reeds to match those already in place. He was whistling a tune while Flash just stood around trying to be nonchalant. It became clear Jake wanted to know how long it took us to limit out. When he got back to town he could say he'd limited out two hours before the Ole Man.

Meanwhile, for us, nothing was happening. No ducks. No shots. No chance to get out of our misery.

On this day the fall season was at its height. That was easy to see. Dull brown was now bright, the leaves were twirling down, and the puffy clouds were floating high overhead. It was a bluebird day. The ducks might not fly and the Ole Man and I might not get our limit after all. They might stop flying entirely. That would make Jake so happy that he might stop the charade and offer to buy us a drink back in town. If this happened the Ole Man was sure to be in a foul mood.

Jake used up all his blind-repair sequences and now started to "repair" various things on the boat. He hauled it up onshore to examine some imaginary fault. He called Flash over to show him what he'd found. They frittered. They fussed. They laughed. They did everything but point in our direction and guffaw. Jake got out a repair kit, hollered out to the straying Flash about the beauty of the day, and proceeded to repair something or other. With the repair done he sat on the edge of the boat's railing. Flash was lying down on the small sand dune with his feet up on a boulder, enjoying the fall day. Jake leaned back in the bow of the boat with a tipped hat as though he was ready to take a snooze.

We were duckless. None even within our boundary horizon.

Noon was not far away. The luster of dawn long forgotten. The eight o'clock warming coffee was gone. It was near time for lunch. We were stalled. I swear I could smell the fresh bread in the sandwiches we carried in our lunch pack. I was ready to quit hunting for the time being. So what if

Jake beat us. We could take the ribbing and at least act as if it didn't bother us.

Just about the time I was getting ready to find the Ole Man some rope He could hang me with, He nudged me. At first I couldn't see what He saw. I scanned the sky thoroughly, and then I saw them.

On the far side of the bay there were two gray-and-white ghosts coming our way. Two geese! Two geese! Why, if we got these, we would be so far ahead of Jake and Flash we would be absolutely redeemed. Geese are not as common as ducks, and so are high-priority in our area, when they are available. More highly prized. I could practically hear the Ole Man telling Jake, "We waited and took our time to get our waterfowl because I *knew* some geese were on the way." Oh, yeah, baby.

The geese generally fly in patterns that take them over our area of the state, but they rarely land anywhere near our hunting areas. When they do swoop down for a rare visit locally, it is more likely to be near a dairy farmer's cornfield. Getting a shot or two at geese every three years is about all you can usually hope for around here. These bonus geese were perfectly timed, if our shooting was good. If we had taken our duck limit earlier, we would have already packed up and gone home.

As if ordained from above the geese made their way lower and lower, but not within our range. Jake and Flash came alive, but too late as they flared the geese exactly our way. A surprise move. The geese did not see us, and were caught with flared wings pumping for the sky with less than twenty-five yards from their air to our gun barrels. I took the one on the right. The Ole Man fired at the goose to the left. Two shots. Two Canadian geese for us.

The Ole Man couldn't resist it anymore. He hollered out to Jake: "Hey, thanks, you guys. You're perfect decoys, and you sent them our way just right. I've been waiting for them all morning. I knew they were comin'. They're just late, that's all. Thanks again, Jake! Perfect waterfowl assistants.

Do you fetch, too? I'm not going to mess with the rest of my duck limit. This is quite enough for one day, huh, Jake?"

No answer, but I'm sure they heard it all. They disappeared from our line of vision. No surprise there.

Needless to say, Jake has yet to live this down. The Ole Man has told everyone who would listen (and many who would rather not have heard) about Jake and Flash being waterfowl assistants, and how He was now teaching them how to be even better at getting birds to come to us. The story got embellished with many extras as the tale got told again and again. The Ole Man sure enjoyed the twist of fate.

Tonight after remembering this story, he said, "I ought to ask Jake to go goose-huntin' at Black Hole with us this year. Maybe, just maybe, he could get himself a Canadian goose, too."

I reminded Him that duck and goose season were months away, and it was after midnight now. The Ole Man still insisted on calling Jake, right then, to extend a personal invitation.

33

In Favor of Dusty Decoys

HAVE YOU EVER LOOKED AT PIECES of your outdoor equipment with special feelings, remembering the day when . . .

The equipment was part of the scene, part of what happened that day. It's now a treasure, tied to your personal life experience. We all have these personal items in our lives. I own at least one or two rifles I feel that way about. They have gone over hill, through swamp, in snow, in rain, in disgust, in joy, and in times of generally mediocre experiences where nothing special is remembered. The weapon does a chore when asked to perform. Good outdoor equipment is planned and purchased to be a part of the scene for a long time. Nothing cheap and shoddy is considered.

I remember the day deer-hunting when I slipped and fell in a stream while carrying a rifle and scope. The scope stayed waterproof. I cleared the barrel of the gun, checked the scope, and walked only a few yards when a nice buck walked out. The shot was difficult, with a narrow lane between two stands of short pine trees. The rifle and scope performed perfectly. I got my deer for the year.

The 150-grain hand-loaded bullet from the .308 was again successful. The Savage Model 99 lightweight was in the right place; it was not bothered by the dunking, nor had the gun or scope given up the sighted-in point of impact because of a few drops of water. Fortunately, for me, the gun has always performed flawlessly when the going gets tough. I depend on the gun's tenacious quality as a tool with good, utilitarian characteristics. No fancy tooling or special stampings. Just a plain old Model 99 of mass manufacture. I once owned a Model 94 Winchester in the .30-30 caliber. It, too, was a gun of distinction for me. It delivered flawlessly.

Other veteran hunters will have many different choices. In a way we are a walking company advertisement. A product, a performance, a choice, a chance, an experience. But, it's more than the clearly stated details. I can look at the gun in a rack in the den and instantly bring to mind many days when the gun was right there with me.

The Ole Man feels like I do. He cherishes some of His outdoor treasure trove. Truth be known, it's probably from Him that I get the emotional ties to things made of wood, cloth, and metal. He has always preached to the choir about taking care of and maintaining all outdoor gear. Some will be consumable, such as most lures, lines, many casual fishing poles, sometimes a Coleman lantern or stove. But, when it comes to guns and fine, handcrafted fishing rods or decoys, they are lifetime items when possessed by a serious outdoorsman.

When it comes time to throw something away or retire it to a less-active role, it is hard to haul it away to the dump with yesterday's trash. When a plastic floating bait bucket gets a crack in it, the item needs to be replaced. Most glue applications simply extend the life of the bucket marginally, leaving open the prospect it might fail while you're on a long trip to a remote area. Not a fun thought. That's why some things simply get tossed in the dump. Today, with the recycling effort, the plastics of the bait bucket can see a new life. A good idea.

A hunting coat is another life you once lived. It held a compass when you needed a spare. It kept out thousands of hours of cold winds, even when the wind wanted to blow you out of the woods. You were warmed by the wool and cotton layers. The game bag in the rear held lunches, snacks, and often the game you shot while hunting. Anyone with experience knows the feel of a couple of rabbits or grouse swinging back and forth in the game bag as you head home or continue to hunt.

You could always count on a pair of extra gloves, a hand warmer in the vent pocket, or a dog leash and whistle stashed in a side storage pocket. Do you take it to the dump one day when the new one comes? I tend to keep those things in the attic, perhaps too many of them. My wife says I have the collector instinct. If you checked my garage, my attic, my closets, or my cellar, I guess you would agree. I don't seem to be able to part with old friends who've served me well.

The largest collection of such valuable outdoor retirees I know about resides at the Ole Man's house. He has an entire section of the cellar devoted to retired duck decoys. I saw Him down there one day smiling at a dozen broken, shot-up, never-will-float-again-under-any-circumstances decoys, which probably were once reasonable representations of a mallard or black duck. Today, it's often impossible to identify the species the carver was trying to imitate.

I asked Him why He's kept such monstrosities, because they were really just junk.

He scowled and snickered. "You're a bit like Herself, always callin' my most treasured things and trusted associates pieces of junk. Why, these decoys here are still works of art, and deserve to be respected as warriors. Especially, I would think, by the likes of you. They have seen more ducks, witnessed more great shots, and seen more fun than you ever will. I was young when they were. I understand why I keep them." I think He convinced me.

He wasn't finished, however. "They were there when I made the only flat-out double I ever made on geese. Jake was there, too, which makes it even better. He missed everything in sight. I was the master. I couldn't have been any prouder of my decoys and their work. The tollers kept the geese comin' in low and fast so we got off some great shots; at least I did. They rode in the waves with a bounce, making you believe they were really live ducks."

His pause was short, the grin was firm, the memory clear.

"I can remember the time, too, when these decoys were out on Sally's Ledge, where we were sea-ducking. I didn't have any eider duck decoys way back then. Can you imagine? No eider decoys. Well, sir, these decoys right here, they fooled the big eiders. They worked hard to pull it off. I used them for sea ducks for years. I needed the money for other things, and Herself wasn't willing to go on a diet so's I could buy eider decoys. Had a lot of fun with them. I'm sure they enjoyed it, too."

For the next two hours I heard lots of duck tales, most of which took place before I ever met the Ole Man. Each was just as vividly told as the one before. The dusty decoys in the cellar were a stimulus for His brain. A scrapbook of the hunting past, decades ago. He called them "a true history book of great times."

The summation of why these treasured decoys were retired to the cellar and not the dump was found in the story of how they had saved His life.

"Jake and I were hunting eider on Sally's Ledge for about the fifteenth time this season, see. It was a little hard getting out there this particular day. The seas were runnin' a few feet high. But, we went out anyway, knowing full well the near gale would bring lots of passing ducks. The day went well and we got our limits without too much effort, although it was quite a chore to gather up the decoys without smashing into the ledges with the boat. The waves were runnin' very high, the tollers were weaving, bobbing, and getting tangled as we retrieved each one."

His emotions were re-creating the scene from long ago.

"By the time we got off the ledge the sky was black, the seas were building. When the tides were in, the ledge was completely covered. We had to move before they went under the pounding seas.

"We were about three-quarters of the way to shore when our boat started to take in enormous amounts of water over the stern. I mean, we were both bailing for all we were worth, but the trailing sea was filling the boat. Jake had a boat cushion and I had a flotation jacket, which I put on quickly. We knew the sea was helping us get to the beach if we could only stay afloat long enough to get there.

"About a hundred yards out, the boat filled and sank beyond usefulness. My heart was in my mouth when I realized the flotation jacket wasn't working very well. One side was not carrying any ability to float. The stuffing was no good—too old, defective, whatever. I needed more flotation, *now*. It was that bad.

"The decoys came in to save the day. We both grabbed the bag of decoys and sailed to the beach. I bobbed up and down, as did Jake. We must have made a funny sight. But we made the beach safely. A fisherman's wife saw our difficulties develop, and about ten people were waiting when we washed ashore. They waited for the boat to come smashing in, and remarkably, not much was lost. We even got the eiders, because I'd tied the game bag to the rear seat strut. Both shotguns were on the boat's bottom.

"It took about three hours to get the things picked up, because we were about frozen to death in the cold water. Our rescuers and the pickup's heater were almost as much of a lifesaver as the decoys. It was a community effort. But, you must remember, without these decoys here, I never would have made shore. So, I give them a happy home for the rest of my life. It's the least I can do.

"An old guy there told us to be glad these were good cedar decoys. If they were plastic or fiberglass, as badly shot-up as they were, he thought we would have been at the bottom of the ocean right then. Ever since that day, I never hunt with anything but good cedar blocks. Never can tell when they might be needed for extra duty again. I owe these warriors here a lot." He was waving His hands in the direction of the derelicts.

I knew now why He felt as He did. They are not junk. Herself is wrong, clearly.

34

Shootin' Your Wads in Zest

"PULL!"

The birds come out at an angle most shooters find too difficult to keep a perfect score. If the "bird" was straightaway and you missed, you have a reason to be disappointed. If the shot was a crossing left to right or a low-angle miss, it won't be quite as bad. Still, no one likes to miss a shot often missed in the upland hunting season, too. It seems we all have a particular kind of shot, or three, where a miss is more sure than a hit, be it at skeet or partridge.

Skeet's the name of the practice game. It's basically an American-dream way to extend the hunting season for a few extra months every year. (We're all in favor of this, right?) The gunner moves to the locations for shots he knows will simulate field conditions often encountered in the woods with live wild birds. While the clay birds often begin their flight from the ground level, the variations include clay pigeons being sprung from higher angles, too. The "stations" where the hunter/gunner stands to call "Pull!" are placed according to a formula, but many clubs have built in variations. Think of how golf may be played on nine holes, but the layout and circumstances can still vary from club to club.

In 1920 in Andover, Massachusetts, a group of hunters wanted to get in some practice before the open seasons. Skeet was born. The National Skeet Shooting Association headquarters is now in Texas, but the sport is worldwide. To keep the competition equal there is an exact formula for station layouts, but most clubs, in my experience, have casual stations and extras for simulations of local hunting situations.

In the wild the hunter gets a shot, or doesn't; it depends on the shots. But your score on clay birds can vary widely. You can practice hard shots, again and again. It can make you a much better field hunter, and this is exactly why the sportsmen and -women of the world have taken to this year-round activity. Unlimited (except by your time and pocketbook) practice on shotgunning skills.

Skeet shooting, trapshooting with the handheld thrower, and upland bird hunting are three things the Ole Man loves to do. We sometimes load up so many boxes of shells in August, the floor sills under His den begin to buckle with the weight. Or so the Ole Man claims. The reloading equipment, the shot, the wads, the smokeless gunpowder, the immense pile of empty shells—they all take up most of the den when we're getting ready for the fall shooting season.

Thousands of rounds for skeet are loaded while we plan and gab and tell stories and dream. Hundreds of duck loads. Hundreds for grouse, rabbit, or woodcock are also loaded up every August for the annual hunts. Each sport has different needs. We load two or three boxes of #2 steel shot for geese, although we sometimes need very little because we don't see the geese. All of the other sports have different loads; ducks are #6's or #4's, while woodcock are always #7 1/2's. We vary the powder type and charge, too. This is big business; the reloading saves a lot of money.

Herself is often critical of how much it costs. The Ole Man always counters with how much He saves from the retail price. It's always a domestic standoff somewhat akin to a woman going to the shopping malls to "shop the giant sales." It's a yearly dance we all have in our lives.

Herself still likes to put in a few words. "What with the shells, guns, dogs, bells, vet's bills, food for the dogs—I'll bet the basic cost of a single pound of partridge meat would be somewhere around a hundred dollars."

The Ole Man never commented; He was prepared. He knew it was coming. He would later tell me, "A little pain now and I'll still have plenty of shells loaded and ready for all the upcoming hunting expeditions. Sort of like an inoculation. Herself has her say, I pretend to listen, and then I do what is necessary: load plenty of skeet ammo and have plenty on hand to meet the needs for the field."

The Ole Man started this shooting event some three decades ago. The TOSS—or "Tournament of Single Shots"—is really a full two-day shooting affair to find the best preseason scatter-gunning shot in our area. The prize is a case of high base duck loads in your favorite shot size and a case of low base loads for the upland. The real prize is in the bragging rights of the shoot-off. You must use the gun you hunt with, and it's a small town; everyone knows.

Naturally, everyone would love to hunt the whole season with shells bought by other people. In recent years the Ole Man has won, Jake Goodwin has won, Warden Clements won twice, and Flash McLaughlin won a few years back. Last year's tourney saw the Ole Man win in the very last round. Low man gets to clean up and "police" the shooting site after everyone leaves. He also gets to haul the trash to the dump next week. Locally, we call this "Low Man to the Dump," and everyone laughs. I have avoided this designation, so far.

There have been times when the Low Man attracts more attention than the winner—the butt of the joke about being a slave or a manservant. Poor shooters work hard to avoid the bottom standing.

This weekend of fun calls for each contender to shoot ten rounds of twenty-five stations each day. By the conclusion on Sunday, each contestant will have a score based on his five hundred individual shots. It's a big, big event. Last year's event was cut short in the middle of Sunday afternoon. The final tally for everyone was based on 450 shots.

Saturday morning of the TOSS came bright, clear, and beautiful. Jake cooked bacon on the camp stove before first light, with the added smell of coffee brewing. Toast by the loaf, eggs by the dozen; there was food enough for the whole clan, most camped in the field or in the yard at Home Base, our beloved duck-hunting cabin on the backwaters of Merrymeeting Bay.

Full dawn brought a typical Maine fall day. Early frost, warming rather quickly, slight breeze, lots of sun. Everyone was busy getting their guns and shells ready. Every dirty

dish was left in place. Every bed unmade in the camp. Every empty bottle or can from Saturday night's celebration was scattered around, too. The unswept floors and clutter made Home Base look like Hades. All in place for the Low Man's cleanup.

As is traditional, the last year's champion gets the first shot, so the Ole Man was the first one to holler "Pull!" The bird scaled out and He missed it on the first try; His second barrel caught the clay bird dead center. A cheer went up. He got half a point. Two full points if you "kill" the bird on the first shot. If you miss the bird with two shots, you subtract two points from your score. Getting the first-shot kill is nearly mandatory to make the top-shooter ranks. That's also why the tournament is called Tournament of Single Shots. You can't miss many, and if you miss the first shot you must shoot again or the two points will be subtracted anyway. Get a hit on shot number two and at least you salvage a half-point to the good. Once you get in the swing it's easy to keep the scoring straight.

Loren Ritchie and several others qualify for a special rule. They hunt with a single-shot shotgun. Loren's came from his father, so he can fire just one shot without penalty, but, like all single-shot shooters, he cannot get the half-point for a second-shot kill, and he *must* be known to hunt only with a single-shot shotgun when the regular season comes around. Most have doubles, pumps, or semiautomatics.

The Ole Man uses the L. C. Smith He uses for waterfowl. But he has been known to switch—halfway through a round—to the long-barreled Parker. Perfectly legal because He hunts with several shotguns. Everyone knows. He also hunts with a nice Silver Snipe or one of His fine three-barrel European drillings or a couple of Winchesters or Remingtons. All would be legal to use for the TOSS, but He sticks with the Smith or Parker almost exclusively

By the end of round five it was clear Flash McLaughlin was going to be close to the day's Low Man. He was way off, a long fall from champion a few years ago to Low Man on the opening Saturday morning. I was only a little higher than Flash. Jake Goodwin scored 246.5/125. This means he missed almost nothing: a perfect for 125 shots in five rounds would be 250. Jake was close. The Ole Man,

Warden Clements, and Mike Eash were all within range to catch Jake. The rest of us were far away in another shooting-score range entirely. It isn't as easy as it sounds.

Flash got to prepare the meal. Corn on the cob, baked potatoes, hamburgers (actually caribou burgers from the Ole Man's caribou hunt to arctic Quebec), hot biscuits, and coleslaw. For dessert there were three kinds of pie, with the favorite being a monster over two feet across baked by Herself for the tourney. It was made from last year's venison mincemeat. Delicious.

While the men ate, Flash and I got to provide the entertainment by shooting a bonus round allowed to the lowest-scoring gunners. Any points we picked up were added to our score, but our negative numbers were discarded. As I recall, Flash got a full ten points and I did, too. Now, five for twenty-five might not sound like a very good score, but we were the center of attention. It's distracting. All shots were fired from Station Eight, not a good place to shoot from. A hard-slinging, low-angle shot is all that's offered.

The afternoon session on Saturday went a little better for those of us in the lower strata. Flash was sixth. I got up to fifth. The Ole Man was in the lead by three first-shot bonuses over Jake, with Warden Clements in third. Harvey Jameson brought up the rear after a record-setting thirty-one consecutive misses on Station Five.

Our TOSS clan was ready for more Home Base cookery, this time prepared by nursemaid, Low Man, Jameson. He also was privileged to clean the floors and wash the pots, pans, flatware, plates, saucers, cups, and the rest. He was also banned from Old Stump Blower while the others spread the cheer before eating. Some played cribbage, others played poker. Around the kitchen table another group of hunters, fishermen, and liars gathered to talk about the outdoors.

Supper, the evening yarns and tales, then bedtime for all. Camping, tenting, squeezed into Home Base. Wherever. Another full day was coming.

The next dawn found Jake back in the kitchen with bacon, eggs, sausage, coffee, toast, and some leftover pies. The sky turned to deep black right after dawn. A hard wind was coupled with heavy rain pelting down.

Somehow, we all managed to stay inside for a couple extra cups of coffee. It was a late start to the shoot, but one where the Ole Man really showed His expertise. The more straight birds He broke, the louder His tales of joy became.

"Guess you guys can't shoot in the rain and wind. Good duck day, to me. Guess I'm by far the best shooter under field conditions. Guess you guys need bluebird weather to shoot a decent score. Jake, I guess you know you should practice bowing to REAL SHOOTING TALENT, huh?"

The clay pigeons were being blown all over the field, after a flight with odd twists and turns. I brought my gun up once and found the bird traveling as fast westerly as it was straight ahead. Hard shot. Wind force was blowing small branches off the trees and sand was filling the air as small twisters or funnels spun their merry way around us. Your feet needed to be firmly planted. As the morning passed the rain got more torrential, even stinging the face upon impact.

I considered it an honor to be Low Man for the morning. That meant a reprieve while I got the noon meal—indoors. The spirits of the whole group were falling as fast as the rain. This was getting to be like work, and required the grim determination of the normal work week.

By the end of the 450th shot a halt was called. The last few birds were coming out like the ducks of Black Hole do when you have worn an orange hunting cap instead of green or brown. As the Ole Man said, they were leaving the trap at "speeds greater than the shot being blasted down the barrel. The damned things are gaining speed over the shot once they get to thirty yards. At forty yards they are going faster than an *Apollo* rocket. Why, I'll have you know, some granite rocks far across the way are being scarred by incoming clay pigeons."

Trees were being uprooted. A few shingles flew off the roof of Home Base. A part of the dock broke its anchor moorings and floated away. Home Base itself was shaking with every gust. We waited for the word to reassemble for the final two rounds of twenty-five each. But, with the fierce storm not abating, we gave up and simply awarded the Ole Man the winning place—one he'd earned with fantastic shooting. We voted to give him both cases of shotgun shells, even though the whole TOSS tournament was abbreviated. Jake objected but was overruled by the group. We all felt the Ole Man would have won after 500 shots, probably by a wider margin than he was leading by after 450. This wild weather agreed with His shooting skills.

The trip home was an adventure. There were washouts, trees down, blinding rains; closer to town, even the electric wires were down, and an emergency crew was working to restore power. It was a mess. We'd need to look for the Home Base dock or make repairs some other day.

When we got home we found we were shooting trap in a full-blown hurricane. The storm was just approaching its height as we got home. Our wives made some comments about our collective male mentality and seemed to doubt their own choice of male counterparts, given our performances.

But Jake was the one who provided the extra fun for the Weekend. He called a meeting scheduled for the next night, after work. He even offered to buy the drinks. When we were all assembled, Jake started explaining why some of us had delivered a pretty poor shooting performance. "It was the low barometric readings with the hurricane coming. It interfered with our mind's ability to follow targets and make the necessary adjustments, kind of like a home computer with a virus." His whole talk seemed to be saying the Ole Man never really won, and probably even knew the hurricane was coming and so knew He needed to take an early lead.

Finally, the Ole Man asked for the floor. "Hurricane or no hurricane, I could beat the likes of you, Jake Goodwin. If you'd like, I could tell the whole gang about last year at Black Hole when we decided to only shoot at singles. Would you want me to tell them about the score?"

Jake remembered the weekend. He was unable to get a single duck in four days. The Ole Man got His limit easily every morning. What Jake didn't know then, or now, was that the Ole Man had snuck into Jake's house before the hunt last year. He had replaced Jake's normal duck loads with blanks, good hand-loaded heavy blanks. When the hunt started the Ole Man was so sure He was the ultimate winner, He bet Jake a really big handful of cash on the outcome. He even bet an extra amount, enough for a super new fly rod, that He would skunk Jake. The Ole Man won, was happy for weeks, and every time Jake has come to the Ole Man's place since, the Ole Man gets out the new fly rod and lightly oils the guides and fittings.

Jake declined to hear the story again. He bought rounds for everyone and declared the Ole Man the TOSS champ for the second year in a row.

Six months later they were still calling Him the "Hurricane Shooter."

Later He told me Jake woke up one morning to find two cases of shells and a new fly rod on his doorstep. With a wry smile the Ole Man said, "Jake was perplexed with my newfound generosity. He thinks I left those things there, but he can't prove it, and is suspicious about the motivation. I told him I just felt sorry he was always the runner-up."

35

Corn Not Meant for Man

IN STATES WHERE DAIRY FARMING IS IMPORTANT, the corn crop is often tied to small farms. The acreage devoted to corn is some of the finest available to the farmer, because corn and corn silage is an important feed source for his cows.

In New England and many other locales, the raccoon is an enemy of the dairy farmer, robbing him of a significant portion of his mature crop. They can ruin more in a single night than the average family could eat in a year. The "cow corn" is tasty to the masked bandit. The reason for the severity of the corn damage is that coons have a habit of "sampling" the corn over a period of a couple of weeks, before it's sweet enough for them to seriously attack. If it is not quite ready for their tastes, they still do damage by knocking down enough samples to make the farmer's machine harvest less productive.

A mother raccoon with a litter of five or six youngsters all sampling and finally eating in a field of corn nightly will make a mess. The local farmers often seek out hunters with hounds. Coon hunting can be excellent training for future bear dogs, occasional bobcat dogs, or simply for those who enjoy raccoon hunting.

The farmer calls to ask for help. The hunters will carry a .22 revolver or automatic sidearm. Add a dog or two with instincts to hunt coon and you are in business. Since it's after dark you need a good three-cell flashlight. Hunting at night is a different experience. Fun, but not everyone's cup of tea.

My introduction to raccoon hunting came early in September one evening when I stopped at the Ole Man's house. Without further ado He asked, "Got your flashlight ready?" I asked, "For what?" He was ignoring me. "You'll need an extra leash for the dog just in case you're the one to pick him up. Don't forget a spare bulb and a few extra batteries, too. Walking a mile or two in the woods at midnight on a dark night will make you a believer in lots of light." I assumed we were off on some kind of outdoor adventure.

I was in the battered Jeep before I knew we were going out for coons. The Jeep made the climb to Eddie Sleeper's back field in record time. "Throw out the anchor!" Eddie would call out every time we reached a farm gate. We came to a temporary halt every time Eddie needed to swing open a barbed-wire gate to control his huge herd of cows. All the fences were electric, so you needed to be careful to hold the colorful yellow rubber sleeve and not touch the bare wire. This lesson I learned the hard way, just once, early on. You can get the jolt of your life grabbing the bare wires of a farmer's electric fence.

Cows know—I don't know how—when the electricity is turned off. I have seen them plow right through an electric fence where the power was just shut off a half-hour before. They knew the wire strands were powerless. One old

farmer told me he knew cows smelled electricity and therefore knew when it wasn't operating. I don't use my nose. I
believe it's on and avoid coming in contact with bare wires.

At the last gate leading directly to Eddie's sixty-acre
cornfield, we stopped right after the gate. We let Mandy
and Tramp out to explore. Mandy is a right nice-looking
blue-tick bitch who has been a great hunter in addition to
whelping some first-rate bobcat hounds. She even looks like
a talented hunter. Tramp is a tramp. His heritage is something three Philadelphia lawyers couldn't untangle. Both
dogs are owned by Mike Merry, another dairy farmer, who
was also jammed into the old Jeep.

Tramp yipped to mark the first coon scent. He was about
a quarter-mile away already. He was not only a skilled
hunter, but a very, very fast hound. The Ole Man and I
walked one side of the corn while Mike and Eddie walked
the far edge. At this point in a hunt it is hard to see which
way a chase will develop—straight line to a tree, across the
corn, circles in the lowland farming fringe. Hard to tell.

By the time Mandy chimed in, the chase was developing
in the opposite direction from all four hunters. The unexpected is almost expected in raccoon hunting. I have seen
some take to a tree in fifty yards. Others have gone mile
after mile until you are sure the hounds must be chasing a
black bear. Still, when found, with the faithful hounds
"marking" the tree with a baying sound, it is just a raccoon
who decided to check out things in another county.

The Ole Man was sure He knew where the hunt was
headed. "There's a swamp down on the far end where the

cedars start marking some wetland. They'll head for one of those orphan maples from the old forest. It means a hard shot to bring one down."

The sound of the hound music on the trail always excites me, especially as the scent gets hot. It sasses you by being both interesting and wild. I know of no other sound quite like the hound hard on a fresh trail. The stillness of the night adds an element of mystery to the moment. It's primitive, beautiful, fulfilling, energy-absorbing, and wily, stated in a near echo. If you have never heard it, you are missing something in the outdoor world.

The coon crossed a half-mile of real estate to the edge of the cedar swamp where it scurried up an ancient old maple orphan. He went to the very top where he was waiting for us. The dogs marked the tree with a changed voice. They waited for our arrival. Tramp has a quick *chop, chop, chop* voice that means "The raccoon is in this tree, boys!" He is always right.

To the sound of curses and more curses and swishing corn and broken cedar limbs we finally arrived. The Ole Man hollered out to the other hunters. The dogs barked *tree*. It was a night of sounds. When all were assembled we switched on the lights to search the treetop. It was there, an old boar, way up at the top. The circles of flashlight combined with the flash of fire from the handguns. The coon fell dead at our feet. The dogs were allowed to feel their claim and we picked up the coon to move on.

Environmentalists tell us that sound is a very harsh pollution. I agree. The sound of buses, trucks, trains, airplanes, and urban sounds are really pollution. The sound of hounds is music. I learned this from the Ole Man.

Dyed-in-the-wool hound men will stay up for hours discussing the different strains of canine voices they have heard on the trail. The strike dog, the follower-but-fighter, the lone wolf, the hunting bellow, the hot track, the cold trail marker, the warming up, the yip of excitement, and the treeing call to arms.

Whatever your persuasion, the sound of the hound hunt at night is worth the tree-limbs-in-the-eyes, stumble-over-everything-in-the-dark trip through the nighttime woods.

When we finished the evening of coon hunting with Eddie and Mike, I asked the Ole Man why He didn't own a pair of hounds like these. He mused a bit and said, "Well, you see, it's like this: Herself has tolerated a brace of rabbit hounds, a wonderful bird dog, more guns than I can ever use, some mountains of camping gear, a few boats, thousands in reloading equipment, tons of shells, an extra Leonard fly rod or three, some L.L. Bean bills, Orvis bills, my snowmobile, my all-terrain vehicle, bills you wouldn't believe from Dakin's Sporting Goods, and my time spent with you. I think coon hounds might be stretching my welcome at home a little thin. Besides, what are outdoor friends for? Mike goes rabbit-hunting with my dogs and he hunts partridge over my Brittany."

As usual, the Ole Man made perfect sense.

36

A Case of Cheer

SPRING DOESN'T ALWAYS COME ON TIME. Even in northern
New England you should be able to plant peas before Memo-
rial Day if you're going to have the traditional first harvests
by July Fourth. It's a traditional Yankee dinner to have fresh
peas and a garden salad for the midsummer holiday. Trout or
salmon are the expected main dish. When all the ingredients
are not present, the Ole Man has plenty to say.

There are many April days when the winds are filled
with the warmth of summer. The sky is blue, the nights
warm, and the next day brings a repeat performance. False
summers, they call them. I guess they are. On these days we
sometimes get a bundle of frosty nights, snow squalls, and
outright snowstorms to reward us for our belief that summer has already arrived.

The spring runoff stays around longer. The floods rise
during the day and recede at night. On the depth of the forest floor the skunk cabbage, the grasses, and the ferns,
including the widely sought variety known as "fiddleheads,"
await a little more warmth. They will venture forth soon as a
harbinger of spring. The frost at night is ever a threat right

now. Many springs with a heavy late frost see about a third of the fiddlehead crop turn a very dead black as morning warmth strikes. The plants always generate enough regrowth to regenerate themselves, but the resulting edible fiddleheads are very small and not as desired as the original crop.

A late spring means trout fishing will be slow to develop, too. Flooding water, as it warms, will bring insect hatches and more life to the brook-trout fishery. Members of the "I-can-guess-the-day-the-ice-goes-out" club will be sadly off the mark in a seemingly never-ending winter.

Deer are also affected by lingering winters. They will be seen in open places looking for a windfall of greening grass or leftover apples, fermented and rotted though they may be. The pregnant does need all the nourishment they can find. A slowly developing spring makes them scrounge the fringes for whatever edibles might be available.

Black bears look for critters that died during the winter. Several times I have seen a she bear with cubs practically set up household at the location of a moose that died in the winter. The meat is really carrion, but is relished by the bear as she guards against intruding coyotes or fox. Most years the bears will feast off the winter kills, but quickly move on to green sprouts as soon as they are available.

This is the time of year where bears can be the biggest nuisance because they will seek food at locations that bring them in direct conflict with people. Green grass on the lawn of the high school, unattended garbage bags in the backyard, spoiled food such as a farmer's cast-off potatoes, farm dumps—all sorts of "foods" the bear will seek out until natural foods are ready.

For the outdoorsman who has his heart set on a mess of fiddleheads and fresh brook trout for supper, but arrives at Swift Brook to find the water flowing five feet above normal fishing levels, the delay is threatening his sanity, too. My wife says the hardest days of our marriage are "the days—I hope not weeks—when the hunting and fishing seasons are not open yet." I guess I mope around the house and the work site, too. I'd just as soon get fired or divorced or die or—I guess I just feel that I'm not attached to anything. I'm a ship set afloat, set adrift. Bob Dylan called it "no direction known." As soon as the fishing season opens and the real spring arrives, I'm a really upbeat person again.

I never have been able to understand why the best, most active, most youthful, most energetic years of your life have to be spent at the cement factory. And, in your declining years, you are set free to roam while too pooped and

crippled to do much. When you need money the most is when you are young. Families to raise, household goods to buy, a mortgage to pay, vehicles to buy, and outdoor needs to fulfill—all with little money coming to pocket. This is the time of life to establish a career, work overtime, get ahead. Now, is this any way to spend your youth?

I'm afraid someday I will get an L.L. Bean catalog in the mail and find there is nothing there I want to buy. Everything I want is already at home and is filling the closets, cellar, attic, and garage. The best of boots, an extra Silva compass, the heavyweight shirts, the rain suits, the bird-hunting pants, even an extra ax, still unused.

When that day comes I'll assume the death scenario is being played out. If we have accumulated all the outdoor stuff necessary to be competitive outdoors, and even some extras, the journey through life would seem to be nearly over.

The Ole Man sulks about this from time to time. He was doing this more often during the year of the slowly unfolding spring. I stopped in to visit and found the back door wide open. I don't mean the door was left open and unattended. I mean, someone slammed the door hard enough to leave the hinges broken, the door barely left in the frame.

Vic Peavey and the Ole Man were lounging around in the den. Neither of them seemed to have enough energy to even greet me with a "Hi." I walked over to my favorite chair and sat down. A long silence went unbroken. For an hour the only sounds in the den were the occasional snap of burning wood in the fireplace, the ticking of the grandfather clock, and the flipping of magazine pages. It was weird.

I was beginning to feel uncomfortable when He sighed. "I think I ought to fix those hinges before Herself gets home. You know, I already shut the door twice before the wind caught it the last time. That time I really shut the damned door, but good! Lord, don't I wish spring would hurry up and get here, or I'm going to be homeless, fat, and divorced. My nerves have an ever-sharpening edge as the days tick by. Why, I'll tell ya, I even opened a new Orvis catalog and couldn't find anything I wanted to buy. Never thought I'd ever see the day when there was nothin' left to buy. It's almost scary." With that last statement He sagged into His his favorite chair, shoulders drooping, face looking about a hundred years old.

Through the sliding-glass door in the den I could see the outdoors. It was late April and spitting snow. Depressing. I think He honestly forgot about the door hinges, because in another hour Herself was home and working in the kitchen. The fact Herself wasn't fussing about the broken door was a sign she recognized the state of the Ole Man's mental condition. The silence spoke volumes. Not a time to rock the boat. The den action—nah, lack of action—was so down it felt like a weight on the shoulders. Instead of getting higher, excited, or interested as I normally did when I visited the Ole Man, I was now finding it depressing. Even my comments about a trip for togue to Matagamon Lake, or the story I told about the big brook trout in the lower reaches of Swift Brook, failed to get a conversation going. Vic and I talked about April fishing in other years, but the Ole Man never said a word. Usually, He would have added His own stories, and the energy level would have shot upward.

Finally, I couldn't take it anymore. The whole miserable social scene, coupled with the dismal prospects of the weather outside, was too much. I shuffled out the door and scuffed my way home in six inches of newly fallen snow. The walk seemed liked miles. Cabin fever has a lot of parts tending to weigh down the human spirit. Maybe spring really wouldn't come this year. Maybe the eco-freaks were right and the climate was suddenly changing for the worst. Maybe . . . maybe I needed to go to bed. Tomorrow is another day.

Somehow we all managed to get through another week of weather showing little improvement. The water table did drop a little and the skunk cabbage started to seriously break through the ground. I knew full well spring had arrived when I got home from work and found brookies on a stringer at the back door, left there with an illegible note in scrawled handwriting.

I brought the note in and by adjusting the light I was able to make out "If you want some more like these, be ready by five in the morning. Bring your gear and lunch, tell your wife it may be late, not that I care about your domestic affairs, but one more week of winter and I would surely have needed the undertaker or a new housekeeper. Oh, yeah, I almost forgot: I found some new socks I need and ordered a dozen pair from L.L. Bean. They look about perfect for late-season deer hunting. See you in the morning."

I didn't need to guess about the origin of the note, or about getting ready for the morning.

37

Lost Near Second Musquacook

COUSIN RAYMOND AND UNCLE HARRY arrived on the 6:30 p.m. flight. They were routed via New York's JFK, Boston's Logan, and our home airfield. The local facility didn't impress them much, but they were polite about it.

Both men, relatives of the Ole Man, were here to do some fishing in the North Woods. They had heard the tales about the giant brook trout, the high-jumping salmon, and the hefty lakers. All things considered, they were looking forward to their first coldwater fish after a steady diet of bass, catfish, and crappie.

I said "all things considered" because they were somewhat uneasy about the woolly tales the Ole Man wove around our best trips afield. He told about the size of the native blackflies ("They weigh about seven pounds apiece"), or people getting mauled by black bears ("Bears like to chew you up a bit before droppin' you"), or being confronted by moose ("They are as big as a house and will stomp you into the ground if you're not careful"). Then there was the thing about getting lost, for weeks at a time.

On the way home from the airport he laid it on even thicker, making sure they understood that the Ole Man was often the hero in these tales of woe. Jake entered the conversation often as the person who didn't know whether he was afoot or on horseback. I was in the stories as the little lost lamb who found the good shepherd.

It was all in good fun.

The next morning we were all up early. The old Jeep was all packed and ready to go. The canvas canoe was tied to the top. In the back was crammed an assortment of necessary items, like a reflector oven and the food storage box we used as a base. It was the "rear seat" for the two of them to sit on for the trip north. Anyone who knows about World War II vintage Jeeps knows there isn't much extra space for people or baggage. The Ole Man was ingenious when it came to finding spaces to store the gear. The canoe racks were modified to keep several ten-foot tubes, under the cross rail, to store all the necessary fishing rods.

Most of the extra things we loaded were in the "trip trailer" we hauled behind the Jeep. We mounted my canoe on the long wooden trailer. It just cleared the rear of the Jeep. The Ole Man thought of everything. The trailer had high sides, two doors on each side, and extra storage racks built to hold the tent poles and bulky things galore. When ready to go the trailer looked bigger than the Jeep.

In short, the whole troop had the look of seasoned veterans. Felt hats, canvas stream boots, dungarees, heavy cotton flannel shirts that had at least thirty machine washings to make them soft. Raymond and Harry were given some of the Ole Man's "best" duds to wear. He said, "I don't want my relatives looking like some fool dudes from the city." They looked good.

We were bound for a very remote section of the North Woods. Neither the Ole Man nor I had been there in years. The area we chose was loosely defined by Big Black Brook. At least this was to be our final destination, after a day or two of a shakedown on a good salmon lake. We chose Big Square Lake for the salmon workout. We knew there were big landlocks there.

We didn't catch any huge fish on Square, but Raymond and Harry were extremely happy with a pair of three-pounders and the species' great fighting abilities. The weather was good and the lakeshore vista was truly beautiful.

The Ole Man was pleased with himself. The fishing was good, the food was campfire-perfect, the weather was cooperating, and the blackflies were out in force.

With the salmon under our belt we headed out for the togue of Second Musquacook Lake. At the very end of this road were the native brook trout of Big Black Brook. We were to spend four days, at least, at Musquacook. It is located in the heart of the forest tracts noted for pulp, lumber, and dense forest growth. Some call it the "spruce and fir capital of northern New England." Only northern Quebec or New Brunswick might have more softwood trees in the inventory. It is a wild commercial forest with great acreage, the size of which is beyond the imagination of many. This area has about four million acres.

I think we crossed every acre.

Once we left the main tarred roads at Ashland the logging interests became apparent. Every vehicle we saw was a log truck of huge size carrying bulging tree-length loads. Occasionally we saw pickup trucks with chain saws, barrels of oil and fuel, and toolboxes for the crews working with different types of equipment to harvest trees, such as feller-bunchers, grapple skidders, or the mobile chippers. The more we traveled , the narrower the roads became and the fewer people we saw. Civilization was left far behind. That's a feeling most outdoorsmen love to feel, as you are on your own with the modern world left behind, except for what you carry with you. Forget anything? It's too late now. You'll have to make do.

By noon we were somewhere near our destination. I say "somewhere" because I really have no idea where we were. Logging roads were recently cut, or were cut, used, and abandoned, creating a literal maze of intersecting roads. Neither the Ole Man nor I were sure of the location where we stopped for lunch. Nothing jogged our memory. Roads grow full of small saplings, quickly. The new roads were confusing our memories. The brook where we ate lunch was incredibly clear and probably trout-filled. Harry and Raymond quickly caught our lunch, proving the area has plenty of fishable waters.

As we were getting ready to board the Jeep for the rest of the journey, Harry turned to the Ole Man and asked a

question I would have loved to have asked: "How far to Second Musquacook?" The Ole Man was quick with a "Not too far." I noticed he offered no other details.

With the passage of time and a few more logging roads I noticed the Ole Man was getting quieter and more sullen all the time. He approached each new crossroad as if looking for a road sign. There were none. No familiar road markings, no people to ask, no sign we had ever been here before.

At three p.m. he stopped "for a little stretch." The rest of us did the stretch thing, but He finally got out maps. The Ole Man was never going to admit He was lost; getting out the maps was a rare-enough event in my days afield with Him. There were clues as to where "we probably were right now." I was not convinced, and even the Kansas City relatives were doubtful. Even so, the Ole Man assured us the country still looked familiar. He knew the sandbar at Second Musquacook would soon be appearing on our right.

After an hour another crossroad came in sight. It looked as if it had not been used in a decade or so. But the alternatives looked even worse. We took the crossroad and sloshed along in four-wheel-drive high range until we came to a brook. There was a bridge there at one time, but only the rotting timbers were left, and the Jeep needed to ford the stream all on its own. The water looked deep. The Ole Man shifted to low range. I thought sure He would admit defeat and say He was lost, but, no, ahead we went. We barely scraped through to face an uphill climb needing all the Jeep possessed.

After the washed-out bridge the road got worse and narrowed to a small mountain path with washouts every fifty yards. Slow going. At the top of the "mountain" my worst fears were realized: The road suddenly stopped. There was nowhere to go but back the way we'd come. The end was a big circle where the logging trucks loaded the trees the skidders hauled out to lay in piles. It was a long time since it had been active. Now, we needed to reverse directions. We were lost "somewhere near Second Musquacook."

All the Ole Man said was "Guess I took the wrong turn at the last crossroad." If He meant the last "real" crossroad, it was fifteen miles back. If He meant the last grown-over, leftover, never-used crossroad, it was the one on the other side of the washed-out bridge. Back we went.

I was going to remind Him that the last time we'd gone to Second Musquacook, we'd used a station wagon with two-wheel-drive and never even needed to slow down to get to the lakeside. After a few thoughts, I decided to forgo the reminder.

Our return trip to the unused crossroad was at double speed, with the old Jeep squatting on spring frames from time to time. Our only holdup was when the trip trailer got hung up on a rock in the middle of the brook with no bridge. That halting lurch also caused another problem when the bottle of Old Stump Blower under the seat somehow got loose and broke as it slammed forward. There were blue words about that.

The trailer we pried with a long pole and set it over the rock. We did, of course, get wet.

After a run up the other possibility of the crossroad we were again dead-ended and finally forced to return to where we'd eaten lunch. The visitors bailed out of the Jeep and were soon fishing brook trout. Just about a hundred yards below in the brook they came to a spot where the waters widened into a deadwater at the edge of a wide heath. The water was deep, and the cedars mixed with alders overhanging the deadwater made for some mighty interesting native brook-trout waters. Lunker country.

The Ole Man and I put up the tent, built a nice campfire, got a meal together, and slouched down over a map to try and figure out where we'd gone wrong. When the visitors came back they each held up a brookie of two pounds, or better. Even a disgusted Ole Man had to agree that these trout were something special. The visiting relatives were ecstatic. They dug out cameras and took some pictures of themselves with their fish. The native trout were beautifully colored.

After a pleasant meal spiced with fresh fish and some great campfire tales, the conversation got around to "Where the hell are we?" The relatives went to bed with that question not answered. The Ole Man said to me, "I'm totally lost, and if you *ever* say anything about this to that Jake Goodwin, I swear I'll break every fly rod you own."

Now, we got out the maps and seriously looked at all the possibilities. Every clue was added. The maze of roads we knew and the ones on our (outdated) maps were superseded by new roads. We were lost because the roads and maps were not as shown. A lot had happened since our maps were made. All we knew for sure was that the sun sets in the west, and how many miles we'd traveled that day from the time we left Ashland. By checking that mileage we should be approaching Quebec City if we traveled in a straight line. But our line of travel was more circular than straight. We were still in the United States. I think.

There were millions of acres, and we were reduced to saying, "Remember the little odd-shaped pond with the wide brook we passed?" "Oh, yeah." No help there. There were dozens and dozens of little ponds and little brooks. We each postulated a few "possible locations," but at the end of the night we still did not have a clue. We needed to do some major retracing. We could skip the legendary Big

Black Brook and do our brook-trout fishing right here. There were obvious advantages to that prospect.

When dawn came the visitors took out their rods to "explore this brook's deadwater a little more." They were still excited with the trout fishery they'd discovered the day before. Their first go at nice brook trout was a very pleasant memory. As it turned out, that day and the next three days were some of the best brook-trout fishing I'd ever seen, bar none. I'd even compare it favorably to our summer trip to Labrador. We decided to let them have their beloved deadwater and the Ole Man and I took to exploring the upstream part of the brook.

We stopped at a waterfall for a pipe of tobacco. The Ole Man called this brook the No-Name Heaven Brook, and commented on its great ability to produce terrific fishing. He said, "I wish I knew where in blazes we were, and then we could slip over to Second Musquacook for togue for a few days. It would successfully complete their trip. I guess we need to bungle back toward Ashland until we bump into a logger to get directions on these newfangled roads."

We were late getting back to camp. Our visitors were already there with supper cooking over the campfire. They were excited about something and came walking up to meet us. Raymond started right in. "We found the way! We got a guy to give us the directions. He even wrote them down. We can drive right to Second Musq—whatever you call that lake. The guy came in by another road. Oh, by the way, he said he knew you right well."

With that Raymond handed over the written directions. Even I recognized the handwriting, especially the huge *Jake* scrawled at the bottom of the page.

As if he didn't know enough to keep his mouth shut at a time like this, Raymond added, "By the by, this here brook is Big Black Brook. We been getting fantastic fishing because we were right on the legendary brook all the time!"

What cousin Raymond lacked, Uncle Harry doubled with a choice comment: "That Jake is a real nice guy. He even offered to guide all four of us *for free*. Of course, we told him we were being kindly guided by our good relative, the Ole Man. Jake sure got a chuckle out of that . . . yeah, he surely did. He said he'd take a Leonard fly rod if you wanted this kept quiet. I don't rightly know what he meant by that, but he said you would."

After the earthquake the rest of the trip to Second Musquacook for lake trout went pretty well.

38

No TVs Allowed; No Electricity, Either

SOMETIMES THE OLE MAN SHUFFLED AROUND. Normally, He just walked, ran, or crawled. But, on certain days, He shuffled from place to place. It always meant the world was badly beating Him in His quest to make sure nothing ever changed.

It was on a shuffling day in early March when I went for this particular visit. I'd barely closed the door before I wished I had waited for another time. He was on a binge of reading books on arctic life and Inuit and ancient travelers. The arctic project, in itself, was good, but He was reading the books now, as He often did, to escape life in the worka-day world where life was not an exciting adventure.

"I'm going on a caribou hunt this fall in the Ungava Bay area of arctic Quebec. Want to come? I've got to find an out-fitter who still hunts with the fly camp, one like the classic sporting operations of the 1940s, when there was no TV or electricity in the hinterland. They used wood for cooking and heat. They used candles, Aladdin lanterns, with the old gasoline Coleman lanterns for light. I want a hunt like that."

Major money would need to be spent to see this through. The arctic travel, hunt, camp is not cheap. I was going to ask Him if He wanted to give up His Orvis graphite rod or a small trolling outboard motor for the lake fishing He loved to do. But, instead, I just bit my tongue. I humored Him, and along the way, I began to get excited about the arctic trip, too.

Something in the outdoorsman leads us over the ridge, the next hill, the swamp, the mountain, the river, and the pond. This something is where the fishing is better at the other end of the lake, or the deer have bigger racks in the next county. Something urges us to join the adventures of those who first explored Africa, Alaska, or the far-flung anthills of St. Louis. There is always the thrill of standing on the highest hill, being the first to conquer a boundary, imaginary or real.

About 70 percent of the fun came from writing letters to the prospective outfitters and waiting for the replies. When the mail came every day I rushed to the mailbox with anticipation and expectations. The chore of writing inquiry letters fell to me because the Ole Man was busy "planning other aspects of the trip. You can act like a secretary." Finally, there came a response I was sure meant we had found the right outfitter.

The letter and brochure described Quebec's arctic Kaniapiskau (there are several accepted spellings) River in the Ungava region. The camp was run by Montagnais Indians, who we all knew, by reputation, were no-nonsense, capable guides. Although they had some nice tent-platform camps with stoves, central dining at the lodge, and an electric generator, they also ran twenty-one primitive outpost camps for caribou. The brochure said: "We have thousands of caribou near our outpost camps, where you can experience the hunt of a past century, with no electricity, running water, or indoor plumbing. This is not for everyone. Only veteran outdoorsmen should apply."

This sounded ideal for our hunt. I immediately took the brochure to the Ole Man. In two days we had booked an outpost camp off the Kaniapiskau River for a few weeks in September. Between the booking time in April and the actual hunting trip in September is what the Ole Man calls "the sweet time of blissful dreams and serious planning." A day of togue fishing close to home was filled with comments like, "I wonder if we should get some better maps of the upper Kaniapiskau region of Ungava?" Or, it might be, "If that Woolrich jacket wasn't so red I'd take that for my arctic hunting coat. But probably I'll bring my foul-weather duck-hunting jacket so I won't spook the caribou."

It was the real stuff of life.

As the time drew down to only a week from departure, we were ugly and uptight around work, excited, unhappy, moody, ready to quit work early, and unsettled at home. The Ole Man's wife, Herself, summed it up quite well: "If I didn't know better myself, I'd be thinking you were getting ready for the senior prom and a movie queen was coming to take you away. Now, go in the den and get out of my way, the both of you; some of us have to work for a living. I've got things to do!"

I checked my gear about a thousand times, but the night we left I gathered the flight bags, sleeping bags, guns, and everything else in a single heap. The kitchen floor looked small when I was finished. Actually, our kitchen was over-size, but with three weeks of "things" for two men on an arctic caribou hunting trip, all laid out on the floor, it was a major job for anyone to get a glass of milk from the refrigerator—which was about thirty miles from Labrador according to the maps I had spread out on the floor.

There was a single heap I called "camp comforts," things like a pair of well-worn moccasins. I never went anywhere without them. I even thought to bring my best Case knife, one my father had given me about thirty years before. It was useful for cutting an apple into slices or gutting a partridge back home, or cleaning a mess of Dolly Varden trout in Nulato, Alaska. It saw action in a multitude of locations and served many purposes.

After fondly staring at my most prized possessions, I was urged by my wife to get them all out of the way or she was going to move them "somewhere, until the Ole Man comes over and you two boys leave to go play in the mud and snow up north." I agreed, but went over my checklist one more time as I packed everything for the last time.

After a sleepless start on the night we departed, the big jet seemed to make us more comfortable. We both snoozed our way to Montreal where another plane would be taking us to the northern Quebec city of Schefferville, where a bush plane would carry us the third and last leg. Hopefully, our luggage would all be joining us.

We arrived on time in Schefferville on the Quebec-Labrador border. Schefferville's only reason to be is a huge mass of iron mines. The ore is carried south to the St. Lawrence River via a small railway, which will take passengers, but only on a miner's schedule. No ore, no trip.

We went to Schefferville's floatplane base and began our trip to arctic waters. The pilot was all business, but we felt more comfortable around him because he wore jeans, sneakers, and talked guns with us. "What are you guys bringing for guns?" he asked. A good question to bring up. I brought my much-favored 7mm Remington Magnum in the Remington

Model 700, left-handed bolt-action. It had performed well on many hunts before. I was hoping to add a memory.

The Ole Man was kicking high and willing to be as friendly as possible. "I got my deer rifle from Maine, the one I shot a nice buck with at four hundred yards in Jim Braley's big potato field. It was a classic hunting bull's-eye that sooner or later everyone will know about." With that He tapped His case holding a prewar Winchester Model 70 in .30-06 with a lot of love and appreciation.

It was nearly sundown when we glided to a stop on the upper Kaniapiskau River. Ungava Bay of the Arctic Ocean was only thirty more miles north. The treeless barrens were a beautiful, wild, unoccupied, roadless, endless track of the Canadian Arctic. On the way here we had seen several bands of caribou from the air. On the ground the tracks were easy to find, even around the water's edge, where our floats were tied to a tiny dock.

We met Joe, our Indian guide, and bid farewell to the pilot, who said he needed to get home before the arctic night settled in around Schefferville. He would be home in time to watch the late news. We watched him taxi, take off, swing around, and tilt his wings. We now had as much as three weeks in the wild Arctic.

Joe led us to the "outpost" cabin. It was about ten feet square. My wife would have croaked right there. But, to us, it looked good. The guide's faded blue tent was set up about fifty feet away, near a small spring on a little knoll. This was home. Joe said, "We've got the best place to hunt—the best in town."

Our cabin had a stovepipe sticking through the roof and there was smoke coming from a fire inside. The walls were unpeeled spruce logs notched on both ends, probably hauled or flown here strapped to the floatplane's struts. The roof was cedar shakes and the floor was common spruce and pine boards, obviously brought in by air or water.

Inside were bunk beds, cooking stove, woodpile (including kindling), and a small sink. The water was stored in a holding tank outside and pumped from the river by hand, as needed. There was also a tiny counter, shelves above with dishes and a pot or two. There was plenty of wall space taken with canned or boxed foods. The stove held the frying pans, and there were hooks on the wall to hang clothes. A rope was dangling from one wall. The other end when tied to a spike was our clothes-drying rack. There was a roll of toilet paper on a nail by the door. All was in place—the outpost cabin as promised.

Joe made a fresh pot of coffee. The stove was putting out plenty of heat against the settling chill outdoors. We were ready for our first meal. Joe dished up beans, bacon (canned, of course), hot biscuits he made himself, and a can of peaches for dessert. With the meal done, he cleaned up the dishes and said he would see us "early in the morning. Must get early start. Long day." With that he left for his tent.

The night was in the chilly thirties as we stood outside, looking at the stars. Inside we were thrilled. It was soon lights out, but we talked in the dark for a while, into the night. The Ole Man said, "Them stars don't look too different from the ones we see back at Swift Brook, but the view around here in the quiet of the North sure looks peaceful. And, you know, even if we never get a caribou, the whole trip will be worth it. This is a wild, beautiful, new, unspoiled land, something that's getting downright hard to find back home."

We drifted off to sleep in the land of no TVs and no electricity. We slept with the occasional wolf call and the knowledge that caribou were not far away.

We both got bull caribou, and would love to return there again—right after our trip to Colorado for mule deer and elk.

39

The GPS Needs a Regular Compass

THE USE OF GPS HAS ENSURED an explosive growth industry. In 1973 the US Department of Defense acknowledged in an announcement the outline of the "US military development of a global positioning system for precise knowledge of the relationship of where military targets and personnel were placed on the globe, and thus giving our military tremendous assistance in deploying our forces."

The Ole Man's response was quickly offered: "Anyone not yet asleep could be forgiven for dozing off. I thought some fishermen who were egghead militaries last summer told us this junk would *revolutionize* fishing. I think they were dead wrong, and here I believed they were smart folks. Guess not."

By the late 1990s even the Ole Man perked up with new GPS thoughts and actions, although He thought the use of downriggers was "nearly immoral," and the rapid growth of electronic fish finders was "something a decent soul would never touch. Every last one of those electronic gadgets needs to be outlawed—just like dynamite can't be used to

stun the entire trout population in a small pond!" He was
red-faced, filled with venom. His thinking applied to fish
finders and their often coupled use with downriggers, but
did not now apply to all GPS applications.

The success of Jake Goodwin last summer at Whitney
Cove on West Grand Lake was "not acceptable—not at all.
If a blasted fool like him can return every time to the *exact
spot* where he had success before, then decent fishermen like
me and you have to have the same tools, electrical or not."

What Jake did was pull up beside the Ole Man and me
trolling near the Whitney bedrock ridges and holler out, "I
painted a big X on the side of my boat to mark the exact
spot where I've been catching the trophy togue. When I get
there we just have to keep circling and the fish jump in the
boat without a struggle." Jake kept gesturing as though he
was hauling in a real monster fish and then pointing to the
X on the boat. His companion today was Pete Qualey, who
added in a spirited but softer tone, "He's got a new GPS
tracker that stores places you want to remember, and then
when you come back out, the screen shows you exactly
where you found success the last time. Perfectly legal and
very, very, very accurate. You ought to get one and become
a champion fisherman like Jake!"

They spun around without waiting for our response and
roared wide-open to a spot about a mile away, where the
bottom was littered with big boulders, making it extremely
difficult to successfully troll through without getting hung
up on bottom. Murray Spoons get caught in the rocky
structure about every hundred yards, or so it seems. Losing

a spoon, several swivels, a rudder, and your pride is expensive. But there is pride in not getting caught on bottom. The loss of $20 for the six-inch silver spoon fades when compared to the hoots, jokes, and name-calling that would result daily when you got back in town, most especially at work. Getting hung up on bottom was an amateur's signature move. Experienced trollers who knew the bottom of the big lakes avoided rocky, boulder-strewn bottoms at all cost. But now, with far more advanced electronic fish finders and the GPS spot-marking option saving the information, it made the old way obsolete for all but the diehards.

I knew the Ole Man would find a justification for his own electronic purchases. Right now His mood was black, deeply filled with great anger. Getting beat once was hard to accept, but the prospect of getting outdone *every* time out was not acceptable—now, or ever. A mood-changing strike hit on the Ole Man's pole. It was the big *thump-de-thump-thump* of a bragging fish. There was a grin and a coming grimace as the fish was on and then shook the live bait hook loose.

Slack lines should mean a return to grumbles and doomsday thoughts. I was surprised when the Ole Man developed the demeanor of a man having inspirational thoughts. He simply said, "I'm going to buy one of those tools, and it's going to be soon." We never even finished fishing.

A few hours later we had the boat loaded on the trailer, appearing to be bound for home. We passed the home turn-offs and wound up in a large parking lot not too far from Dakin's Sporting Goods. The Ole Man had a mission. He was not to be denied. Fish finders were still "the work of the

Devil," and downriggers were for "the terminally lazy," but suddenly, GPS electronics were now called "fishing tools— like using an electric drill or a circular saw . . . electrical tools that help you mark a spot on the map, not at all like fish finders, taking pictures of the fish so you can hit them with dynamite or shamefully use downriggers to sneak up beside them. There's no sport in that. Clearly they need to be illegal. GPS simply acts like a tool—a map. It doesn't take photographs of fish; just acts like a road map when you take it out of the glove compartment of your Jeep."

I sort of agreed, and we entered Dakin's on a buying spree.

The Ole Man bought two GPS devices. "I've been study- ing this for years, these advanced electrical tools to improve the sports of fishin' and huntin'. I want to practice at Matagamon or maybe Shin Pond before I challenge Good- win at a really big Maine lake, but I've been readin', and I've got some DVD stuff about using them most effectively—as a fishing tool, of course. I ain't about to go whole hog in any annual competition until I'm all-fired sure to win. It wouldn't be fair."

So, throughout the summer He used the GPS to return time after time to exact locations; however, we found there was more to successfully concluding such trial runs. The fish were not all stupid. They lived hour by hour in a vary- ing environment that required they move with the smelts and minnows. Schools of both did not stay in any one watery environment too long. If a new hatch of insects or other feed came to be, then the big fish moved there for the

next meal. You can GPS it just so much. It *is* a tool; it is *not* the ultimate answer to all fishing success.

We spent the summer being given lessons in GPS-ology. We found that there are places where ground structure of the lake bottom means a place for small critters to hide consistently, and therefore a place where we should fish— just not all the time, or we would quickly disturb the dynamics of that location. We had to be wise.

Once Jake found out the Ole Man was fishing with GPS as a location and directional marker, he had no new challenges to brag about on the big waters. They both had good days with success and days of angling winds sagging to an immediate state of the becalmed. A salty fisherman would refer to it as the Equatorial Doldrums. Not much moving.

Toward the end of the season we kept almost no fish to eat; everything was photographed, digital postal scales used, and we kept electronic records, with the fish returned to the waters.

There was a hoop-dee-doo about Labor Day weekend. It started as a classic test of who was the best fisherman. After camping and fishing on Saturday and Sunday, it looked interesting. On Saturday the Ole Man had a nice, sassy, seven-pound lake trout. I had a twenty-inch, probably two-pound, brook trout. Jake, fishing alone, couldn't beat that, but on Sunday he got a nine-pound lake trout that we agreed from his digital photos was bigger than anything we had taken. Over the Sunday-night campfire they both told jokes and tales, mixed with an Old Stump Blower drink or two. They both made a promise to catch the "biggest and best" on the holiday Monday.

Labor Day Monday dawned blustery and dark, not terrific fishing for trollers. Nobody caught a decent fish—we thought—until we got back to the boat ramp and found George McManus and his wife Lolly. They had been staying at Mic Murphy's Fire Cove camp. On Saturday and Sunday our tallies were similar, but on the holiday-ending Monday, Lolly had landed a whopper salmon so big that *she* wanted it mounted for the den. A Man Cave with a female "best of" trophy on the wall? George was okay with it.

He said, "This landlocked salmon weighs an unbelievable eight pounds and eleven ounces." With obvious pride he added, "And listen to this, boys: Lolly caught it on a Gray Ghost. No live shiner. Nothing fancy, just a regular old worn Ghost. I'll tell you, guys, I was sweating getting it in the net, but she held the rod tip high, played out the backing line just like a pro. She kept the pressure on when he flopped around. It took a good twenty minutes to a half-hour, and then the old monster just let me scoop him up in the extended telescopic landing net. Wow! What a fish."

We opened the cooler to look. It was a huge freshwater trophy salmon. Lolly accepted our congratulations, and with a smile finalized it by adding, "I offered hubby George some fishing lessons this winter. That was a Gray Ghost I tied myself last winter!" And turning directly to Jake Goodwin and the Ole Man, she said, "I've even got time to teach you ole fuddy-duddies a thing or two. Maybe we could get together a special class for some older beginners. What do you think, boys?"

It was a great sight to behold. The speechlessness was obvious. A fitting close to the summer fishing season, a Labor Day tale still told annually over a wide part of northern Maine.

As time slipped by more toward the fall hunting, I began to wonder what use the Ole Man would make of the pocket-size GPS he'd bought for hunting. I did watch two videos with Him that provided some basic things to do and other things to surely avoid. I was surprised to see that the Maine Department of Inland Fisheries and Wildlife had officially made a recommendation that all GPS hunters *carry a good magnetic compass* with them at all times. They added, "The new technology can be confusing and sometimes *just plain wrong.* The backup compass is something you want to always carry on deep-woods hunting trips, and even on ventures closer to home. Be careful out there."

The Ole Man said, "Ain't that a hoot—a real hooty-hoot-hoot. The great wardens will be coming out to check on us with great new technology, and, in case it's a total flop, they want us to carry the old-fashioned, tried-and-true, absolutely perfect pocket compass to find out where 'North' really is. What a world we live in. It's absolutely crazy. First, a woman catches the biggest landlocked salmon caught around here in years, and then the Maine Warden Service tells us not to rely on the high-tech GPS. Boy, if that ain't a hoot."

The number of women who hunt, fish, and trap in Maine has risen every year for a couple of decades. The percentages may not rival that of men, but the rate of increase is eye-opening. There are more girls who want to be wardens, too. Some of the pioneer Maine wardens who were females are now retiring.

The Ole Man was surprisingly impressed with a female warden the first time we were checked in on the Allagash while fishing Chamberlain Lake. Only when she skillfully drew her boat up close and asked for licenses did we know it was a female warden.

She said, "How you doing, boys? I see you have your life vests, but, for safety's sake, we recommend actually wearing them at all times while you're in the boat. You don't legally have to do anything but use them as bow stuffers, but I need to advise you to wear them. The choice is yours." She checked our coolers and, satisfied that everything was legal, she drifted away to travel up the lake.

I was expecting a holy terror of a fit from the Ole Man. Instead, He said, "I surely never thought I'd ever live long enough to see that, but, I mean, holy cow, she wasn't a damned bit different than a man warden. Although I would say she smelled better." He smiled from ear to ear, knowing that wasn't at all what I'd expected.

I wasn't sure myself, at the very beginning, that a woman, even an armed woman, could handle confrontational situations all alone a hundred miles back in the North Maine Woods, where there's more than four million acres of commercial timberland filled with loggers and sportsmen, both widely scattered. The women of the Maine Warden Service perform perfectly. Now, if you get checked by a warden, you get checked by a warden. No one even mentions the sex of the warden, and that's the way it ought to be.

I was just surprised that the Ole Man felt that way until Herself one day afterwards casually said, "I have a distant niece who just joined the Maine Warden Service way down by Bethel, on the New Hampshire border. She has wanted to do that since junior high. She went in the army, finished an associate's degree in law enforcement, and got into a warden class last fall. She finished third in her class."

Later when He and I were in the den alone, the Ole Man said, "I told you the world's changin'. I don't know whether it's good or bad. I guess I'm just about equal either way you want to think about it." He had that far-off look in his eyes and a wrinkled brow to boot. I was just about to speak when he chimed in with this connection: "When the GPS needs a regular compass and women wardens check your fishing license and a lady angler gets the biggest real trophy fish of the year, I guess we have to say welcome aboard. The world changes a little every time the sun comes up; otherwise, Mount Katahdin might still be covered with two miles of solid glacier ice, and we'd have nowhere to go hunting or fishing. That'd be a real disaster, yes, it would. This other stuff is pretty small potatoes, I think."

40

Not Enough Tackle

THE PILOT AGREED TO TAKE US IN TO LONG POND. It was
fabulous brook-trout water where the spring-run fish often
weighed in at three pounds, and sometimes more. A real
bonanza. The pond received little notice from the angling
herd because it was too remote and extremely hard to reach.

Floatplane pilots didn't much like it, either, because there
was a high ridge on one accessible side, a shallow water
depth on the other, and the pond was right at the minimum
for safe landings and takeoffs. In hot summer weather the
"lift"—the air flowing over the wings—was not good, and
some days, no veteran pilot would land there because the
takeoff was impossible. Wind was also a factor because
downsloping from the mountains and ridges pushed planes
down, unless it was an early-morning thermal.

Ground access was barred by two unbridged rivers, a
swamp, a game preserve without roads, and a non-friendly
large landowner who gated roads coming anywhere near
Long Pond.

So, the sporting community largely fished elsewhere,
even though some state fisheries reports called it one of the

best coldwater brook-trout fisheries in the state. I think the mystery of it added an aura we found so compelling it was in a must-do category all its own.

Our pilot agreed to take us there in his Piper Super Cub. One trip in for each of us. The Ole Man's a white-knuckle flyer, but He said, "Getting in is easy. If we crash coming out, at least we'll have caught some great brook trout. If the lift isn't good on our scheduled day to come out, then we'll have to fish some more. All in all, a pretty good deal."

The Super Cub was especially equipped with light floats, a special high-performance carburetor for max horse-power—a nice STOL (short takeoff and landing) airplane. With the big engine, stubby wings, and solid design, it was up for the job.

Most pilots will say the Super Cub is a great bush plane as long as it isn't overloaded and the pilot is quick at the controls. No novices in close quarters. If the pond had been normal in length and level of difficulty, we could have taken the pilot, the Ole Man, and me with the canoe strapped to the struts. This Long Pond flight meant splitting the load. We didn't need an overloaded, unstable floatplane. I don't want to visit the spruce forest from a faulty flight. Not even for three-pound brook trout.

Since we were going for a full week, we took dehydrated foods, split the load for each flight, and went easy on heavy gear. I took my Primus single-burner stove instead of the big two-burner Coleman. We cut our camping comforts and shortened our list of fishing gear. I even left home my tripod and one of two cameras. I cut the list of lenses from seven to two: normal and moderate telephoto. No wide-angle or portrait lenses. Keeping the weight down. I did take an extra tip for my Orvis Battenkill and extra flies, both dry and wet.

As I looked at the puny pile of fishing gear laid out on the dock before we took off, I felt sure it represented more gear than you needed for a day's outing, but certainly nowhere near enough stuff for camping, eating, and fishing for an entire week. Even the Ole Man checked His stuff to be sure everything was there.

My favorite flashlight is a big, square rig lacking in beauty, but world-class in reliability and candlepower. As I write this now, there are three of them, all in perfect working order, set out on my desk. They use a very large six-volt battery and while heavy, they get the job done. The batteries last a long time, can be recharged, and give steady light. No LEDs or other newfangled blue lights here.

On this flight, to save weight, I took only a small light that I stored in my shirt pocket. Not quite a penlight, but not my favored square lantern, either. Not exactly what I wanted, but the pilot had cautioned us to "save all the weight you can. Landing at Long Pond is not hard. Getting out of there is a scheme based on minimum weight." He jokingly added, "On the day we get you out of there, be sure to drink no more than two cups of coffee." I think it was a joke.

The name Long Pond is a joke, too, I would guess. It is oblong in shape, but "long"? Not long enough, and yet this lone lack of access was the thing keeping the pond practically unfished.

Pilots have a term for floatplane flying called "getting up on the step," where the floats sit on top of the water, not settled down into the water. To achieve this is similar to an outboard motor getting a boat up on the surface and not just sitting deadweight in the water. A heavily loaded floatplane squats in the water until the pilot calls for full power, to first drag the plane forward and then begin the lift as the float "sits up on the step." That's one step from flight. The plane is actually ready to leave the water's surface at the proper air speed.

Our man was a long time getting our load to "full step." The Ole Man stayed at the dock. I was on the first flight with the canoe; He would come next with the camping gear. The floatplane base is located on a large body of water. There is plenty of room to taxi, to take off, to land, and yet we were using a lot of water to get airborne. Long Pond, on the other hand, was named by someone who had already walked twenty miles on the day he'd chosen that name, and He didn't want to walk around another piece of submerged real estate on that day. Maybe it was named after John J. Long . . . In any case, no one alive today knows why it holds such a relatively inaccurate name.

Once we lumbered into the air I forgot my reservations because I was too busy gawking out the window at some of the lands and waters where we hunt and fish. As we passed over Swift Brook, I couldn't help but remind myself there were brook trout in this brook that probably rivaled anything at Long Pond. But, it's the grass-is-greener thing. There is the traveler's mentality that says "Maybe I should have taken the less-risky route," but this, too, passes as the plane flies on toward the destination.

For the most part, the two-hour flight was uneventfully smooth. We did get some rough air over the Penobscot River watershed, but it quickly passed. The sky was clear, the engine droned on. When we circled Long Pond for the actual final approach for a landing, I saw how small Long Pond really is out my passenger window.

Once we'd landed safely, the pilot wished me well and went to get the Ole Man and the camping gear. I got the canoe out, paddled around, set up a campfire ring, hauled and cut firewood, and found a really nice spring. Someone had enhanced it by rocking it up, to keep debris from falling in when you filled a container of water. The water was sparkling-clear and tasted excellent.

I was just beginning to wonder where they were when I heard the Super Cub coming and saw it circle for a landing. The pilot said, "See you in seven days. I hope we have good weather." Empty, both times leaving Long Pond, the plane zipped along, up on the step, flew nearly at a 45-degree angle, or so it looked, clearing the trees easily. Would it be that way with us aboard on the flight out? I wondered.

As soon as the plane was gone the Ole Man said, "We didn't seem to get airborne very quickly back at the base, did we?" I guess He was wondering about the return trip, too.

I knew during the next week that this thought would be framed again and again in my mind, whether I acknowledged it or not. With the junk we carried—the camping gear, the canoe, the two men—there was quite a load. I hoped for great lift conditions on the day we left. We both knew the pilot knew his business. He'd flown in the military, and as a civilian he had been flying for thirty years. Surely he knew whether Long Pond takeoffs were safe or not. Ya gotta believe.

Still, we remembered how hesitant he was when we'd first discussed taking us here. "Can't say that I want to. If there's a cross wind, you'll have to wait an extra day or two.

I need a day of maximum lift, and Long Pond can be tricky. I won't fly unless the margin of error is in my favor. Too many guys, guys I knew well, have bought the farm by being careless. I *won't* come to get you until the weather is right." We said we understood.

The only thing we heard was that he would take us to Long Pond. We ignored the warnings and cautions. Now, as we set up the tent and got camp fully operational, we thought about little else except the flight one week hence. When we went out to go fishing it was even more obvious. The Ole Man got a solid strike from a fat, native brook trout. When He edged it over the side for a quick picture before releasing it, He said, "Suppose anyone will ever get to see that picture you're takin'?"

A shiver went up my spine. Never in all the years I knew Him was there ever such an inference. Life was precious. There was a cloud hovering over us, implying we might have forced the pilot's ego to get us here, "where no man ever goes." If we didn't do something quickly, the whole trip would be scuttled while we solemnly waited for the returning plane in seven days, in the same frame of mind as the condemned prisoner awaits his date with the executioner.

My mind filled with images of an aborted takeoff and a sudden crash into the heavy evergreen trees surrounding the pond. Perhaps a big hemlock would do me in. A shiver went up my spine. I even remembered seeing some big rock maples sticking into the sky near the liftoff point. Maybe they would be my fate.

It was a quiet lunch. Neither of us commented on the lovely weather, the wild, enchanting setting, the fabulous fishing; it was all background. Something needed to change our doomsday thoughts. Maybe we just possessed overactive imaginations. When we'd asked other pilots, they'd all said to contact the one we engaged. They all said he was the best, and occasionally flew someone into Long Pond, and while the Super Cub could have taken the Ole Man, myself, the canoe, and the gear in one flight, our cautious pilot would stay conservative and insist on two flights each way. It cost us more, but those were his rules, and we abided by them.

As the day progressed we decided to make our best effort to enjoy the week. By the next morning we were genuinely having fun. The fishing was as good as it gets. The brook trout were cooperative, the weather was sunny, breezy, mild, and the camping vista was just unbeatable. By the end of the week it was hard to imagine we were ever troubled by any thoughts of impending doom. We were solidly upbeat, even talking about making this trip an annual event.

When we heard the drone of the floatplane on our appointed departure day, it was different. Soon, we could see why. There were two Super Cubs. We would be returning to the base without a long wait. Once they pulled up beside us the pilot we hired said, "The weather is perfect for a good lift, and Jimmy here, a man with more experience than I have, offered to bring his plane along for a look at the scenery. You all ready?" We were.

In a matter of minutes we were all airborne. There was clearance to spare on takeoff, and now we drifted home in dual STOL craft. The moral of all of this? We've now been going to Long Pond annually for the past ten years, and we've thoroughly enjoyed each and every trip. Twice we have added a day or so to the trip because the pilot said the conditions were not good. We gladly stayed put for another day of fishing. The fishing gear we brought on the first trip proved minimal, but adequate, and we have taken the same spare tackle every year since.

We know fishing. The pilot knows flying. We let him do his job, and we always do ours. He flies. We fish. Never once has he accused us of having too little tackle.

41

Lessons for a Shiverer

HOME BASE IS A WELCOMING SIGHT after a week of being confined to factory work or office work, or work anywhere the ducks don't fly. I cannot really explain the thrill I get from watching a lone black duck go about his routine business. Magic is watching these ducks take off from a wilderness bay, a marshy saltwater flat, a pothole, a beaver dam, or just right here at home at Black Hole.

It's as simple and as complicated as that. It exists every year, every day of open water, and yet the whole mixture of environmental and human factors blended together is difficult to explain. The urge to get out the shotgun soars through your body. The small limits, the cold air, the combination of sleet, snow, and rain—something the Ole Man calls *slain*—all are parts of this mystery of life.

If your best friend came over at four a.m. and asked you to go to work early, at double pay, you would groan, moan, and tell him to go to hell. The whole idea of going to work at that early hour is just not for you. But, with a day of duck hunting ahead, the alarm rings at four a.m. and you jump out of bed. It's as though someone was going to make you a millionaire.

That happens especially on a November morning when the slain comes driving down, the winds are up, and you're at Home Base, expecting a day of waterfowling. Morning moans at you, the white pine by the bedroom window creaks and groans from wind and sleet-filled air. The outhouse door flaps in the wind, and you still feel inspired to enjoy the day. All around there are sounds to awaken everyone and everything that isn't dead.

The ducks will surely be flying. You know a full thermos of hot java will slide down by eight, or a break in the action about then. And, you know once the coffee is gone, there won't be much warmth until the day is done and you have returned to the comforts of Home Base. Or, maybe it will be an early run because you have limited out on the legal amount of ducks you can take in one day. Nonhunters might read that to say all hunters are desperately waiting for the end of the day. They would be wrong. A basketball player knows when the game will be over, too, but that doesn't mean he doesn't enjoy playing the game, even when the going gets tough.

Back in the camp, still under the spell of anticipation, the duck hunter has other sounds to keep him company. The coffee has aroma and bubbles in the background as it comes to a boil, even as the rainy mix slashes away at the cedar shakes on the roof above. The bacon sizzles in the frying pan and smells as breakfast only can when it's prepared in a backwoods sporting camp. The Ole Man shuffles around camp and gets out his special duck-hunting gear.

He will wear His waders today, all day. The rain poncho covers the top part and the waders cover the rest. On top He has a roll-up type of felt hat that has been made more or less waterproof. It's a faded forest green. Under this will be layers of wool and cotton, what the skiers and snowshoers or mountain climbers all call "layering." The air spaces between layers keep the body breathing, but warm. A happy duck hunter when facing a miserably cold November dawn of slain.

At least one or two layers are wind-resistant and water-shielding, at least in theory. I still shiver. My teeth chatter and my lower back gets cramped. It isn't as though I came unprepared, yet sometimes, the Ole Man will whisper, "Will you stay still and keep those teeth silent? You'll scare the ducks." So, I try to shiver quietly.

Slain was beating down hard on one such day I have in mind. All night the wind howled over Home Base. It was so noisy I tossed and turned. Open season was two weeks ago, and there were still plenty of hunting days ahead. I must admit, there was a bit of hesitation when I left the warm bed that morning and my feet made contact with the camp's wooden floor. *Brrr!*

After all, this was a vacation, and we should be taking it easy. Instead, we were "working" from dawn to dusk. On the days when we limited out early on ducks, we spent the rest of the day beating the bush for woodcock and partridge until sunset. If the duck hunting was slow, we hung

with it until dark, or until the legal closing time, often getting back to camp a half-hour after full blackness. We both cleaned the game birds. It was always the number-one item on the evening's agenda. The Ole Man started the portable gas generator and made sure the freezer was getting ready for some new entries. I checked for coals in the fireplace or stove, or both. I added the wood.

Now, we got to cleaning the birds, packaging, labeling, and gabbing about the day's hunt. My next job was to check the stove and fireplace and make any necessary adjustments. I also made the coffee. The Ole Man liked to do the cooking. He was a fine cook, taking it as seriously as He did hunting or fishing.

I thought of all these steps on the big slain day. It was going to be a long, long day. The Ole Man got out His

Norwegian socks and a well-worn, heavy, green plaid wool shirt. No one said anything; although we weren't too happy to think about the slain beating us in the face every time we looked at the beaver house at Black Hole, or the other cold-weather factors, mostly we thought about the good fortune of excellent duck hunting in the day ahead. The wind would drive the sleet right into the cracks between our teeth, or at least it would seem that way. Yet, we both anticipated the gunning action.

After breakfast we took the day pack, the guns, shells, and the other gear to the waiting boat. The decoys were already kept loaded. A flick of the wrist would start the prop and whisk us out around the point into the full fury of the storm. From there it would be some long minutes just holding on, hoping for smaller waves, watching for duck activity in the increasingly lightening sky. On arrival at Black Hole we needed to get the tollers set out. We were practiced. It didn't take long.

On a day like today we liked to set the decoys a bit closer to shore to simulate the real ducks sitting just a few feet closer to the safety of the feed beds. We have observed this behavior time and time again. At least it holds true for puddle ducks. Sea ducks like the wily eider are more likely to raft up in stormy weather and stay farther out, away from the ledges we hunt.

With all the tollers out, dawn arrived, and a small flock of teal nearly took our hats off. We never got a shot off as they wheeled as a wedge and struck for the far side of the marsh. Our next customers were three barreling black ducks who were not that lucky. They set their wings for our decoys just as we stood up together and got two of them.

In ten minutes a flock of Canadian geese warmed our toes, but kept on course with the lonesome talk they do so well. It sounds like a death in the family, and the family stays high and moves, as one unit, on and on. They have a north wind at their tail. Time to make the miles.

The lone male woodie became our visual thrill for the day. He folded his wings on a pretty crossing shot from left to right. I was just about to tell the Ole Man He'd missed the bird when the second shot rang out and the bird fell to the water in the midst of our decoys.

"Just gettin' the range on the first shot," the Ole Man said, adding, "Those feathers will sure make some nice trout flies."

The male wood duck has to be one of nature's most beautifully colored creatures. This specimen was no exception. The bright purples and tans, the mix of various shades of white—all were exquisite. All the colors of the rainbow are sandwiched on a medium-size bird, painted like a Rembrandt, only better. We always savor the meat, collect the feathers, take pictures of the feather coloration, and admire the bird's savvy. When we have a photo show, we always include the male wood duck with shots of the autumn colors, to provide a background for our photo presentations. It warms a February night.

After our wood duck the flights slowed down for us. Then, it reached a standstill. Only then did I notice the biting wind. It was fierce. Funny how the action of anticipation allows discomfort to pass with barely a notice. I'd forgotten my mittens; my fingers were white. I suddenly was shivering from a wave dumping a half-ton of November water over the bow and down my rain slicker, both inside and out. This actually happened on the way to Black Hole. I never noticed in the flash of the moment.

I have been told this not noticing is similar to firing an African big-game caliber in a gravel pit back home or on safari. You notice in practice, not in action. In the gravel pit you notice heavy recoil. With a live water buffalo in Namibia, you never even feel it. Same goes for duck hunting.

My teeth started chattering by nine. By noon my grasp on reality was slipping. My wife's comment that I "didn't know enough to get out of the rain" was coming to mind. Somewhere around two, the ducks started to return, and I got a nice drake pintail. Suddenly, the chill was gone, my sore muscles didn't ache, and my teeth were not playing beaver. The cold hours in between were forgotten, along with the other fleeting seconds I wished to sweep away. The ducks were there. The return was on time for the evening flights.

We didn't quite limit out on that day, but around the fireplace that night, we shot more ducks than ever lived on the Atlantic flyway since Eric the Red was a teenager. And we talked incessantly about having some luck tomorrow.

The Ole Man summed things up: "I'll bet you forget your mittens and hope for slain in your dreams tonight. Ducks in the chill of November—I wonder what the poor folks are doin' today."

42

When Hell Freezes Over

DEER SEASON WAS NEARLY THREE WEEKS OLD. There would be just one more week. Neither the Ole Man nor I had shot a deer. I missed an easy shot at a nice buck lying down on a squally, snow-covered morning. My excuse was inattention, surprise (the deer was looking away from me), poor shooting, a hurried shot, a human comedy of errors. Maybe it was my gray hair.

The Ole Man was just not right this year. No luck. A slight cold started about opening day and was still hanging on, dragging Him down, even if He wouldn't admit it. The Alton Bog had been His favorite hunting place for decades. The vast sweep of the cedars, a few birches, some marshy peat stretches where your boots can get sucked off if you're not careful. In the years before 1900, this bog was the last stand of the eastern caribou. It still has the arctic caribou country look (with those dwarfed trees), but it's now favored by massive deer herds. Moose hold sway there, too.

The only trouble with hunting The Bog was access. It took hard work to get there. Casual hunters need not apply. And a hefty bagged buck was a hell of a drag out of the

340

quagmire. Some seasons you needed tall, waterproof foot-wear to wade through several overflows where the water was knee-deep. The glory of hunting The Bog was twofold: Many, many deer, and *no other hunters*. Because the hunting access was hard, we just never saw competition.

These trials and tribulations have never bothered us before. On this Sunday before the last week of the season, I was determined to hunt The Bog most, if not all, of the last week of open gunning. There was a lot of walking venison there. With this in mind I went to face the Ole Man. I wanted to hunt The Bog; we each had a single week of vacation left; it was the best place to be the last week. I was determined. The deer would have seen almost no pressure. They were prime pickings. The gang of road hunters would have driven the deer into the depths of our beloved, swampy bog.

My previous success in confrontations with the Ole Man was limited. He was stubborn, ornery, opinionated, verbal, convincing, willing to go the distance. Yet, this time I was ready for battle. All season the Ole Man had avoided The Bog. No explanation of why He wouldn't hunt there. He just said, "I got better ideas, better places." He knew that wasn't true.

I think He recognized my feelings when I knocked on the door. It had been years since I had done that. I never knocked. This was formal. I usually just barged in unan-nounced and headed for the den. When Herself answered the knock she was quite surprised. "Oh, it's you," she said. "I didn't know the door was locked."

I never let on that the door was undoubtedly not locked, and that the reason for knocking was because I wanted to make a formal entrance, to appear to have the upper hand.

He was looking over some maps when I walked into the den. They were quadrangles of a backcountry section of the upper reaches of Swift Brook. It was an ominous opening to the evening.

I didn't help things any when I asked how His head cold was now.

"Why, balls of fire, you'd think I was an old goat in a nursing home the way everyone carries on. I'm feelin' fine. Now, let's get on with the huntin' plans—or did you come here to discuss your great knowledge of medicine?"

I knew of no retreat. After asking for a run of Old Stump Blower, I settled into the black recliner by the roaring fire in the fireplace and asked, "Where do you think we ought to go huntin' this week?" I was hoping He would say the Alton Bog, or at least be noncommittal. I wasn't going to be lucky.

"Well, the way I see it, there is only one place where I think we can see some deer that haven't been spooked by an overload of hunters. The outback on the upper Swift Brook." He expected me to say okay, but I felt it was now or never.

"What's wrong with The Bog? We haven't even been there once all season. I'm sure the deer will not be spooked there."

He feigned adjusting the logs in the fire, shuffled across to His chair, and finally answered, "Swift Brook is better. The Bog has seen better days as a great deer cover. Swift Brook is getting better all the time. In The Bog the covers we used to tramp through are all grown up and the deer have left the area. We have many other choices, places where it's prime time."

I knew this was all hogwash. The Bog was as good a deer cover as anywhere in the woods of New England. Water, resting choices of dense cover, small hardwood saplings, raspberry bushes, cedar stands long gone uncut to keep out the heavy winds of winter, fringe feed along the alders, little hills to sleep away the day, trails to the various other cover options. It is ideal. *The deer were there.*

I said as much. "The Bog is *the* place to go this week, and you know it, Ole Man. Why are you fighting it? What the hell gives?"

When He didn't answer immediately I felt uneasy with the silence, and went on. "You have hunted The Bog for forty-five years. Every year if you really need a deer, you return there—always—and you always get your buck. Why is this year different? Now you're telling me somewhere else is suddenly better. I've got to be honest with you: I want to hunt The Bog this week. I've got confidence there. I've had many successes there. I know the country." With my pitch complete, I refilled my glass.

"Okay, okay! It's The Bog. If you wanted to hunt there why didn't you just say so, without all the shenanigans? It's all right with me. Just don't complain none about the cold water in your boots. Or, about the work it takes to get a deer out of there. And, by the way, it's forty-six years I have hunted The Bog."

After that the conversation was none too friendly. I got the feeling I was getting the bum's rush and quickly made an excuse to leave. I felt somewhat good; at least I'd stood my ground and won, even if the win was a mite hollow. I won. With a slight jounce to my step I made my way home to get things ready for the morning's hunt at The Bog. It was comforting.

344

At four the next morning I was ready to go. The Ole Man was ten minutes late. He said it was a cold morning, which it was. With the temperature hovering at 20 degrees, the old Jeep protested by almost not starting. That was unusual. The Jeep never failed. Finally, it came to life. I was as ready as a young pointer on his first real hunt. We were going to The Bog. Deer were there. We needed two.

The morning was frosty. There was actually ice along the trail. Mornings for a week and more were hanging in the teens and twenties. It would be noisy around water-filled bog springs today.

We parked the vehicle on an old logging road, the same place the Ole Man's father used to tie off his horses to go deer hunting more than seventy years ago. The logging road had been used commercially several times since the era of the Ole Man's father, but it was now in a state of growing back to wildness yet again. The logging road was now more of a trail the trusty Jeep could follow. It made a perpendicular intersect with the paved road. The loggers had pointed it directly at the heart of The Bog, but had stopped far short of actually going there.

I grabbed my gun and my day pack, dug out a flashlight. Dawn was still some time in the future. We needed flashlights to traipse through the water, the alders, and the cedars until getting out to where the deer would be. By then it would be dawn. Trudging through the alders and water overflows was trouble enough. We carried only what we planned to use for the day, nothing extra.

The first twenty minutes went rather well. We crossed the first two water holes and still each had one dry foot. Sometimes we both get our feet wet and need to stop to wring out our cotton and wool socks before the day's hunt. Some other times we bring waders and leave them on the other side where we put on our hunting boots. Today, the water was just a bit higher than we thought it would be. Thus, slightly wet feet. The ground was hard in some places. The ice was coming for the winter.

We always stop after the water holes for a "catch-your-breath-one-minute" break. Today, it stretched to fifteen minutes as the Ole Man outlined a change in plans. He wanted to hunt a fringe area of The Bog on our way in. He told me to go ahead and He would hunt slowly as soon as it got light. I was to meet Him at The Swamp for lunch.

I thought it was a little peculiar, but I took off, trying to plan my hunt once it got to be legal shooting time. Because The Swamp was the Ole Man's favorite hunting area, I decided to go there straightaway. I always liked hunting there, too. The last few years the Ole Man's "favorite spots" seemed to be moving around. I just accepted it.

With ten minutes to go for legal shooting time, I was seated exactly in the middle of a narrow neck of cedars between two islands of sapling hardwoods. Both islands were fringed with raspberry bushes and thorn plum trees. The deer often feed there, sleep there, and often walk through from one island to the other. It's been a habit for generations of deer who have lived here.

I considered it a prime location to just sit and see what the deer might be doing here this year, this day, this hour. The deer could cross the area by walking in the boggy swamp, but it wasn't likely. For man or beast, it takes a lot of wet-foot work to get there and back. It's easier to just use the higher solid ground.

At dawn I was able to see fresh deer tracks all around me. I was right! This was *the* place to be. There were so many tracks, it looked as though a deer convention was held right in the few feet I could see from my perch. My excitement and anticipation was high, even if it was only "track soup." There was bound to be a good buck in with this many deer, and there were several very large tracks. "Antler soup," too.

The first deer after dawn to pass by was a lone spike-horn. He walked within fifty feet of me and disappeared toward the other wooded island. My seat at the nosepiece of land was looking even better. The deer avoided the swamp to keep dry feet on the higher ground. It not only made sense in theory, it was a demonstrated fact. I was sorely tempted to blast the lone spike-horn because of the dearth of deer I had sighted all season. After all, this was the last week. But, in the end, I let him walk away unscathed. I still had five more days to hunt The Bog, if necessary.

It was just about seven a.m. when *the* buck came into view. I'd heard him twice before, but had been unable to see him. Now he was rubbing his antlers on a small hardwood about two hundred yards away. He was not very quiet or careful about it. After what seemed like an eternity of silence, he was finally here.

Through my scope I could see his fine rack and graceful but heavy body, through the trees out front as he made his approach. He was about fifty yards from me when he stopped and raised his head. The 7mm Remington Magnum in the left-handed Model 700 sent the 150-grain bullet zinging through the air. Before the echo of the bellowing shot, the deer's eyes were glazing over. He fell without ever knowing danger was near.

He was a huge deer. The full twelve points in a near-perfect rack and a body to match. He was the trophy I had hunted a lifetime to get. By far, the biggest, nicest rack of antlers, and by far the heaviest weight. I guessed he would dress out at 250 pounds. When we later weighed him he went 234 pounds on state-certified scales. A big deer.

To say I was pleased was a total understatement.

While I was dressing out the deer, I kept hoping the Ole Man would show up. He must have heard the shot. It was a quiet morning. I knew the drag back to the Jeep—three miles away—was going to be torture. The deer was big, the drag was tough, and there was an underlayment of shell ice forming wherever there was water. I knew I could use some help.

My dream was answered. The Ole Man came shuffling up the trail, just as I was finishing field-dressing the whitetail.

"Damned nice deer! Real, real nice deer! Now, that's what I'd call a trophy buck. Congratulations!" His praise shocked me. He never, never made remarks like that.

I wiped my hands in the grass and sat down for a minute's rest. He was obviously thinking, and said, "You know, I've never told you this before, but there's an easier way to get a

348

deer outta here. When the ground starts to freeze a little, as it's been doing on these real frosty nights, there's a deer trail out across the old heath that will shorten the drag by half, maybe two-thirds. I think with this deer here we ought to try it out today. I've only seen it used one time before, a long, long time ago. Once you get away from those organic springs where the decaying vegetation adds heat, the going gets better. I think we should try it." He was sure.

The Ole Man was giving up His hunt for the day. I would have done the same thing, of course, if He had shot a buck. This was a two-man chore, and a rough one for two to drag this creature from the woods of the Alton Bog. I needed the help. The Ole Man would still have five days to hunt after today. If He got a deer, I would certainly help Him get it out of the woods.

We were ready to start the drag. Right from the start the work was even harder than I'd anticipated. It seemed about the best we could do was drag for 150 feet, rest, and start all over again. After a half-hour I could still see the area where the deer had walked up to me—distant, but not too far. After an hour I carried the rifles ahead while the Ole Man rested, and when I leisurely got back, we dragged some more.

There was no chance to get an ATV in here, or I would have certainly tried. Our luck with the chilly weather was still holding. The gray clouds overhead held back the sun, assuring us the ice layer under our feet would not melt. We broke through plenty of times around boggy springs, but stayed on top once we got to the Main Beaver Flowage. The water there is three feet, but the mud would easily

triple the footage, making it an impossible passage. As it
was, we both were wet to the knees and tired.

Main Beaver Flowage is nearly a half-mile wide at the
point where we edged across. We were saving ground and
making headway. The ice here was strong enough to slide
the deer along while we both broke through every five
steps. It was easier than the marsh grass trudging because
the deer was sliding. It now seemed the Ole Man was not
doing His part. I was surprised. I began to feel resentment
because I was taking the lead and He was just stumbling
along behind, not much pulling on the deer at all. I wasn't
about to stop and accuse Him of slacking, but the farther
we traveled, the more I knew He was not doing His share.

When I glanced over at Him I saw the sweat was just
flowing off Him like a river cresting in spring. His cheeks
were bright red. I was a little scared. It never occurred to
me, until right then, that a man of His age, whatever it was,
might be pushing Himself too hard to exert the energy it
required to haul the giant buck. He could have a heart
attack out here in The Bog.

As I carefully watched I saw He was putting out a lot of
effort, but only getting a little bit of power. The Ole Man
was an old man. I saw it for the first time. He wasn't just
aging, He was aged . . . old. Suddenly, I realized why He no
longer wanted to hunt The Bog anymore. This was why the
easier access of Swift Brook was attractive to Him. The Bog
was too much effort for His over-the-hill body to endure.

I found myself calling early halts to the next drag. I
feigned cramped muscles. Actually, I was embarrassed by

my lack of sensitivity. I just always saw the Ole Man as an institution—everlasting. Never-changing. Even with shorter drags I could see the day was really taking a toll on Him.

In the early noon hours we finally reached the far side of The Bog and an easy haul to the waiting Jeep. When the deer was placed in the back of the vehicle and the guns were safely stored, we both paused for a sigh of relief. I was glad to see Him breathing normally, even if He was tired. I was tired, too. That was a lot of work.

The Ole Man broke the silence with, "You know, don't ya? I've been thinking about it now for about the last three hours. I'm too old for this. I just can't do it anymore. I can't hunt The Bog like I used to. I couldn't even keep up with you this morning on the trail in. I just faked a hunt along the fringe. I didn't want to admit it yet. I thought I could hide it for another year. Then, damned if you went and got that big buck and dragged both me and the deer out of The Bog.

"This is exactly why I wanted to hunt Swift Brook. I been planning it ever since we flew over that country on the way in to fish Long Pond. Remember? Well, the last time I ever dragged a deer out the way we came today was a deer my father shot, his last one from The Bog. He never hunted there again."

The Ole Man was speaking again, in His questions-without-answers style, suggesting, "Now, The Bog is yours. Take good care of it. I'll be hunting tomorrow, on the upper reaches of Swift Brook."

I'll always remember that day.

About the Author

DAVE O'CONNOR was born to the Maine outdoor life more than seven decades ago. He spent the first part in the northern Penobscot town of Millinocket, or at South Twin Lake. More recently, he's lived in Sherman and Island Falls in Aroostook County, with twenty years in between, in Stacyville—a town everyone believes is in Aroostook, but is actually located in the extreme northern part of Penobscot County.

Dave has spent time in all fifty states and in the Canadian provinces, hunting, fishing, taking photos, camping, boating, canoeing, climbing, and hiking, sleeping many hundreds of nights in the back of a pickup truck or cabin, and thousands of nights in a tent.

He has been a regular columnist for the *Northwoods Sporting Journal* for more than twenty years, and has written outdoor articles for hundreds of national, regional, and weekly publications, including the NRA's *American Hunter* and *American Rifleman* magazines, *Guns & Ammo*, *Organic Gardening*, *Boys' Life*, *Outdoor Life*, *Sports Afield*, *Maine Life*, *Yankee*, *Down East*, and *Fur-Fish-Game*, the place where paid writing first became possible for Dave when they published one of his stories in October of 1962. Outdoor writing has been a big part of his life, with one of his stories published every month since then.